SPECULATION

IN

PRE–CHRISTIAN PHILOSOPHY

SPECULATION AND REVELATION
IN THE HISTORY OF PHILOSOPHY

SPECULATION
IN
PRE-CHRISTIAN
PHILOSOPHY

by

RICHARD KRONER

Philadelphia
THE WESTMINSTER PRESS

Library of Congress Catalog Card Number: 56-9575

PRINTED IN THE UNITED STATES OF AMERICA

To My Wife

who in perfect loyalty stood by my side for more than
fifty years blessed with that love which combines Eros
and Agape

CONTENTS

FOREWORD   9

INTRODUCTION TO *Speculation and
Revelation in the History of Philosophy*

I. Speculation and Revelation   17
II. Perspective of the History of Philosophy   30

SPECULATION IN PRE-CHRISTIAN PHILOSOPHY

I. Speculation and the Greek Mind   45
II. Preparation of the Gospel   60
III. The Rise of Cosmology   73
IV. Ascent to the Invisible   87
V. The Foundation of Ontology   102
VI. From Dogmatism to Skepticism   117
VII. Socrates   133
VIII. The Cosmos of the Ideas   152
    A. The Heritage
    B. Ontology of the Ideas
    C. Cosmotheology
IX. The Consummation of Greek Thought   183
    A. General Character of the Philosophy of Aristotle
    B. Metaphysical Principles
    C. Theology
    D. Transition from Aristotle to the Stoa
X. Speculation and Religion in Stoicism   223
Index   241

FOREWORD

THE following discussion is the outcome of lectures I delivered for many years at Union Theological Seminary in New York, and also at the School of Theology in Temple University, Philadelphia. When I left New York in 1952, the students urged me to publish my course on "The History of Philosophy from the Christian Point of View." This volume does not exactly render what I used to say in that course (which somehow changed as to its content from year to year). However, what I am offering now grew out from my lectures.

The relation between speculation and revelation appeared to me on an ever increasing scale to be the nerve center in the history of philosophy from the beginnings up to Hegel, whose system I believe was the last great attempt to find a reconciliation between these rival contenders.

Although the Greeks did not yet know revelation in the Biblical sense, and although their speculation originated independently of this contrast, still there is an element in Greek speculation that corresponds to revelation — a fundamental vision not derived, and indeed not derivable, from any empirical observation or rational analysis of facts observed, but, rather, intuitively conceived. What is commonly called Greek ontology was from the beginnings not only a strictly logical, but also a religious, concern. Many books of recent years have made it abundantly clear that the Greeks from the time of their earliest speculation tried to create a substitute for the religion of their nation, with which the thinkers were no longer satisfied.

When Thales set out to discover the ground of all things, he was fully aware that he thereby put aside the traditional (Homeric as well as Dionysian) polytheism and offered instead a speculative

9

monotheism. His water principle was by no means a naturalistic or materialistic design in the sense in which modern science would understand it. It was rather a very mysterious stuff, to be identified neither with the water we can perceive nor with the H_2O of chemistry today, but the aboriginal and eternal essence of the universe, which took the place of the deity (as later sources would even insist he had stated it himself). This water was " seen " with the eyes of his speculative mind. He could not possibly have demonstrated by reason that water was what he believed it to be, however many reasons he may have given for this contention.

Now it is true that Thales, as well as all his successors, wanted to assert that speculation is able to discover the nature of things without relying upon any religious source whatsoever, and that their principles did " reveal " this fundamental " nature." Nevertheless, their philosophic thought was speculative precisely in so far as there was an underlying vision at work in their thinking — an analogue to the revealed truth on which Christian thinkers later relied. I try to show in my book what the origin of this underlying vision was and how it can be understood as rooted in the Greek spirit.

This book represents only the first of three volumes in which I hope to discuss the development of speculation and revelation from the pre-Christian, through the deliberately Christian age, up to the modern age of philosophy. We commonly distinguish these three ages in the history of European philosophy; and this distinction illustrates perhaps better than anything else the thesis defended in my book: that it is the relation between speculation and revelation, or between the secular and the sacred approach to the Ultimate or the Absolute, which determines the character of philosophic systems.

The distinction between the three ages is based upon the fact that the Greeks did not yet know anything about Biblical revelation, whereas the philosophers in the second age (one would suitably call it the age of Roman Catholic philosophy) did know it and therefore reasoned about the relation between the two sources of truth (reason and faith or the natural and the divine light within knowledge). Philosophical speculation in the third (the " Protestant ") age tended to emancipate itself from the bondage of Biblical revelation (positivism and " analytical " philosophy today are the " last " manifestations of this endeavor) and to establish purely " scientific " systems.

However, the very attempt to emancipate itself from revelation characterizes the substance of modern thought. In fact, this emancipation never fully succeeded; it is rather the tension between speculation and revelation that is the mark of " protestant " philosophy — often more " protesting " than confessing, until it finally rejected any bond with revelation or faith.

Greek speculation is not only pre-Christian; it is outright un-Christian. The very undertaking to discover the root of all things by means of human intuition and hypothesis is radically un-Biblical or even anti-Biblical. It is hardly necessary today to emphasize this fact. Indeed, Kierkegaard has made it so compellingly evident that one has to be blind or deaf not to recognize it. It is, however, a historical fact that not only did Greek speculation approach the advent of the gospel in its own way but also Christian dogma and theology in turn were deeply influenced by Greek speculation and would never have arisen without its influence. This alarming interdependence (alarming only for our modern philosophers who had completely disregarded it) demonstrates victoriously that the relation between speculation and revelation is of central significance in the history of Western thought and life.

How could Plato ever have gained the power over Christian thought that he actually did gain, if such a close interdependence between Greek speculation and Biblical revelation had not existed? Clement of Alexandria was the first thinker to realize this close kinship, and he introduced thus the marriage between Platonism and Christianity which lasted more than a thousand years. Even Thomas Aquinas was much more tinged by Platonic idealism (or, as the medieval scholastics named it, Platonic realism) than has been commonly acknowledged.

In three volumes, I expect to deal with the three ages in which the relation between speculation and revelation underwent significant transformations. In the first, the pre-Christian age, speculation developed as a protest against Greek polytheism out of a peculiar half-mythological, half-intellectual intuition which took the place of a religious revelation in the Biblical sense. The second age generated a kind of Christian speculation, in which the Greek inheritance was of the uttermost import, so that one sometimes does not really know whether a thinker was more deeply engaged in Platonic or Aris-

totelian metaphysics or in Christian thought. The third age, the age
in which Protestantism was intellectually the leading power, generated a speculation that did not appeal to Christian revelation, but
nevertheless could not dissociate itself fully from the predominating
spirit of this revelation. Thus, modern systems show an oscillation
between the fight against this spirit and the ambition to interpret
Christian revelation by secular speculation as Hegel most impressively did.

The series of which the first volume, *Speculation in Pre-Christian
Philosophy,* is here presented deals with the historical development of
the relation between speculation and revelation. I hope that I shall
be able to finish the two other volumes in a not too distant time. In a
way the whole development culminates in Kant's Critical philosophy,
because Kant saw more clearly than any other thinker before him
that the limitation of reason for the sake of faith was the primary
and central task of European philosophy. I admit that this evaluation
involves a systematic and not merely a historical answer to the question of how speculation and revelation are fundamentally related to
each other. Is there a permanent rivalry between the two approaches
to ultimate truth? Or is it possible to settle the dispute between them
in a final form? If so, in what way? Has one of the opponents the
supremacy, so that the other would be reconciled to the first one by
some kind of subordination? Or is it possible to maintain equal
rights on both sides and yet bring about a lasting peace?

My discussion will treat all these questions only in so far as history
itself has given its answers. However, a certain appraisal of these answers is indispensable not only for the selection of those systems
which I regard as most significant, but also for the purpose of interpretation. One cannot understand philosophic systems without siding
with and against them; only so an intelligible interpretation can be
offered. The reader will find more on this issue in the subsequent
text.

Kant, I believe, has given the most profound and the best substan-
tiated solution of the central problem, but he has not satisfactorily
understood the function of revelation; he thought it possible to ce-
ment faith by means of Practical Reason. I do not share in this decision. But this critical remark if pursued would lead me to a systematical inquiry which I do not intend to undertake in this work. I

hope I shall eventually write another book giving my own solution of the crucial problem.

I wish to thank first my students who have encouraged me to publish these lectures and who have contributed through their often most intelligent and penetrating questions or objections to the final result. I cannot call all of them by name, but I feel that I should express my special gratefulness to Miss Mary Stuart, who not only prompted me several times to publish this interpretation of the " history of philosophy seen from the Christian point of view," but also read the first draft and told me frankly what she would like to have changed in it.

I owe gratitude to Professor Freeman, of Wilson College, who took the trouble to correct the English of my manuscript and weeded out my Germanisms with pitiless but gracious mind.

I also am thankful to Miss Gloria Livermore, Professor of Classical Literature at Wilson College, who polished once more the style of my book and gave it the finish that I should never have been able to accomplish myself, and to Dr. John E. Skinner, Professor of Bible at the School of Theology of Temple University, who helped me in correcting the proofs.

Philadelphia

RICHARD KRONER

Introduction to

SPECULATION AND REVELATION
IN THE
HISTORY OF PHILOSOPHY

I

SPECULATION AND REVELATION

THE concern of speculation is the ultimate problem of philosophy, the philosophical absolute. Speculation is peculiar to metaphysics. In the course of the history of philosophy, metaphysical systems have been constructed in which questions have been discussed such as: What is the ground of all existence? What is the relation between being and becoming? Is reality governed by one single power or is it divided into several different and independent realms? Is there a fundamental division between reality and appearance? Metaphysics is the most central, the most important, the most profound, the most widely desired, and the most admired of all the philosophic disciplines. And yet, paradoxically, it is also the most questionable. It is the most uncertain, the most obscure, the most despised, and the least reliable of all the sciences. Metaphysics is the heart of all philosophic thought. But does this heart really beat and pulsate? At its inception philosophy was confident that it could solve the ultimate problem; from its beginning it was metaphysical. Thales never doubted that he could answer the question, What is the ultimate basis of all that is? This doubt was not uttered until after centuries of speculation.

Speculation is therefore a kind of intellectual adventure. The first explorer is confident he will find the sought-after shores. At sight of land he trusts that he has reached the goal of his voyage. Later adventurers recognize his mistake. He has discovered some valuable land, but not the ultimate he had sought. Thus the idea of the goal is repeatedly modified; the whole enterprise appears in an ever new and changing light. Speculation is not so sure of its goal and its direction as is an explorer. The explorer can orientate himself by looking at the sun, stars, or his compass. The speculative thinker is without any such aids. No map indicates his direction. Goethe, in his *Faust,* has expressed it for us as follows: " A man that speculates is like a beast on moorlands lean, that round and round some fiend misleads to evil plight, while all about lie pastures fresh and green." To be sure, this is a saying of Mephistopheles! Nevertheless, it is undeniable that speculation, seeking for ultimate truth and reality, often seems to end in a desert of empty terms. The vessel of speculation seems to get lost in the midst of an angry ocean where it is threatened with destruction by tumultuous waves.

Speculation, the product of human reason, is man's adventure. Revelation is the work of God; man is only the receiver. And yet revelation and speculation are not entirely dissimilar. Speculation cannot proceed without an intuition or a vision. Its point of departure is not the result of a deliberate and spontaneous investigation; it is a flash of mind, a dictate of inspiration. No great metaphysical system can ever do without this quasi-revelatory element. Divine revelation, on the other hand, cannot be passively received. There is always some necessary activity on the part of the prophet. God said to Isaiah: " ' Whom shall I send, and who will go for us? ' Then I said, ' Here I am! Send me.' And he said, ' Go, and say to this people: " Hear and hear, but do not understand; see and see, but do not perceive " ' " (Isa. 6:8, 9). The prophet understands and perceives the word of the Lord. All others hear it without comprehension. For this reason the prophet is elected to speak to the people. In spite of what we have been saying, the activity and the kind of inspiration received, prompting the action of the speculating philosopher and the elected prophet, are clearly distinct. Speculation is not merely the work of reason; it is also the work of an intuition. Nevertheless, reasoning is at the bottom of speculation. And although the prophet is also active, nonetheless he carries out the mission commanded by the Lord and speaks what the Lord suggests.

In many respects speculation and revelation belong to different spheres. Speculation is a method by which truth is known. The truth that speculation knows is scientific, i.e., " theoretical," detached, demonstrative, impersonal; it is disengaged from the thinking subject, as an individual. The truth mediated by revelation, in contrast, is " practical," " committing," undemonstrable, personal — in short, religious; it is addressed to man as an individual. And yet rivalry exists between the two spheres, because the truth of both claims ultimacy. The question of primacy is therefore inevitable. Ultimacy cannot be shared — it is indivisible; two ultimates are mutually exclusive. Which truth is higher, that of speculation or that of revelation? How can they live together? How are they correctly related to each other? If we call the ultimate divine, then are things divine known more adequately, more profoundly, and more completely by speculation or by revelation?

Biblical religion is more averse to speculation and metaphysics than any other religion. Brahmanism and Buddhism are themselves partly speculative. Their concept of the divine is not so personal and so untheoretical as is the living God of the Bible. The Upanishads and the conversations of Buddha contain much that could be called philosophical reasoning. Confucianism and Taoism are even more outspokenly metaphysical or ethical. Biblical religion alone is personal; it is more purely religious than other religions. The chasm between speculation and Biblical revelation is, therefore, of a peculiar depth and significance; their antagonism is particularly acute and apparently irreconcilable.

God the Creator of heaven and earth is so exalted above the reach of man that any endeavor to make him the object of investigation and of a theory is not only hopeless but also simply irreverent. It is incompatible with his unspeakable majesty and his incomparable sovereignty. If this transcendent Lord rules the world, as he has created it and sustains it, then all merely human effort to know his nature is absurd. The only acceptable human attitude toward this King of Kings is obedience, reverence, adoration, fear, and love. The story of the Fall has revealed that man is forbidden to know the truth as God knows it. The desire to be on the level of God is the greatest and most fateful temptation. From the very outset the Bible makes it clear that man can never traverse the distance between God and himself. Humanity is, in the first place, limited by the limitations of human knowledge. Metaphysics is excluded in principle. Speculation is condemned before it arises. The serpent in paradise, appealing to man's desire to know as much as God knows, is, as it were, the spirit of speculation. According to the Bible, God alone can bridge the infinite distance between himself and man. Thus any inquiry into things divine is precluded at the outset. God does not incline himself to man in order to inform him about his nature. God turns to man to command, to advise, to warn, to guide, to punish, to reward, to console, to support, and finally, to forgive and redeem him. Such divine actions do not provide metaphysical instructions or theological information; they are personal, practical, deliberate, and are directed toward man's moral and spiritual welfare, toward his education and salvation. Metaphysical and theological information is not only denied to man; it is incompatible with the true relationship between the Creator and the creature, between the infinite and the finite self, between the supreme lawgiver, ruler, and judge, and ourselves, who are subject to God's law, government, and judgment. Our theoretical knowledge is necessarily restricted to finite things and concepts; only such can be investigated and known in a scientific, objective, and impersonal way. God cannot be known objectively; like man, he is himself a subject. God is infinite and, therefore, beyond the ever-finite categories of human thought.

Because of the untheoretical character of revelation, mystery surrounds the Infinite. Revelation does not disclose this mystery; it only heightens and intensifies it. All personal relations are mysterious inasmuch as they are not scientifically knowable. To be comprehended they must be experienced in a living way. And if this be true of relationships between human persons, then how much more so if the person involved is not finite but infinite! The personal character of God prohibits any speculative approach to the Ultimate as revealed in the Bible. God reveals himself, i.e., his actions and ends, not in a theological system, but in the epic narrative or dramatic dialogue. Revealed truth is not concerned, therefore, with God's metaphysical nature but with his will and intention. Every concept of God is consequently un-Biblical. The Word of God is not conceptual but commanding, directing, admonishing, judging, acquitting. It is not the word of a thinker but of a living spirit, an acting person, a willing Lord who has the power to enact what he wills. The Bible is definitely not a metaphysical textbook. It is the report of God's holy will and work and of man's response and destiny in consequence of his relationship to the Supreme Being.

Even dogmatics is a questionable science. It tries to make the will and actions of God more systematic and logically consistent than the Bible does. The dogmatician may think that he is loyal to the original spirit of the Word of God. He may believe that systematization only translates the personal style and the dramatic procedure of God's dealing with man into the language of logical thinking. But if the epic and dramatic form of the narrative is the only adequate style in which the will and deeds of God can be related, then such a systematization is certainly less adequate. It transposes the living truth to a level on which it is no longer living. Such a rearrangement kills the spirit and destroys life. The living God cannot be enshrined in a logical system, even when it is based upon the Bible itself. God cannot be grasped by means of concepts, even when such concepts pretend to comprehend what is told in a nonconceptual form. The conceptual and the nonconceptual cannot be simply equated to each other either in a speculative or in a dogmatic fashion. God could have revealed himself in a dogmatic fashion but he did not, and must therefore have had his reasons for not doing so. Dogmatics is after all man's work. The gulf between speculation and revelation can never be bridged. If a kind of philosophy or theology is implied in the Bible, it is not revealed in a doctrinal form, and it cannot be so rendered without undergoing an essential transformation. The doctrinal form is alien to revelation and therefore changes its original meaning. Form and content are closely bound up with each other in revelation as well as in epic or in drama. Those who wish to establish a Christian philosophy must take this momentous difference into account. Abraham, Moses, Amos, Isaiah, Paul, and Jesus were not philosophic teachers. The prophetic, the mystical, the personal tone in which they spoke was more adequate to the content of their message than the doctrinal and logical method of philosophy. There is no equation between the two forms, just as there is none between the two contents.

And yet in spite of this diversity of form and content there is undeniably a competition between the two powers, a competition leading to strife, victory, defeat, combination, and compromise. This diversity does not exclude all contact and unity. Some point of contact, and consequently some possibility of competition, always exists between opposites. The living God of the Bible deters all conceptual knowledge, and yet in some way he stands for that ultimate truth which speculation tries to grasp in its own right. In spite of the diversity, separating their form and content, speculation and revelation meet. The religious and the speculative Ultimate are in the final analysis the same Absolute.

The two powers encounter and compete with each other in the history of philosophy. In the Greek epoch speculation prevailed over Greek religion. Because the latter was primitive and in many respects insufficient, philosophy assailed it and was victorious, though never completely. Religion defeated speculation in the form of Christian philosophy and Christian theology (dogmatics), although these sciences somehow unite religion and speculation. The later revival of an independent speculation, however, finally threatened the integrity of both revelation and theology. Since the Renaissance, speculation is again on the march, ignoring or directly suppressing Christian philosophy. The supplanted religious forces came to the fore only in Pascal and Kierkegaard who attacked speculation on its own ground. The fight continues, testifying to the competitive character of speculation and revelation, philosophy and religion.

This rivalry is further disclosed by the fact that metaphysical systems are commonly distinguished or classified in accordance with their basic solution of the theological problem, as atheistic, pantheistic, or theistic. This division is not complete, but it aptly strikes the central difference between the various systems. The " philosophy " implied in revelation is very often designated by the term theistic, thereby distinguishing Biblical religion from nontheistic (though not necessarily atheistic) religions. And theistic religions are further divided into monotheistic and polytheistic types. Such customary designations show the clashing and competitive nature of speculation and religion. Pantheism and atheism are denounced by the Bible believer as being hostile to the revealed God almost as vehemently as polytheism. Greek speculation inclined from its very beginning toward pantheism, whereas Christian philosophy, adopting the Biblical position, always maintained a theistic view. And even when speculation turned to a kind of theism, its concept of God was never quite in agreement with the God of faith.

Certain basic features and certain key figures within the realm of revelation and speculation indicate and confirm the inevitability of a clash. Although repudiated by speculation, Greek religion nevertheless exercised an indirect influence; speculation assumed a quasi-religious authority and appearance. Some of the most ancient thinkers, like Parmenides, Pythagoras (or his followers who lived together in a kind of religious community), and Empedocles (who claimed to be of divine origin), spoke in a solemn, almost hierarchical, style. They did not yet apply a rational method, but they pronounced in a dictatorial manner what they considered to be ultimately true. Parmenides, the founder of ontology and the first "rationalist," was also a poet. Feeling himself to be an inspired prophet, Parmenides wrote his doctrine in the form of a poem; introducing it by mythological symbolism, he regarded his wisdom as divine revelation and not as the result of his own labor.

The strange "method" of Socrates has in another way some kinship with religious manifestations. Socrates did not write at all. He spoke directly to his fellow citizens and entangled them in the snare of embarrassing questions, questions that went straight to the heart of their moral personality. He needed the support of others, for allegedly he did not know the truth but only sought it. Socrates developed his own views in conversations, but he seldom, if ever, reached a doctrinal and conceptual conclusion. Socrates represented a living philosophy: philosophy should not be verified by reasoning alone but by the very life of man. Socrates himself set the example.[1] And Plato, the great pupil of Socrates, did not proceed in a manner that we would today call scientific. By depicting the personality of Socrates and relating his conversation in a quasi-dramatic style, Plato imitated the immediacy of life and the actuality of concrete situations in which such conversations took place. Similarly, the cynics were half-religious figures who by their mode of life demonstrated their attitude toward its meaning. And the Stoics sought the outright transformation of philosophy into a kind of religion.

Biblical revelation, on the other hand, undoubtedly shows a trait of rationality. The books of Moses, the historical, the prophetic, and even the proverbial and quasi-doctrinal books, are not speculative in the Greek sense, and yet moral reason has a part in Biblical wisdom. The term "holiness" originally had no moral, but only a sacramental, connotation. Gradually, however, it assumed that of moral purity, and perfection. Monotheism in itself has an affinity for the oneness of reason. And if, as Socrates and Kant claim, moral reason is supe-

---

[1] Cf. Plato's dialogue *Laches,* 188: "I compare the man and his words and note the harmony. . . . Socrates has in his own life a harmony of words and deeds."

rior to speculative and theoretical reason, then Biblical " philosophy " may be nearer to the philosophical truth than speculative systems of metaphysics.

Such considerations make intelligible the competition and strife between speculation and revelation. They disclose the reason why this rivalry could become the very center of the history of philosophy, exhibiting its various aspects in the different epochs and periods. Moreover, the question has to be raised whether speculation ever existed, and, in fact, can exist, without a certain religious foundation or source. In our time the thesis has been defended that a religious " ground motive " was always operative within metaphysical systems and that the history of philosophy can be best understood and interpreted when we reflect upon this motive and make it overt. Only then can the ground motive of a Christian philosophy be rightly appreciated. After such reflection full justice can be done to a Christian philosophy in its struggle with other philosophical systems and schools. The representative of this thesis, Herman Dooyeweerd, asserts that all Greek speculation was based upon the contrast of matter and form, a contrast that has a religious origin and significance.[2]

According to Dooyeweerd, " matter " is rooted in the Dionysian and Orphic religion, which venerated Mother Earth and believed in the divinity of a universal stream of life out of which are generated transitory individuals subject to necessity and death. This religion found its speculative expression in the Ionian philosophical systems from Thales to Heraclitus. Its counterpart, the cultural religion of the personal and individually shaped Olympic gods, prevailed in Homer and was represented philosophically by the motive of form. The contrast between those two religious types is the background of Greek speculation. To quote Dooyeweerd: " The autonomy which philosophical *theoria* demanded, in opposition to popular belief, implied . . . only an emancipation from the mythological form. . . . It did not at all imply a loosening of philosophic thought from the central religious ground motive which was born out of the counter of the culture religion with the older religion of life." [3]

Since I shall subsequently deal with these problems in the text, I

[2] *A New Critique of Theoretical Thought.* Vol. I. *The Necessary Presuppositions of Philosophy.* 1953.
[3] *Op. cit.,* p. 62.

shall postpone a discussion of this philosophy of the history of phi-losophy. Undoubtedly, Greek speculation arose out of a religious tradition. It did not proceed, however, from the contrast between Dionysian and Apollonian mythology alone, but also from the con-trast between religion and science. Greek speculation was an attempt to reconcile these two sources on a higher plane; it sought to trans-form the religious creeds by making them scientific. It must be noted, that both types of Greek religion, the Dionysian and the Apollonian, were obviously deficient morally and rationally (theoretically). From the outset Greek philosophy sought to remedy this defect. It was, therefore, critical with respect to religion, even to the point of being hostile. A second important consideration, which I shall subsequently enlarge upon, is the fact that Greek philosophy had its roots in the main Greek attitude with respect to the world and to life, an at-titude that was not religious but artistic. And this aesthetic propen-sity of the Greeks shaped their religion to such a degree that it deter-mined the very form of their gods, as well as the accounts of their exploits. Greek religion was more artistic than religious. Hence within Greek civilization philosophy could desert religion with greater facility than is possible in the Christian Era. The peculiar character of religion gave speculation an unusual chance to develop.

Christian philosophy arose from the necessity of defending the Christian faith against the attacks of Greek speculative systems. In contrast, ancient philosophy from its very inception attacked the gods and the faith of the populace. Christian philosophy, resolute in its intention to adhere to Biblical revelation and even to the Church and its dogmas, was never free, in the Greek sense; unable to unfold in speculative systems, it could only adapt its thought to the religious sources out of which it arose. The Greek thinker was an individual, an adventurer, and a conqueror. As such he really was autonomous. His thought was the product of an autonomous *theōria,* recognizing no other authority than the facts of empirical observation and such inferences as could be deduced from them. Of course certain ideas inherited from the popular religion, of a more or less mythical na-ture, as well as moral values partly sanctified by that religious tradi-tion, were assimilated in his thinking. It may well be the case that the worship of earth and fertility in a Dionysian cult facilitated the rise of Ionian natural philosophy, although, as we shall see, the word

" nature " in Ionian speculation has to be interpreted carefully. The Platonic realm of ideas may have had something to do with the polytheism of the Olympic religion. But all this is highly conjectural. The fact that Greek thinkers were independent personalities, relying upon their own experience, insight, and judgment, is much more important and impressive. Heraclitus, for instance, was not in any way dependent upon the Dionysian cult, but spurned " the night revelers, Magi, bacchants, maenads, and initiated, and held their practices to be unholy." [4] And even if the contrast of matter and form ever had a religious connotation, it was not expressed philosophically or expounded philosophically; such connotation had been lost entirely in the scheme of Aristotle. As far as I can see, there is no religious ground motive within Aristotle's system. I shall show that Aristotle's emphasis upon form is not religious but aesthetic in origin. Even though the Greeks originated the idea of autonomous *theōria,* they did not formulate the ideal of autonomy because their religion was not dogmatic; it did not censor their thought. Even though some philosophers, like Anaxagoras and, notably, Socrates, were persecuted because they violated popular religious sentiment, the Greeks were entirely free to think and to teach. In both the aforementioned cases of persecution, political reasons were involved. The charge of impiety was either secondary or a mere pretext. By introducing the idea of heresy, the Christian Church alone seriously restricted the freedom of thought. Against the background of ecclesiastical imperialism, at the dawn of modern times, after the power of Rome over intellectual and spiritual life had been broken, autonomy was demanded and practiced.

Dooyeweerd does not reflect upon the difference between a religious motive, deliberately assumed and ostentatiously proclaimed by a philosopher, and historical conditions more or less unconsciously influencing individual thought or communal thinking. Even if we accept the hypothesis that Ionian speculation was an outcome of Dionysian or Chthonic cults, it would not necessarily follow that a religious ground motive determined that speculation in the same way as Dooyeweerd would let the Christian faith determine his own philosophical thought. It is of course true that thought, thinking, and

[4] Fr. 14. In Fr. 15 he identifies Dionysos and Hades. (Fragments according to H. Diels.)

thinker never develop in an empty realm. There is always a certain atmosphere, cultural, political, moral, and spiritual, conditioning their development. This atmosphere, however, has to be distinguished carefully from a philosophical principle, programmatically depriving thought of its prerogative to rely upon its own judgment and of its ability to reflect independently of any religious source. When the Ionians first spoke of the " arche," they intended to assert the very independent character of their thought, reserving to themselves the right to declare, on the basis of their own insight, independently of any previous religious doctrine or mythos, what the principle of the universe is. Of course from a historical point of view their conceptions were not unimpressed and unconditioned by previous statements or doctrines. Dooyeweerd recognizes in principle the ascendancy of Biblical doctrine over philosophic thought. From the Greek point of view such a recognition is thoroughly unphilosophic. This historical fact at least proves that it is illegitimate to ignore the difference between historical conditions and philosophic presuppositions.

In opposition to medieval theonomy and ecclesiastical sovereignty over philosophic thought, modern times proclaimed the autonomy of pure reason. Modern times thereby did, and yet did not, return to the ancient position. Inasmuch as it no longer tolerated the tutelage and censorship of thought, modern times returned. But the wheel of history can never be turned back. Even when things bygone are reborn or reclaimed, they are no longer what they have been before. Greek religion could not be resuscitated any more than Christianity could be annihilated by the decree of some friends of antiquity. Moreover, in modern times, emphasis was laid upon the investigation of natural (physical) processes. It was not so much philosophic speculation that reasserted its ancient freedom from religious authority. Of course this reassertion also occurred. But it was primarily in the field of mathematical physics that scholasticism and Aristotelianism were simultaneously overthrown. The autonomy of reason proclaimed by mathematical physics was the innovation that released the avalanche of modern autonomous thought. Philosophy only subsequently and under the sway of physics was hurled into that current.

By criticizing ancient speculation as severely as scholasticism, Galileo Galilei introduced a new " arche " into European thought. In the field of natural sciences he defended the autonomy of mathematical analysis and calculus in opposition to the primacy of both speculation and revelation. This was the turning point in the development of thought from the Middle Ages to modern autonomy. Descartes only applied the principle of Galileo to epistemology and metaphysics. Up until Kant's *Critique of Pure Reason,* the ideal of mathematical exactitude and demonstrability, and its philosophic counterpart, conquered the minds of modern thinkers. It is true, as Dooyeweerd maintains, that in Kant a quasi-religious feeling was unfolding which stressed and overstressed the autonomy and freedom of moral reason. But again one should not ignore the vast difference between this feeling and the proclamation of the primacy of a religious motive in a philosophic foundation. It is precisely the difference between a quasi-religious and a genuinely religious, between an ethical and a Biblical principle, which creates an abyss between the intentions of Kant and those of Christian philosophy. Although the religious spirit of Kant's work varies profoundly from that of Greek speculation, still the autonomy principle of Kant is more cognate to that of the Greeks than to any religious principle.

The contrast between speculation and revelation should not be obscured or eradicated by the fact that all philosophy is indeed influenced by the circumstances and atmosphere of the period and even of the nation in which its arises. The effect of Christianity upon the formation of philosophic systems was altogether different from the effect produced by Greek religion and modern ideals. It is precisely this difference that really matters, for it determines and elucidates the relation between speculation and revelation. The contrast between these two great spiritual and intellectual powers, the one springing from Greek soil, the other from the Holy Land, can only be fully understood and appraised if we study its historical developments. Both streams, that of Greek speculation and that of prophetic revelation, join in the period in which Christianity was born, and the whole subsequent development of thought bears the traces of this momentous event. While the Middle Ages believed in the reconciliation of these opposites, though under the sway of the Christian faith and the Roman Church, modern times, no longer sharing this hope and aim, declared that faith is faith and therefore ought not to be allowed to meddle with speculation.

The new outlook was sponsored by the Reformation. The Roman Church was not extinguished, but its unique power was broken; cultural initiative and creativity passed from Rome to Protestant countries. The following discussion will tell the story of this development of Western thought from the perspective of the contrast between speculation and revelation. This historical discussion cannot solve the philosophic problem involved, but it may clarify the issues. And thus it may indirectly prepare a solution suited to our own needs and sorrows.

II

PERSPECTIVE OF THE HISTORY OF PHILOSOPHY

THE contrast between speculation and revelation will be the perspective of the following historical discussion. But is not history an objective science which does not tolerate any " perspective "? Does the history of philosophy permit a special perspective without becoming distorted or arbitrary? A perspective seems to imply a subjective attitude, a prejudice encroaching upon facts and thereby modifying their meaning according to its own point of view. If history in general is an objective science, relating facts without bias and without any subjective ingredient, then the history of philosophical facts cannot be any exception. Ranke used to say that history wants to know how things really happened and nothing more. In protest against any speculative interpretation of history, such as that of Hegel and his school, Ranke thereby excluded in principle any special position or perspective from which things were to be seen and understood.

No longer are we inclined to believe in the possibility and, indeed, in the desirability of such an objective conception of history. We are now too deeply convinced that man can never escape the conditions and the spirit of his age and civilization. He cannot even evade his own individual character, faith, and ideals. We can no longer deem it possible for man to abstract from such conditions in dealing with human affairs of the past. In this respect there is a profound and pointed difference between the natural and the historical sciences. Natural processes have no meaning in the sense in which human action and creations have meaning or are meaningful. Natural objects are simply there. They occur, but they do not claim to express volitions or mind, purpose or ideals, as do human actions and the products of human creativity. When we encounter the human mind and its expressions, we cannot refrain from looking at them through our own mind, interpreting them along the lines of our own purposes or creeds. Not even Ranke could abstract from his own mind in referring to the past. As historians we do not simply deal with facts but also with acts; indeed, the facts themselves involve action on the part of man and are therefore meaningful — i.e., historical and not physical facts. I cannot be an objective scientist when I contemplate the scene on which people act and suffer, strive and succeed or fail, produce and create, judge and are judged, defeat and are defeated. This scene is not merely an objective ground on which objective causes operate and objective effects are brought about. It is rather the scene on which people think and plan, feel and wish — people like ourselves, who under other circumstances and in other atmospheres faced similar tasks and problems. Motivated by similar passions and values, they pursued similar ends and aims and were in every respect like us in their human nobility, frailty, ambitions, pride, ignorance, and wisdom.

If this is true with respect to political and social history, how much more so with respect to the history of thought, where the innermost mind of man manifests itself, and where the meaning of life and the world is discussed and announced. Certainly, a Roman Catholic cannot look at the history of the popes with the same spiritual eyes as a Protestant; a monarchist cannot look at the French Revolution with the eyes of a socialist, and so on. The facts themselves look as the person looks at them. Therefore, history looks always as intelligent as the person is who looks at the "facts." The situation is intensified in the realm of the history of thought. A Platonist would by inner necessity write another account of Aristotle's system than an Aristotelian or Kantian; a Kantian would understand Hegel in a way totally different from that of a Hegelian, and a materialist would comprehend both Kant and Hegel in his own terms, as did Friedrich Albert Lange in his history of materialism. An objective history of philosophic thought is impossible. History would lose all intelligible coherence and even all meaning if one should try to write it in a neutral or merely factual manner. The "facts" would no longer be intelligible thoughts which were meaningful in the mind of their creators, but they would degenerate into curious remarks or unintelligible systems of words, as is unfortunately the actual case in some books dealing with the history of philosophy.

It is not possible to write political history without any political interest, experience, judgment, and opinion. It is even more impossible to write the history of philosophy without philosophical comprehension, and that means without a certain philosophic point of view. Only such a point of view permits the selection of thinkers as well as of thoughts out of the mass of books composed in the past. Only such a perspective permits the comprehension of the relation between systems and epochs. The Kantians of the nineteenth century frequently believed that Kant had created the only scientific and objective system ever achieved. They therefore thought themselves able to take a perfectly scientific and objective position with respect to all other systems; and in consequence they deemed themselves able to write history in such a scientific and objective sense. But they were completely mistaken, for they produced only historical treatises from a Kantian perspective, whereas the Hegelian historians had produced theirs from the Hegelian point of view.

Only in this partial sight can the significance and the truth of the systems be illuminated. For the historical truth about philosophic systems can be discovered only in an intimate connection with their philosophic truth, and how will one understand and appraise that philosophic truth without being a philosopher and without philosophizing? The history of philosophy assumes an intelligent appearance if and only if it simultaneously receives both historical and philosophical treatment. When filling its proper function, a history of philosophy is both a historical and a philosophical work.

The history of philosophy cannot, therefore, be more objective and impartial than philosophy itself. Modern philosophy strove after scientific truth; it aimed at the same objectivity characteristic of the natural sciences and responsible for their success and trustworthiness. Philosophy is, however, not a natural science. The ideal of scientific exactitude and demonstrability can, therefore, not simply be borrowed from the natural sciences and applied to such a different task as that of philosophy.

Descartes, Spinoza, and Leibniz employed the same method, or at least followed the same regulative ideal of mathematical demonstration. Nevertheless, their systems differ widely in outlook, spirit, and result, as did the national backgrounds, destinies, intellectual surroundings, and character of the authors. Philosophy is ever dependent upon such conditions.

One is forced, therefore, to concede the validity of the conclusion that philosophy is a very questionable science. But its character merely corresponds to the questionable nature of our world and of our own existence. Our world is not only mathematical; it is also mysterious. And it is this second feature that arouses philosophic interest and labor. It is ridiculous to demand the same method for philosophy and for mathematics. Even such great thinkers as Descartes, Spinoza, and Leibniz, insisting upon the mathematical ideal, unsuccessfully aimed at a mathematical method in philosophy. The metaphysics of Descartes and Spinoza, and the monadology of Leibniz are not based upon the mathematical method, even though they proclaimed such a method to be ideal. But it is necessary to terminate our introductory discussion of this problem.

Of course a certain objective basis for the history of philosophy does exist. It is of great importance to study and investigate the " facts," in so far as they can be known in an objective fashion. Since this is today overstressed I need not dwell upon this point. Various kinds of data have to be ascertained before any interpretation is in order. Often the lack of certainty about such data makes interpretation difficult and uncertain. Nevertheless the converse is not true: the certainty about facts does not facilitate the task of interpretation. Plato or Aristotle are as differently interpreted as Parmenides or Heraclitus, although we know the " letter " of Plato and Aristotle infinitely better than we know that of Parmenides and Heraclitus. Correct data can, of course, contribute to the certainty of the interpretation, and under certain circumstances may even suggest a modification or correction of interpretation. But the perspective underlying the interpretation is itself the result of the philosophic position taken by the historian.

But does not our perspective, underlying the following picture of the main trends and schools of philosophy, altogether transcend the philosophic horizon? Does not revelation belong more to dogmatic theology than to metaphysics? Therefore, does not our perspective, the relation between speculation and revelation, from the outset mix theology with philosophy? And does this not mean that the facts will be distorted, or will at least appear in an alien light? Is not the interpretation of philosophic concepts thereby endangered and alienated from their own proper outlook?

Such would be the case if, and only if, philosophy and religion were foreign to each other, without any common interest or connecting tie. But, as we have attempted to demonstrate, the very opposite is true. In spite of obvious differences, the same ultimate concern exists in both speculation and revelation: the preoccupation with ultimate truth and ultimate reality. Moreover, during its thousand-year reign Christian philosophy intimately united speculation and revelation, thereby showing the inner relation between these two sources of truth, and demonstrating that philosophy can consider both simultaneously. The long standing of a Christian philosophy, even when rejected, convincingly illustrates the point that revelation, though transcending the horizon of philosophy, does not lie completely beyond the compass of speculative thought. At least the problem of the relation between speculation and revelation can no longer be ignored. The history of medieval thought should remind us of the urgency of its solution.

It is a memorable and formidable fact worthy of deep consideration that the short first chapter of Genesis has had such a tremendous effect upon the human mind in general and particularly upon the philosophical mind. If one reflects upon the immense labor spent by Greek thinkers to discover the essence of the divine and its relation to cosmic reality, he cannot help feeling amazed at the enormous influence of Genesis on the trend of speculation in the Christian Era. And when you are convinced that the figure of the living God, portrayed in Gen., ch. 1, is of more relevance than the figure of the demiurge in the *Timaeus,* and than that of Pure Form in Aristotle's *Metaphysics,* you must then ponder on this superiority. You cannot avoid asking whether revelation is perhaps a more reliable source of information about the divine, better adopted to the penetration of the mystery surrounding it, than is speculation, in the Greek sense and on the Greek level. Should such be the case, then the relation between speculation and revelation must necessarily appear in a new light, too much neglected in modern times and too little respected by all modern thinkers, except men like Pascal and Kierkegaard. The latter's critique of Hegel's metaphysics has stirred our philosophic conscience. Even if Kierkegaard did not rightly measure the greatness and profundity of the German metaphysician, it remains forever of the utmost importance that in his critique the Christian faith assumed a new weight in opposition to the force exerted by speculation. Modern speculative philosophy has undergone its " last judgment " in Kierkegaard's critique.

We are not permitted to forget the inner defect in so-called Christian philosophy, a defect that brought about the final downfall of that once so powerful movement. And even apart from the fact that religious reasons prevent such a step, we should not try to ignore this downfall by returning to the Middle Ages. There is a deep necessity in the development of thought, a necessity not only of causes and effects but rather of questions and answers, of problems and solutions. The history of philosophy is like a long conversation in which many minds in many periods participate. Although there is much that is accidental in the conversation, and much that is not to the point, still there is an inner consistency and inner progress in its development. Only this conception makes a real history of philosophy possible and meaningful. Hegel was right at least in this respect, although he was not sufficiently critical in his own discussion of historical systems, and was too convinced that the inner necessity of historical development agreed fully with the necessity of his own dialectical method.

The relation between speculation and revelation simply does not allow us to base speculation on revelation, thereby apparently making revelation a principle of speculation. It does not permit us to take from revelation the principles of speculation, as did the Middle Ages until Thomas Aquinas emancipated natural theology, only to substitute the authority of Aristotle for that of revelation. But it does remind us of the limits of speculation, and therefore it furnishes us with the best perspective for the understanding of the history of philosophy.

Ancient speculation did not succeed in thinking out the divine mystery, because the right approach to it is not theoretical, logical, and rational, but is practical, devotional, religious, and spiritual. This fundamental insight makes it plain that the language of the Bible, better than that of philosophic thought, can open the horizon to a legitimate knowledge of the divine, which knowledge serves the moral and religious needs of man and not the impersonal inquiry into an objective truth. It also makes it clear that the epic and the dramatic are the proper medium of communicating the nature of the Ultimate, impenetrable to theoretical analysis and synthesis. The history of philosophic speculation discloses this insight and has therefore to be interpreted from this perspective.

The commonly accepted division of the history of philosophy into three periods is valid only from this perspective, since this very division is based upon the relation between speculation and revelation. Ancient thought developed independently of revelation; medieval thought depended upon revelation; modern thought was built upon the principle of the separation of speculation and revelation or upon the subordination of revelation to speculation. Only this different conception of the relation between speculation and revelation verifies the distinction of these three main epochs and shows thereby that in fact no other perspective can explain and justify the general acceptance of the division.

One might say revelation is the silent and concealed judge of all speculation, precisely because it is not speculative itself, but beyond and above all speculation. Revelation dominates the scene from behind the horizon of thought, just because it can never be resolved into thought. It reveals what cannot be analyzed or demonstrated and what therefore is the supreme basis, the ultimate goal, and the eternal center of all that can be analyzed and demonstrated. Its relation to speculation is therefore paradoxical. Revelation is potent only so long as it is not drawn into the argument; it dominates the field only so long as it does not enter it.

The paradoxical part revelation plays within speculation is definitely corroborated in the three main periods by the different attitude and destiny of thought. Antiquity, completely unaware of revelation, was able to philosophize in the freest and boldest form, but the true God remained hidden. Plato came the nearest to seeing that there was a mystery he could not penetrate. Accordingly, he spoke mysteriously of that supreme but incomprehensible ground, center, and goal of reality, using the form of myth wherever his recognition of the creative purpose of the universe reached its highest peak. Antiquity in its entirety felt that something evaded logical analysis, lying completely beyond speculation. In the Christian epoch (more correctly called " Roman Catholic ") revelation was acknowledged as a source of truth, outshining Greek speculation, and adding the knowledge of that something which Greek thought had tried vainly to grasp. But in that epoch philosophy enjoyed less freedom, displayed less creativity and adventurousness than before or since. In modern times, religiously determined by Protestantism, although not all its great figures were Protestants, philosophy was again free, but not to the same degree as it had been in Greece. For now the truth of revelation was more or less acknowledged and influential, though not in the direct manner of the " Roman Catholic " epoch. While surpassing that of the Middle Ages, speculation was consequently not so original and powerful as it had been in antiquity. Philosophy was most successful and penetrating when it became critical of " pure reason." For then it established its own principle.

It is the incomparable charm and the unique greatness of Greek speculation that the adventure of seeking ultimate truth could be performed without any external or internal hindrance. The Greek mind was entirely free. Hegel has called the state of Hellenic culture the " paradise of mind." This is particularly true with respect to the state of the thinking mind, which, unimpeded by State or Church, was free to investigate and inquire, to argue and assert whatever seemed true to it. Therefore, philosophy flourished, especially at its beginning, in the colonies of Asia Minor and Italy, where these conditions were particularly favorable and where a pioneer spirit was naturally most at home. Athens began to participate in the philosophic conversation only in its later development, making a completely new start with Socrates. Athens began to take part after its democratic institutions had reached their most glorious and powerful zenith.

The character of Greek speculation, though determined by geographical, political, and social conditions, cannot be derived from them, as some historians, notably Theodor Gomperz, have tried to suggest. The " paradise of the mind " originated from the fact that the Greeks philosophized on the basis of their national culture, in an age in which religion had not yet reached the state of Christianity. Their mind was natural and naïve in Schiller's sense of these terms.[5] It was the mind of a people most gifted in cultural activity, especially

[5] Cf. Schiller, *Über naive und sentimentalische Dichtung.*

in the field of artistic creativity. The Greeks were eminently sensitive, that is to say, not sensuous or sensual only, but endowed with the capacity of combining both sensuality and spirituality. Their spirit was bound by their senses, but their sensuality was highly spiritual. They did not yet know the antagonism of the two. And this was the secret of their ingenuity in all realms of cultural activity. But when they were compared with Christian nations, it was also the source of their shortcomings and defects.

The Greek mind was perhaps the most brilliant, most subtle, and most penetrating mind we know, but it was essentially pre-Christian. Greek philosophy derived all its virtues and results from this pre-Christian character. It was sensitive and sensuous, but it was also intellectual and rational, as these contrasting features were combined in their artistic culture. It was thoroughly contemplative, and therefore predestined for speculation. This speculation departed from the visible universe as the natural basis for thought and ascended to the heights of invisible forces controlling and governing the world of sense. Greek philosophy was consequently cosmocentric. It originated from the visible and it issued in the invisible features of the world in which we live as beings endowed with senses, but also with intellect and reason. There was nothing in all Greek speculation that transcended this cosmic whole. The horizon of the cosmos was also the horizon of their thought. Even Plato and Aristotle, for all the intellectual spirituality of their principles and arguments, were rooted in the intuition of that all-embracing totality, perceptible to our senses and comprehensible to our mind. The existence of this comprehensive whole was assumed as self-evident. It was the background, the basis, the final end, of all their philosophic adventures and discoveries.

The Christian mind, on the contrary, was no longer so naïve, natural, aesthetic, and so artistically creative. Rather, it was ruled by the spirit of Biblical revelation. The very first words of the Bible: " In the beginning God created the heaven and the earth," conditioned and governed Christian thought and mastered Christian speculation, if one is permitted to speak about speculation in this new sense. The fundamental character of Christian philosophy has to be understood in the light of the fundamental duality set by the first words of Genesis: the duality of the Creator and the creation, and, within the creation, that of the heaven and the earth. These fundamental opposites forever destroyed the unity of the Greek cosmos. It is amazing that so few words were able and destined to have such a formidable and consequential effect. They completely revolutionized all philosophic categories from top to bottom. Instead of the one cosmos we now have two entities: the world, whether of sense or of intellect, whether sensible or intelligible, and God, who created it and who rules and sustains it. Aristotle had separated the divine mind from the natural world, but, even so, together they form one greater whole, just as the human body and the human soul together form the human entity. Aristotle's god is not the creator of nature but he exists side by side with it. It is the mind of the world, a cosmic mind. The wholeness and unity of the cosmos covers and holds together both world and mind.

The Christian mind is no longer aesthetic, natural, and naïve; it is driven out from the Greek paradise. It knows sin as the barrier between God and man, between the creation and the human creature. The Creator is radically transcendent. He is invisible in a sense not yet conceived by the Greeks. He transcends not only the horizon of the visible universe, but also the horizon of the thinking mind, the horizon of thought. In the natural theology of Aquinas, the character of God as Creator was not comprehended: this theology fell back to Aristotelian and Neoplatonic schemes. Christian philosophy is thoroughly theocentric in a manner that Greek speculation could not have been. God begins and consummates all that is. World and man are absolutely subordinated, without any power that is merely their own. Indeed, God takes the place of what had been the cosmos in Greek speculation. He is the "Cosmos of the cosmos," to use a phrase applied by Clement of Alexandria to the Christian Logos.

According to the Greek mind, the gods and man were merely parts or manifestations of cosmic forces; their existence was entirely immanent within the whole. According to the Christian scheme, the world and men are dependent upon the Creator God and, as Paul said at Athens, in some way they are immanent within his superior being. This is not a pantheistic idea. Rather, world and man, though derived from the will and action of the Creator, nevertheless have a certain independence within the scope of God's omnipotent and ubiquitous spirit. While Greek speculation was cosmomonistic,

Christian philosophy is dualistic. The creation has preserved a remnant of its cosmic glory: it embraces everything created and is in that restricted sense still a whole or a universe, relatively complete in itself and relatively independent. The same is true, and in an even more serious way, with respect to man. He is free to obey or to disobey the will of his Maker and is thus susceptible to temptation.

Whereas Greek speculation was aesthetic and naïve, Christian philosophy is ethical and reflective; it reflects upon man's sinfulness as the source of the evils that befall him and as the dynamics of history guided by God's eternal counsel. While Greek speculation is basically unhistorical, Christian philosophy has a historical outlook. There is a beginning and there is an end of all that is. The creation moves from the one to the other. As God was all in all at the beginning, so he will be all in all at the end. While the Greek cosmos is harmonious and therefore a whole in itself, the Christian scheme shows a certain tension between God and his creation, between God and man.

God is One and everything is created by him and governed by him, but because of the basic duality of Creator and creature, Christian philosophy is not monistic, but dualistic. Greek cosmology, no longer the only center and root of thought, is not entirely eradicated. It continues to exist, though under the ascendancy and control of theology.

Modern philosophy is distinguished from both ancient and Christian (Roman Catholic) philosophy in that it centers in the mind, reason, and consciousness of man. The cosmos, degraded by Christian philosophy to the subordinate place of creation, is now even more degraded; it is conceived as the subhuman section of the universe. It is now made the object of a new science (*scienza nuova*), which controls and construes it by means of mathematical analysis. It now becomes " nature " in the modern sense. The ancient cosmos, demolished to the point where it has even lost its wholeness and unity, disintegrates into an infinity of innumerable worlds (Giordano Bruno). There is, however, still a kind of glory in Bruno's idea of such an infinity: he could still worship this plurality as the mirror and symbol of the spiritual infinity, retained from his Christian faith. But step by step the modern mind dismissed even this remnant of cosmic enthusiasm. It became reconciled to the idea that the world is nothing but matter, mathematically ordered; to be known by means of the correct world equation, comprehending all that is — at least all that is visible, while the invisible part of the ancient cosmos now degenerated into the content of the human mind alone.

Whereas antiquity did not yet envisage revelation in the Biblical sense, and whereas the medieval mind reconciled and even unified revelation and speculation, modern philosophy completely separated these two sources of ultimate truth, leaving revelation to systematic Christian theology and speculation to a metaphysics growing out of the new science of nature. However, this Solomonic judgment dangerously rends the human mind. Neither systematic theology nor scientific metaphysics can find rest with a good intellectual conscience. Metaphysics cannot completely forget the God of revelation and it tries to transform his figure into a rational concept, as Whitehead has recently done. And Christian theology either resigns in a petrified dogmatics or again, following the example of Melanchthon, attempts to recover the synthesis of the Middle Ages, though now on a Protestant level.

The dominant note of modern philosophy is its ambition to vie with the natural sciences in exactitude and rationality. The spirit of ancient philosophy is determined by its aesthetic trend, that of medieval philosophy by its religious origin and that of modern philosophy by its connection with the natural sciences. But in each case the relation between speculation and revelation gives the perspective necessary for an understanding of the whole development and for assessment of the value and function of each period.

SPECULATION

IN

PRE-CHRISTIAN PHILOSOPHY

I

SPECULATION AND THE GREEK MIND

THE connection between speculation and Greek culture in general is very close. No other nation, no other background, no other period in the history of Europe could possibly have produced the same enterprise of philosophic search and venture. Such a speculative surge could arise only in a nation endowed with the same extraordinary gift for imaginative creation, with the political and social background of Greek life, and existing in an age in which both science and religion were rather primitive. To bring about the conditions favorable for the growth of such speculative world explanations as those of the early Ionian thinkers, the mind had to be inclined toward an imaginative production of metaphorical conceptions concerning the powers that determine and rule the visible world; life had to be free enough to permit the development of such conceptions; science had to be in the stage of immaturity, and religion in that of insufficient and unsatisfactory ideas about the deity. Of course these conditions alone could not bring about the wonder of the early systems. In the last analysis its rise simply cannot be explained. Only the unique and astounding genius of the Greeks can account for it — the same genius that produced the greatest fine arts ever seen, the marvel of Homer and all the other early poets, the wisdom of a Solon and a Pericles, and the enormous versatility and sagacity of the people in general.

The basic gift, and the moving force, of Greek culture and of the speculative enterprise itself was the eminent creativity of imagination, which made its religion richer than any other religion, in stories and tales and in the representation of individual gods, half-gods, heroes, and caricatures. It made the political scene as eventful, changing, and exciting as Thucydides describes it. And it made the orators

45

as powerful as Demosthenes. It made their works of art and poetry more consummate and enjoyable than those of any other nation. It made the theater a place where the nation celebrated its greatest creations of imaginative drama and where the people contemplated themselves in the mirror of tragedy and comedy. And for all time it made their scientific and philosophic discoveries and constructions a model of mankind's attempt to find out the truth.

It is hard and perhaps even impossible to realize and to appreciate fully what it meant to initiate the long series of philosophic systems comprising the history of that enterprise. It was in a sense a *creatio ex nihilo*. Although Homer, Hesiod, Solon, and Pindar can be called forerunners of the philosophers, still the gap between their creations and wisdom and the speculative systems is so huge that we are inclined to think of the latter as marking a completely new beginning. But although speculation was something absolutely new, not only in the history of Greek culture, but also in the history of mankind, still this innovation was not inconsistent with the Greek mind; it was in line with the whole trend of their imagination and their creations. In our time this inner coherence of all Greek productions has been strongly brought out, so that the history of philosophy no longer appears as an isolated phenomenon but rather as a link in the context of Greek life and activity in general.[1]

While the peculiarity of the Greek mind was formerly found in its artistic qualities and in the corresponding strength of creative imagination, Werner Jaeger has recently stressed the significance of the polis, the city-state, which enabled the Greeks to act in all the other fields of their civilization, thereby encouraging them to promote scientific investigation and speculative construction, as it had inspired their artistic genius and poetic vision. Undoubtedly the classical view of German humanism almost entirely overlooked this political aspect of Greek culture; it gave an altogether too romantic picture of Greek character and life. Men like Hölderlin glorified and exalted the beauty and splendor of Hellenic existence, entirely omitting the darker aspects of its deeds and morals. Hölderlin is an extreme in

[1] See especially Werner Jaeger, *Paideia;* Herman Fränkel, *Dichtung und Philosophie des frühen Griechentums;* W. Nestle, *Griechische Geistesgeschichte von Homer bis Lukian;* F.-J. V. Rintelen, *Von Dionysos zu Apollo;* Julius Stenzel, *Metaphysik des Altertums;* Fr. Nietzsche, *Early Greek Philosophy* (tr. by Maxim A. Muegge, 1924).

this respect, but it was generally held that the Greeks were the nation of aesthetic idealism, a nation which by its poetic power had beautified everything, even the gloomy facts of life and history. Thus they invented tragedy, which transformed the most gruesome and most villainous actions into an enjoyable spectacle, adorned by the most refined charm of language and the most ingenuous composition of events. They had thereby placated even the most horrible destiny, using it as material for aesthetic pleasure.

To offset this classical glorification, Jacob Burckhardt brought into prominence, in the nineteenth century, the sinister side of Greek life and politics. Without any mitigation he exposed the cruelty, barbarism, and superstition of its religious life, social conditions, and customs. And this darker aspect counterbalanced the beauty and fascination of its artistic works and the spiritual prominence of its philosophic systems. Werner Jaeger, Julius Stenzel, and others, though influenced by this more realistic interpretation and estimation, began to inquire into the Greek scene *sine ira et studio,* without any prejudice. They soon discovered that the political, moral, and educational conditions are the presuppositions and the roots of the greatness of the Greeks. To gain a fair and correct picture of the Greek mind and culture, they should be put in the foreground. Jaeger even goes so far as to assert that philosophy sprang directly from the Greek life in the polis, from its laws and its social activities. He insists that cosmocentric intuition did not originate in the observation of the visible universe, but rather in the contemplation of the social community. " The center of gravity of Greek life lies in the polis. It is the polis which includes and defines every form of social and intellectual activity. In early Greek history, every branch of intellectual life grows straight from the same root, the life of the community. . . . Thus to describe the Greek polis is to describe the whole of Greek life." [2] Referring to the famous fragment of Anaximander concerning the justice done to all things according to the order of time, Jaeger writes: " This is the origin of the philosophical idea of the cosmos: for the word originally signifies the right order in a state or other community." Anaximander projected the idea of a political cosmos upon the whole of nature. Here " we can see the close connection between the origins of Ionian philosophy and the birth of the consti-

[2] *Paideia,* I (1945), p. 78.

tutional city-state." [3] Dike (Justice) is older than Logos (Reason).

I do not dare to contradict so great an authority as Jaeger. His arguments are as persuasive as his statements are learned and eloquent. He is certainly right in tracing Greek accomplishments back to their political institutions and to their community spirit. Pericles in his funeral speech, as reported by Thucydides, emphasized the same point. It is the city that he praises for all the glory that meant Athenian culture. The city has provided the means for the mind to refresh itself. The city, Pericles says in his oration, celebrates games and sacrifices. "We throw open our city to the world, and never by alien acts exclude foreigners from any opportunity of learning or observing, although the eyes of an enemy may occasionally profit by our liberality, trusting less in system and policy than to the native spirit of our citizens; while in education, where our rivals from their very cradles by a painful discipline seek after manliness, at Athens we live exactly as we please. . . . In short, I say, as a city we are the school of Hellas. . . ." [4] Who can doubt that this proud declaration was not an empty boast but corresponded exactly with the facts?

The question about the origin of speculation, however, cannot rest upon the historical conditions that made its rise possible and real. The liberality of the city-state fostered intellectual and artistic life, but the intellectual and artistic mind of the Ionians and Athenians in turn also fostered liberality and democratic institutions. It would be hazardous to decide which of the two was more original, the primary cause of material and spiritual wealth. My problem is not solely and primarily concerned with temporal causality and sequence, but rather with the deepest root of all Greek creations and accomplishments, especially with the root of speculation, which undoubtedly arose only within the city-state and was protected by its wealth and power. In that sense the polis is older than philosophy. But is it not possible that both the city and philosophy were equally rooted in a common spirit, also manifested in religion, the fine arts, poetry, music, the epic, and the drama? And is it not probable that, as the German classicists asserted, aesthetic imagination and contemplation is the fundamental tendency responsible for the most outstanding qualities of the Greeks in all realms? Is it not probable that even the peculiar political acumen and versatility originated from the same artistic abilities that led

[3] *Loc. cit.*, p. 110.   [4] Book II, ch. VI.

to the creation of works called "artistic" in the proper sense? Dike was older than Logos . . . but was not Logos already operative in what religion called Dike, and was not Dike called Dike precisely because the poetic imagination of Hesiod had personified the spirit of Justice?

Greek culture was not so disintegrated and divided as modern culture. Its ramifications and manifestations shared a common ground. The opposition between the gods and man in Greek thought was not yet so radical as the contrast between God and man in the Biblical faith. Analogously, the contrast between revelation and speculation had not yet appeared within the Greek mind; the Greeks still lived in a spiritual paradise completely unaware of the Fall and of sin, of Satan and hell. Likewise, the various realms and spheres of spiritual activity were not yet so dissipated and so autonomous as in the modern age. Culture in all its directions was one great substantial whole. Politics and religion, the arts and the sciences were bound together by the same mind, as the melodies in a composition and the colors in a picture.

It is not by chance that the preceding metaphorical expressions are taken from the sphere of the arts. Jaeger is undoubtedly right in maintaining that the city harbored the arts and sciences, as it harbored industry, and labor, craft, engineering, education, and administration. In a certain sense the state completely represented the totality of culture. Nevertheless, this totality cannot be called political with the same justification as it can be called "artistic," in the peculiar Greek sense of the term. That culture was integrated, still united in its inner mind; that the Greeks were still religiously and morally naïve, points to the aesthetic element as the most substantial and all-uniting root of their entire "cosmos." Jaeger may be correct in holding that this most characteristic word first signified the community as such; nevertheless, the word also had an aesthetic meaning.[5] Of course the city, inasmuch as it was well ordered, could be called a cosmos, but it was the element of good order that generated this application, not the specifically political order.[6] The various

[5] The lexicon of Liddell and Scott translates *kosmos* first as "order" and second as "ornament, decoration, embellishment." It registers this second meaning as already present in Homer and Hesiod.

[6] "The polis," Plato insists, is "the image of the most beautiful and best life" (*Laws*, VII, ch. 19, p. 817B).

kinds of order were not so differentiated as they are today. The political order was at the same time the order of religion. Both were ordered by institutions and procedures in which the arts and artistic customs played an important part, e.g., festivals, the chorus, solemn processions, and so on.

The aesthetic is closely united with the natural and the naïve. In the aesthetic sphere the mind is a totality, not yet split up into sensuality and spirituality, perception and conception, contemplation and action. It is a contemplative activity that generates poetry and works of art. This contemplative activity was, I take it, at the bottom of all the Greeks thought, felt, desired, and did, as a nation. From this basic and deepest source sprang speculation. There is a striking kinship between artistic contemplation, scientific observation, and philosophic speculation, all of which presuppose and manifest an impersonal, disengaged, objective, or " theoretical " attitude of the mind. It is remarkable that even in the field of politics, where passion and interests are in the foreground, only seldom regulated by wisdom and prudence, these properties played an important role in Athenian conduct, as the figures of Solon and Pericles show, and as is proved by the amazingly objective historical picture given by Thucydides. The stark poetical trait in Greek religion points to the same basic attitude disclosed by the artistic perfection of their religious statues and temples.

Speculation is the daughter of religion. It could best develop in a nation whose religion was so freely enriched by imagination. Speculation continued, though on another level and in another direction, what religious imagination had begun. As Homer and Hesiod had " speculated " in poetic fashion about the gods, their deeds, passions, quarrels, plots, friendship, and enmity with men, so the philosophers speculated, not without a considerable amount of free imagination, about the forces symbolically represented by the gods. In their own rational way the philosophers wanted to rectify and to deepen the stories about the gods. But the contemplative attitude applied to this new purpose had been applied by their forerunners to the biography and theogony of the divine personages. It was the same mythical medium through which the philosophers approached religious truth, only now rationalized and scientifically controlled. Here I fully agree with Jaeger when he says: " There is no discontinuity between Ionian natural philosophy and the Homeric epics. . . . Actually it is not easy to say how the Homeric idea that ocean is the origin of everything differs from the doctrine of Thales that water is the basic principle of the universe. Hesiod's *Theogony*, again, is a rational system, deliberately built by logical inquiry into the origin and nature of the world. Yet within that system the old force of mythological thought is still active: it lives on in what we think of as 'scientific' philosophy, in the work of Ionian 'physicists'; and without it we could not explain the astonishing ability of the early scientific age to create great new philosophical systems." [7]

Indeed, Hesiod is a transition between the epic and the speculative systems. He is not so epical as Homer; Hesiod's interest is not merely in the narrative, it is already quasi-scientific, the interest of a man who wants to know the truth about the gods without the interference of fanciful stories and novel embellishment. But Hesiod did not fully attain this end and perhaps he did not desire to do so. Unlike Thales, he was not yet a rational thinker but was still something of a poet. It is not to be overlooked, however, that Thales was still influenced by his forerunners.

Thales' Water is by no means a chemical element; it is, as it were, a mythical water that mysteriously transforms itself into all the other materials of the physical world. Thales could not possibly have observed, even less experimented, in order to reach his conclusion that water is the arche, the original substance of all that is. He depended rather upon his imagination, though based probably on some observations; in a bold stroke of the mind he pronounced water to be what he was seeking for: the ground of the universe, the first cause of the spectacle that unfolds before our eyes.

Even so Thales' advance is enormous, creating a gulf between himself and Hesiod that is not to be ignored. What tremendous boldness! Imagine proclaiming one of the visible things in this visible world to be the invisible force behind the scenes. Although perhaps without reflecting explicitly upon the degree of conjecture implied, his thesis amounted to the daring assertion that the human mind is able to discover such a secret force, thereby transcending all perception and all sense experience. Thales could not have thought that sense experience alone provided a basis for his discovery. The au-

[7] *Paideia*, I (1945), p. 151.

dacity in proclaiming something resembling water, which we can perceive, to be the Absolute (even though he did not yet know that term) is so enormous that it defies all explanation, psychological or otherwise.

Speculation is a completely new branch of the tree of Greek imagination and contemplation, but it is also a branch of the same tree on which had previously grown mythical religion, in its poetical and artistic richness. To understand the " birth of speculation from the spirit of myth " one other link, namely, science, must be interposed between poetical stories and artistic portraits of the mythical gods and the speculative activity of the first metaphysicians. The role of science in the development of Ionian natural philosophy has often been exaggerated to an extent leading to incorrect interpretations, as I shall subsequently show; nevertheless, science was a stage in the development of speculation.

Speculation might even be defined as a scientific, i.e., methodical, rational, and conceptual, transformation of religious images. In the Greek epoch this led to a radical demolition and complete abolition of the traditional religion, whereas, in the epoch of Roman Catholic Christianity it led to a defense of the faith, partially based on Greek speculation, by means of dogmas and dogmatic theology. Greek religion was not sublime and ethical enough to withstand the corroding influence of speculation, and was, therefore, finally destroyed by it. Speculation, being more spiritual in intent than mythical religion, was victorious in the end. Unlike its Biblical counterpart, mythical religion did not furnish the human mind and heart with a deity that could satisfy the demands of moral purity and holiness. The mythical gods, though adorned by fantasy and artistic creativity, were nevertheless feeble in a religious and metaphysical respect. Like all other beings and entities, they were intracosmic; indeed, except for their immortality, they were not much elevated above the human plane. And even their immortality was a questionable endowment if we consider their frailty and imperfection. It was not a true and spiritual infinity of mind, character, and intellect, but was rather a semieternal everlasting finitude.

Compared with gods so weak and finite, the speculative concept of the cosmos, probably first pronounced by Anaximander, was by far superior. Polytheism, because of the personality of its gods, is in a sense more akin to Biblical monotheism than is pantheism. It is in this respect more genuinely religious, but pantheism is more sublime and majestic. The cosmos surpasses at least all things finite. In this respect it resembles the Creator God even more than Zeus, who lacked omniscience, and who in spite of physical power possessed a character that was by no means a model of self-control and inner strength. The cosmos at least transcends everything else. It is omnipotent and eternal in a sense in which the immortal gods are not.[8] Even in the Bible, in spite of the personality of its God, there is a drop of pantheism. Some of the psalms, The Book of Job, and the Logos of the Fourth Gospel strongly bring out this element.[9]

Cosmocentric speculation was originally based upon the perception of the physical world surrounding us, especially upon the perception of the immense vault of the sky, which even prompted a Kant to exclaim that the starry heavens above arouse as much admiration and veneration as the moral law within the human mind. This sublimity, felt by everyone today not yet corrupted by astronomical theory, generated cosmocentric speculation. If Jaeger is right in saying that the word "cosmos" was first applied to the city-community, a new and decisive step was taken when speculation transferred this term and its meaning to the universe. Only then did it take on the new significance that created cosmological metaphysics. Then for the first time it received metaphorical connotation in comparison with the political unit, thereby making it a speculative term. The political cosmos was *only then* exalted to the level of the All.

That this term had the origin attributed to it by Jaeger is nevertheless of importance. For it reminds us that the cosmos was not only the physical world, but had from the beginning a richer and deeper content, including all that man can think of, appreciate, live for, and admire, love, and revere. The cosmos was not only material and physical, but it was also an ethical and a spiritual entity, in all respects supreme and all-embracing.

Therefore, it might be perfectly true that the concept of the cosmos, as Anaximander understood it, had the connotation of a vast com-

[8] Heraclitus emphasized that the "cosmos is the same for all and that neither one of the gods nor of men has made it, but that it was always" (Fr. 30). Notice that Heraclitus puts men on the same level as the gods, if compared with the cosmos transcending both.

[9] Cf. Allan G. Galloway, *The Cosmic Christ.* 1951.

munity to which the gods as well as man belonged. A famous passage in Plato's *Gorgias* suggests this origin of the idea of the cosmos: "Some wise men tell us that friendship and community and order-liness (*kosmiotes*) and moderation bind together heaven and earth, gods and men, and that this whole is therefore called order (*kosmos*), not disorder (*akosmia*)."[10] These words show at least that from the beginning, ethical, political, and social relations were included in the concept of the All; the very feeling of friendship was regarded as the bond that holds together all that is.[11]

The idea of the cosmos, however, not only had such an ethical significance, but it was also attractive in an aesthetic sense. It furnished the human mind with the means to gather together in the image of one great unity the vast variety of visible and invisible contents of the human experience. This function of the term agreed with the basic attitude of the Greeks. The order to which it points and which it expresses was the order of beauty. This order, even more than the excellence of sublimity, best corresponded to the fundamental valuation of their mind. If the word "divine" points to the highest value, then beauty had to be regarded as divine. But only Plato abstractly conceived of the beautiful as being the highest. In the beginning of Greek speculation (and, indeed, throughout its development) the cosmos took the place of that which is beautiful in an ultimate and unsurpassable sense.

Although the Greeks officially and explicitly worshiped gods, secretly and implicitly they worshiped beauty as the most divine thing in the world. Only because they cherished this valuation, could they indulge in so many tales and legends about the gods. Only because in their hearts they venerated beauty, could they tolerate the moral weakness and even wickedness of their gods. Only because they regarded the beautiful as the height of all that is desirable, admirable, and venerable could they revere a poet as greatly as they revered Homer. Homer could, therefore, take the place assumed by the Bible in Christian nations. Indeed, Homer was their Bible. Homer was not simply enjoyed and esteemed as Shakespeare or Goethe, but he was supposedly the wisest teacher, possessing the sum total of all knowl-

---

[10] P. 508.

[11] Jaeger mentions that the idea of the cosmos began to hold sway in Homer (*Paideia*, I, p. 35).

edge of the gods and the human soul.[12]

What we need is a word to designate the world depicted by Homer, a world in which everything was so similar to everything else that it could be described by a simile. In the world of Homer, nature and man so resemble each other that a metaphor is the most beautiful and also the most adequate expression of the essence of both. In Homer's world, the gods are as natural as man and man is as divine as the gods; beauty reigns as the supreme standard, the secret spirit directing and controlling both verse and the conveyed content. To grasp such a world what better term could come to our minds than the word that speculation chose to signify the All, namely, the word " cosmos "? Indeed, this world was the prototype of what the early cosmologists meant. Homer in this sense was as cosmocentric as Anaximander, Heraclitus, Xenophanes, and Parmenides.

Beauty is the key to the understanding of the mentality of the Greek world. Winckelmann, Lessing, Goethe, and Hegel were right in their synoptic vision, although modern science rightly corrected their all too optimistic conception of what the Greeks have really been in their behavior, habits, and their social and political life. One has to distinguish their deeds and conduct from their ideals and values. The classical view did not sufficiently respect this distinction and therefore failed to see the full truth about the Greeks. But the classicists had the imagination and inspiration to envisage the order of values the Greeks bore in their hearts. Beauty was the real and the most powerful deity that they worshiped and adored. Their official gods were nothing but the visible form in which they tried to express their inner cult of beauty. Hegel has described the religion of the Greeks as the religion of beauty. In essence he is right. This was their religion, its substance and its core. When the early philosophers exalted the cosmos as the sum total of all that is, when they tried to understand and to conceive its constitution, they worshiped the old deity. The cosmos was the speculative concept of beauty in its actual power and concrete existence; it was beauty as a divine being or entity, embracing all beings and all entities.

Of course, beauty had not yet connoted the modern notion of a

[12] " Poetry was at no time a more urgent need on the earth because the minstrels alone could give an account of the things divine," Jacob Burckhardt says in his *Lectures on the History of Greek Culture.*

special value. It was not yet separated from other values, but was on the contrary the highest value only because it comprised within itself all other values, as the cosmos comprised all other things. The Greeks were the "paradisaical" nation, precisely because they so deeply and sincerely believed beauty to be the essence and substance of all values and even of all things. But this was made conscious only by Plato. Up to him the cosmos took the place of absolute beauty and the absolutely beautiful. On the background of this idea, the poet could play with the stories and adventures of the gods and the sculptor could build his beautiful figures with the certainty that if he did not portray actual beings, he at least depicted their essence in an imaginary form. This unconscious and unexpressed belief was the silent presupposition of Greek religion and Greek art. This secret pantheism behind the overt polytheism came to the fore when the speculative thinkers first conceived of the cosmos as the true reality, revealing thereby the innermost core of the Greek mind and of all its productions and creations. The silent power that had inspired mythological imagination, and had evoked the vast multiplicity of mythological figures and their illustrations in stone and metal, was now made to speak by the philosophers in lucid concepts, transforming the half-mythical vision of the cosmos into the rational language of the logos.

Speculation, the daughter of poetical and mythological fancy and of methodical thinking, is the outcome of a synthesis between an intuitive and an analytical, an imaginative and a critical, activity. More correctly it is an analytical operation that thinks out an underlying intuition. The intuitive object is the cosmos, the beautiful whole of all that is. A thinker analyzes this totality, thereby forming conceptual elements which supposedly constitute and hold together the cosmic All. This analysis led first to the concept of the arche. And this primary and principal element had two functions: to express the essence of the All, and to express the unity of all things. (The discussion of this process and its results will be treated subsequently.)

What is commonly called "pantheism" was never, and could never be, a deification of every detail isolated from the whole. It was rather the deification of the whole. And this deification was the consequence of the worship of beauty. For the whole was contemplated as a whole only because all its parts were regarded as fitting with each other in the way in which the parts of a poem or of a statue fit into the whole work and into the imaginary world therein presented. The secret of the cosmic whole was consciously and fully expressed in the idea of cosmic harmony, as proclaimed by the Pythagoreans; in the idea of a quasi-spherical perfection, as proclaimed by Parmenides; and in the enthusiastic words of Heraclitus: " To the god all things are beautiful and good and just." [13] But it was already unconsciously at work when Homer used his similes and comparisons to show that all things form one great whole, united by their inner and essential kinship. Homer thereby practiced the twofold function of the arche, by which it reveals the essence and the unity of all things belonging to the same underlying totality, a totality in itself beautiful and illuminating the beauty of its every part.

Cosmocentric speculation might be called the private religion of some lonely thinkers who, no longer satisfied with the popular religion of their nation, dared to express what they thought was the essence of religion and its full truth, when the latter is translated from the imaginative language of mythology into the rational or logical language of philosophic thought. But this private religion was in fact the tacit core of the official religion. The Greeks worshiped beauty, whether found in the music of the official dance chorus performing at solemn occasions or in the minstrel songs of the festivals. They worshiped the beauty of the semireligious performances of the theater, instructing them about the government of the world, mirrored in the life, and destiny of kings and heroes. They worshiped the beauty of the marvelous buildings, symbolizing the power and grandeur of their state as much as they served the public cult of the gods. They paid homage to beauty when they took part in the games, exhibiting the physical beauty of the body as well as the moral energy and mobility of the soul. The religion of cosmic beauty was in this sense in no wise private but shared by every Greek; it was the religion of the nation at large, though expressed (and consistently so) by the beautiful in public religion and art.

There is a legendary story (probably of a later origin) that Homer and Hesiod were engaged in a contest in which Hesiod asked Homer to tell him what he thought was the most beautiful to man. Homer is said to have answered in the following way: " When mirth reigns throughout the town, and feasters about the house sit in order to

[13] Fr. 102.

listen to a minstrel; when the tables beside them are laden with bread and meat, and a wine-bearer draws sweet drink from the mixing bowl and fills the cups: This I think in my heart to be most beautiful." The Greek word for " beautiful " (*kalon*) also means, characteristically, " delightful." The historian who records this story adds: " This answer was so admired by the Greeks as to be called ' golden ' by them, and even now at public sacrifices all the guests solemnly recite it before feasts and libations." [14]

I have quoted this story in full because, even though its historical truth is null, I deem it an excellent statement of the general mood and predilection of the Greeks, indicating the esteem in which the poets stood and how the Greeks loved and enjoyed poetry most of all. It summarizes what I have called (with Hegel) the paradise of their mind, their naïveté, their unbroken and aesthetic feeling toward life, and their unofficial but nevertheless very real religion of beauty. It might be instructive to compare such a statement with verses of the Hebrew prophet Amos, which are equally indicative of the Biblical spirit: " I hate, I despise your feasts [says the Lord], and I take no delight in your solemn assemblies. Even though you offer me your burnt offerings . . . , I will not accept them. . . . Take away from me the noise of your songs; to the melody of your harps I will not listen. But let justice roll down like waters, and righteousness like an ever-flowing stream " (Amos 5:21–24).

Perhaps one might object to the comparison of the legend of Homer with the words of Amos on the ground that the legend mirrors popular feelings, whereas the words of Amos express the judgment of a prophet. Such an objection cannot be denied, but it does not invalidate my argument. The popular feelings were expressed according to the legend by no less a personage than Homer, and Homer took the place of a prophet amongst the Greeks; in contrast, the words of Amos, though probably very unpopular, nevertheless express in a striking fashion the spirit of Biblical religion. That the contrast between popular feelings and Homer was not so great as the contrast between man and the Holy Bible is just the point of significance. Only in an age and in a nation as naïve and unbroken as the age and the nation of the Greeks can such harmony exist be-

[14] *Hesiod, The Homeric Hymns and Homerica*, p. 573. The Loeb Classical Library, 1926.

tween the spirit of the greatest of their poets and that of the people, a harmony between the sensuous and spiritual pleasure, between the " will " of the gods and the desire of man. The disharmony between these spheres, on the other hand, illustrates the " break " that underlies the Biblical outlook and message. The difference between Hellenic imagination and God's revelation is illuminated by confronting the Homeric legend and the prophetic announcement.

If any philosopher can be considered a kind of prophet it is Socrates (as we shall see later). And yet the distance between him and a Biblical prophet is enormous. Socrates calls philosophy the noblest music [15] and he himself is called by Plato " the true musician," " attuned to a fairer harmony than that of the lyre or any pleasant instrument of music." [16]

Plato gives the most conspicuous and impressive account of the Greek mind and its " way of life " when he exclaims: " Let our artists be those who are gifted to discern the true nature of the beautiful and the graceful: then will our youth dwell in a land of health and fair sights and sounds, and receive the good in everything; and beauty, the effluence of fair works, shall flow into the eye and ear, like a health-giving breeze from a purer religion, and insensibly draw the soul from earliest years into likeness and sympathy with the beautiful Logos." [17] The inner concord between the religion of beauty and the spirit of speculation could not have been expressed more admirably and more eloquently.

[15] *Phaedo,* p. 61.   [16] *Laches,* p. 188.   [17] *Republic,* III, p. 401.

II

PREPARATION OF THE GOSPEL

I N the fourth century the Church historian Eusebius wrote a book
entitled *Preparation of the Gospel* in which he recorded the religious and philosophical views of the heathen and laid bare their
deficiencies and fallacies. He then showed the superiority of the Bible
and how the Old Testament prepared for the coming of Christ.
And about a hundred years earlier Clement of Alexandria recognized that Greek thought and poetry were not simply defective and
mistaken; they also prepared the way for Biblical faith and the Logos
of the gospel. In his *Exhortations to the Greeks,* Clement rejected
their religious idolatry, but he emphasized that Homer, Hesiod,
Sophocles, Euripides, Socrates, Plato, and many others had had a
presentiment of Biblical truth and some inkling of the living God. In
fact, some of the most ancient thinkers had severely criticized the
mythical gods. And even before Clement, Justin Martyr had
pointed out the same fact. In the age of the apostles, Paul in his
speech at Athens had intimated that by worshiping an " unknown
God " the Greeks somehow admitted that they did not know the
true God. Thus they negatively anticipated revelation.

A seemingly impossible chasm exists between the Greek spirit of
contemplation and the Biblical spirit of action and active faith, between speculation and revelation. And yet the Greeks themselves
have built a connecting link. From the perspective of the entire development of Western history the mission of Greek speculation was
to bring about the destruction of the popular religion, thereby paving
the way for the recognition of the Lord of the Bible. This is the
great tendency of the history of Greek philosophy. If measured
solely in terms of culture, it is a tragic story. The downfall of the
original religion involved the downfall of the entire structure of

Aristotle, upon the duality of form and matter. But even the latter distinction was not satisfactory as an ultimate and definitive solution. For what is the origin of this duality? Is there any way to trace it back to an original unity? And how can the concept of this original unity be gained, since unity is logically the opposite of duality or plurality? All these grave and central questions brought about the final ruin of speculation and coerced the mind to accept another source of truth. The immediate cause of the " degeneration " of philosophy in the final stage of Greek development was an impasse inherent in speculation. Its decline was not due to a lack of great figures or a lack of new creativity. The Hellenic Logos was thus eventually transformed into the Christian Logos.

Speculation and revelation were related to each other, even though revelation played only a negative role in this development. The power of revelation was present from the very beginning, when speculation set out to gain knowledge of the divine, although this power was not yet known as that of revelation. There was within speculation a kind of substitute for revelation, namely, intuition as contrasted with analysis. This intuition was determined by the spirit of the speculative enterprise, i.e., by the spirit of pantheism, which alone corresponded with the source out of which speculation developed, the aesthetic contemplation of the All.

Thus speculation became both the scourge and the cure of a morally and spiritually insufficient religion, a religion relying too much upon human imagination, permeated too much by poetic fancy and artistic images — a religion too naïve and too aesthetic to fulfill the deepest needs of the human heart. But in the end the remedy did not cure radically enough. It was itself prompted by the sickness and it depended upon the spirit that had caused the illness. The religion of the cosmos and of beauty suffered from, and even exaggerated, the very same deficiencies that had restricted the religious value of paganism: it was mainly contemplative, intuitive, speculative, theoretical — an impersonal, intellectual, detached, disinterested, unexistential approach toward the divine mystery. The one-sidedness of the mythological religion could not be remedied by the equally one-sided speculative cosmotheism. This cosmotheism was even more impersonal, more critical and less fanciful, than mythical religion had been.

But in spite of the common denominator of mythology and speculation, there was one great superiority in the logical power of philosophy: its method of analysis and distinction could clarify the issues and thus purify the mind. In that sense philosophy could and
did purge paganism and prepare for the gospel. Tragically it undermined the national soil out of which all the marvelous works of the
Greeks had sprung, out of which philosophy itself had drawn its
strength. In the final analysis it undermined itself. But at the same
time it ripened the capacity of the mind to submit to an instruction
of a higher sort. It matured the religious consciousness to the point
where it could realize that it is wiser to obey the commandments
of a holy God and to appeal to his mercy and grace than to seek to
penetrate to the depths of the deity by theoretical thought. It is to
the eternal glory of Plato that, though representing the unimpeded
confidence of speculation, he nevertheless strongly felt its limitations.
Aristotle, in contrast, fell victim to the temptation of rationalizing
the divine being. Instead of being content to venerate and fear, obey
and love, worship and respect the supreme wisdom, he transformed
it into the content of a metaphysical concept of a pseudo-theological
speculation.

One may boldly affirm that if the thinking mind, the faculty of
speculation, were able to penetrate the divine mystery, Greek as-
siduity, sagacity, profundity, and acumen would have performed
this most desired task. There is a kind of affinity between logical
clarity and moral purity, between speculative profundity and spiritual
sublimity, between the truth attainable by thought and the truth
revealed by God. And to the extent of this affinity, the Greek thinkers
did attain knowledge of the divine being. To that degree Plato
advanced in the direction of revelation. The more consistently speculation proceeded, the more logical its arguments, the more did philosophical concepts approximate to the incomprehensible. There is
an inner coincidence between the truth of one realm and that of
another. What is true in thought cannot be false in faith. And, therefore, as far as thought could go in the right direction, it went at the
same time in the direction of the true faith. It failed only when it
transgressed its limits. But it had to transgress as long as it was
young and naïve, keen on discovering the full, the absolute truth.
Only the experience of uncrossable boundaries could finally break

the uncritical courage and the impetuosity of the speculative adventurer. It was the function and mission of skepticism in the last period of ancient thought to achieve this end.

Clement of Alexandria stated that the Greeks saw the truth " as in a dream." [2] This vision could be attained because of the identity of truth. The limitation of human thought justifies the words of Paul that the wisdom of man is foolishness in the eyes of God, while God's own wisdom appears to man as foolishness. And yet history proves that human wisdom is an avenue toward revealed wisdom. To be sure, the avenue of human thought does not lead to an encounter with the living God. It ends in a blind alley. But man had to enter that alley until he realized that it was blind. Only then was he prepared to receive the message from above. It would be more to the point to say that the Greeks saw the truth, not in a dream, but in the shadow of abstraction. They could not attain to the living God, because this shadow is not the original, not even its concrete image.

Speculation can never be a substitute for religion. Even on the lowest level of superstition and idolatry, religion implies a personal relationship between man and the gods. Speculation, on the contrary, implies an impersonal comprehension or vision and an understanding by critical analysis. It leads, therefore, to an abstract relation between the thinking mind and the Absolute, as its object. The relationship remains abstract and rational even if the Absolute is conceived of by an Aristotle or a Hegel as an absolute or cosmic mind. Man cannot pray to the absolute mind when comprehending it in a conceptual form. He must then make it the object of philosophic intellection and theoretical inquiry. The cosmic mind thus conceived is not God, not even a god: cosmic religion is not properly a religion. Speculation had, therefore, to be frustrated in the end. Parmenides and, in the most subtle and sophisticated way, Hegel both wrongly maintained that the inner unity of the abstract and the concrete could be created by means of speculative method in an abstract, conceptual manner. Such was the erroneous prejudice of all metaphysical theology, and over this prejudice it finally stumbled.

[2] He took this word probably from a passage in Plutarch's *De Isis et Osiris:* " The souls of men while on earth encumbered by bodies and passions can have no companionship with God except in so far as they get a dim dream of him aided by philosophy."

Cosmic religion is impersonal and pantheistic. The mythical gods, in contrast, although the imaginative, poetic, and artistic element predominated in pagan religion, were still the personal gods of religion. To that degree, they were real and alive in the heart of the believer. It was the tragic fate of speculation that it had to decompose and sacrifice the truly religious element, the living relationship between the person and his god, in order to purge the traditional cult by means of theoretical criticism and analysis. Speculation could purify the conception of the deity, but it had thereby to deprive the deity of its religious reality, its power over the human heart and will.

A strange tension existed between the wickedness of the gods as depicted in many stories and drama and the devotion of men less wicked than the gods, at least in their standards of conduct and in their consciousness of ethical norms. An even stranger tension existed between the poetic and artistic liberty of inventing new myths and building new and ever more beautiful statues of the gods, and the sincere piety of the common man in this pagan community of Ionian and Athenian culture. Only a spiritually naïve nation was able to unite these seemingly contradictory features and to adhere to such a union, until the philosophers, by their criticism, and such poets as Euripides, by scornful invective and bitter aspersions, finally destroyed it.

Euripides, like the Sophists, was a confused and somewhat cynical critic, but the censure of philosophers like Xenophanes, Heraclitus, Empedocles, and Plato was seriously motivated by a profound ethical indignation. The latter were honestly convinced that speculative logic could purify the traditional cult by creating higher conceptions. Such philosophers were convinced of the affinity of the logically and the ethically pure; pure thought was allied with pure faith, abstraction and divinity have something in common. The philosophers had good reasons to believe in this inner alliance. Biblical faith also includes a tendency to abstraction. The great sublimity, majesty, and holiness of the Lord God of the Old Testament is because he is so abstracted from the earthly sphere of human life, so rigidly separated from the temporal scene of human frailty and imperfection. This abstract character is at the root of the basic difference between his exalted figure and the earthly figures of the Greek gods. It is the essence of his absolute transcendence, so radically different from the immanent and half-human images of Greek mythological fancy.

The philosophers moved toward the Biblical primacy of the ethical in its contest with the aesthetic. They moved in the direction of a more rigorous separation of "flesh" and spirit, of man and God, of the temporal and the eternal, a separation achieved by means of logical distinction, but also making for the truth of revelation. Speculation thus "prepared" for the gospel. It pointed to the transcendence of the Highest without fully arriving at the Biblical starting point. The employment of logic simultaneously enhanced the ethical standards of religion and applied the latter to the representation of the divine. This trend culminated in Plato. It set in with Xenophanes and Heraclitus. Xenophanes did not yet announce the God of Genesis,[3] but he had an intuition of the oneness and spirituality of the Biblical Creator. "There is one god, the greatest amongst gods and men, not resembling the mortals in figure or in thinking. . . . He sets in motion the All without any toil, by the power of his mind alone.[4] What a sublime image! While preserving a Homeric trait, it reminds one of the psalms. It represents a striking synthesis of Greek and Biblical insight, before Biblical insight was brought to the Greeks.[5]

As various historians[6] have pointed out, early Greek thinkers had a definite theology. The sources are too scarce and too unreliable to indicate certainly whether Thales identified his supreme principle, Water, with the supreme god. But probably in an imaginative manner, permitting also a kind of panpsychism, Thales thought of water as being divine and the creative power of everything else. Xenophanes, a theorist inflamed by the repulsiveness of popular and poetic pictures of the gods, eagerly sought to deprive the latter of their anthropomorphic and finite features. Satirically he said, "If the oxen and lions had hands and could paint and build works like man, they would certainly paint their gods, giving them bodies according to

[3] Cf. Jacob Freudenthal, *Über die Theologie des Xenophanes*, 1886.

[4] Frs. 23 and 25.

[5] About the same time the lyrical poet Simonides wrote verses resembling the psalms. See Herman Fränkel, *loc. cit.*, pp. 392 f.

[6] Notably: Edward Caird, *The Evolution of Theology in the Greek Philosophers*, 1904; James Adam, *The Religious Teachers of Greece*, 1909; Hershel Moore, *The Religious Thought of the Greeks*, 1925; Werner Jaeger, *The Theology of the Early Greek Philosophers*, 1947.

their own form."[7] Nevertheless, the inconsistency mentioned above is to be found even in him. In spite of his criticism, he also paid homage to the gods of the national religion, as his word demonstrates: "It is good always to pay careful respect to the gods."[8] But he especially blamed Homer and Hesiod for having "ascribed to the gods all things that are a shame and disgrace among men."[9]

Xenophanes' zeal for ethical purity joins his zeal for logical abstraction and prompts him to pronounce a kind of monotheism. Heraclitus followed in his footsteps. He also scorns the artistic sensuality of the gods, thereby approaching the Biblical condemnation of the making of graven images or of worshiping wood and stone (Ezek. 20:32). He exclaims: "They pray to these statues, as if a man would converse with buildings; for they know not the true nature of gods."[10] In his early essay on *The Spirit of Christianity,* Hegel takes the part of Greek religion and the adoration of beauty. He speaks ironically of the Old Testament Israelites who did not understand and appreciate the aesthetic note in pagan idolatry and polytheism: "An image of God was just stone or wood to them; 'it sees not,' 'it hears not,' and so on; with such a litany they fancy themselves wonderfully wise; they despise the image . . . and they have no inkling of its deification in the enjoyment of beauty or in a lover's intuition."[11] Unwittingly Hegel is here more Greek than the Greek philosophers who shared the Biblical feeling and reproached their nation for worshiping "stones and wood." While the Greeks prepared for the gospel, Hegel, at this stage of his development, would have gone back to the "paradise of the mind"!

Empedocles, like Xenophanes and Heraclitus, repudiated the mythical gods for the same reason, and with the same emphasis upon the spirituality of the true god, "who is not to be seen or to be grasped with our hands."[12] "His ineffable, holy mind rushes with swift thoughts through the whole cosmos."[13] Here one can learn that the cosmocentric, pantheistic speculation did not exclude the idea

[7] Fr. 15.

[8] Fr. 1, v. 24. His "monotheism" was in fact a monarchic polytheism.

[9] Fr. 11.

[10] Fr. 5.

[11] *Early Theological Writings,* tr. by T. M. Knox, pp. 191 f.

[12] Fr. 133.

[13] Fr. 134.

of a mind immanent within the whole. The early (pre-Socratic) philosophers were by no means naturalists, even less materialists, or "hylozoists." Empedocles was something of a scientist and did think of the cosmos in physical terms. But he was still a mythological thinker whose imagination was not yet checked by empirical observation or controlled by experiment. Empedocles was somehow aware of the contrasting tendencies in his thought: "Although I know that truth inheres in my words, yet it is hard for man to attain to it and the mind does not prove a match for the soaring faith." [14]

The inner conflict between the basically aesthetic trend of the Greek spirit and the effort to purge mythological imagination and poetic abundance of stories about the gods was most consciously and most vigorously felt by Plato, the greatest of the critics. Plato revered Homer as much as any Greek. He loved poetry and was himself a poet of stature. It cut deeply into his heart, when, to exalt his ethical idea of an ideal state and of an ideal religion, he had to attack the beautiful images of the Homeric Olympians. His attack against the Homeric representation of the divine was occasioned by an ethical puritanism or asceticism. It was not a resentment against poetry as such that inspired his polemics in the *Republic,* nor was it only an ironical campaign, as some have suggested. Plato was in deadly earnest; the most central, the most decisive ideal was at stake in the rules prescribed for the lawgiver of the ideal community: the ethical purity and the theological truth of his philosophy.

Plato was ever an ardent admirer of Homer and the tragedians. In an earlier dialogue he called Homer, "the best and most divine of poets," and still in his latest, "the wisest of our poets." [15] His dispute with this venerated poet concerned the transformation of the aesthetic into an ethical outlook, the naïve into a reflective position, the polytheistic into a speculative religion, tending to monotheism and preparing for Christianity. Such was the kernel of his dissent, the eminently important issue of his struggle with the great narrator of human and divine tales. The gravest of all decisions was at stake; the spiritual destiny of mankind was in the balance. Shall the religion of beauty as manifest in statues and temples, in epic and drama, the religion of the entire pagan world, obtain the victory, or

---

[14] Fr. 114.   [15] *Ion,* p. 530, and *Laws,* VI, p. 777.

shall a purer, higher, holier religion arise? Such was the real decision, outshining all ambitions, all smaller issues, even the entire scheme of the ideal state — it was a question of the course of universal history, hinging on the religious decisions of mankind.

Plato was firm. Irony was not in place. Plato faced an issue of the very first order, an ultimate issue not only in the sense of a philosophic, dialectic, or scientific hypothesis, but an ultimate issue concerning man's attitude to himself, his life, and the future of his institutions — an issue concerning the true God. Plato did not waver. He earnestly contended for the coming God and the righteousness and holiness of rules regarded as universally binding. He resembled the Old Testament prophets who unswervingly served and fought for the will and commands of the Lord, whom they regarded as the only true and living God. Such was the very deep reason why Plato had to antagonize the joyful and cheerful world of pagan beauty, so impressively, so seductively depicted by Homer. Therefore he had " to establish a censorship of the writers of fiction." " We shall be silent about the innumerable quarrels of the gods . . . quarreling is unholy." [16]

The " ancient contest between philosophy and poetry " is at bottom not a contest between philosophy and poetry but a contest between philosophy and religion, or between speculative theology and poetic mythology. Plato's own roots lay deep in the mythological culture of his ancestors; his metaphysics was in harmony with the aesthetic trend and cosmological background of the Greek tradition. And yet, as Xenophanes and Heraclitus, Plato was a severe critic of ancient religion. Plato, a philosophic reformer of Greek culture, tried to improve its religious standards, without reflecting on the dangers his work of reform implied for the very foundations of this culture. Unconsciously he prepared the way for the complete demolition of the whole fabric of Greek *paideia,* while his intention was simply to eliminate its abuses and evil consequences. Plato heralded an ethical revolution directed against the aesthetic spirit without knowing that it would necessarily destroy the whole world of pagan civilization and assist in generating a civilization bent not only on reform, but on the overthrow of ancient piety as well as

[16] *Republic,* II, pp. 377 f.

cosmocentric speculation — of the primacy of beauty in the scale of values and of imagination and intuition in the attitude toward ultimate truth and reality.

"Although we are admirers of Homer, we do not admire the lying dream sent by Zeus to Agamemnon. These are the kind of sentiments about the gods that will arouse our anger."[17] "We must beg Homer and the other poets not to be angry, if we strike out these and similar passages, not because they are unpoetical or unattractive to the popular ear, but because the greater the poetical charm of them, the less they are meant for the ears of boys and men. . . ."[18] These quotations clearly illustrate that Plato's real point did not concern the rivalry between poetry and philosophy, but the ethical purge of the mythical imagination, inseparably connected with the imagination of poets and artists. Plato, a Greek in all his inclinations and tendencies of mind and intellect, moved toward a horizon that absolutely transcended the Greek spirit. He was thereby deeply influenced by his relatively un-Greek teacher, Socrates. I shall say more about this relationship later on.

Plato's religious feelings and value-judgments held a middle ground between antiquity and Christianity. This is the key to the fact that Plato has always attracted thinking Christians. For more than a thousand years, beginning with Clement of Alexandria up to the Platonists (the so-called "realists") of the Middle Ages, their minds have been so fascinated that Christian theology stood under Plato's sway. And even in modern times Platonism did not cease to charm Christian thinkers. Such would be inconceivable, if a substantial kinship did not exist between his position and ideals and the Christian faith. Plato stands between the cultural world of pagan naïveté and that of Christian reflection. His philosophy moved from the "paradise of the mind" toward the age in which this paradise was lost. Philosophy is by nature reflective. The philosophizing mind deserts the immediacy of common sense or rather deprives this consciousness of its certainty and complacency. Philosophy was called upon to perform pioneer work in the process of which mankind had to give up its unreflected surety, and its natural attitude in morality and in matters spiritual. It is a miracle that the Hebrews of old had

[17] *Loc. cit.*, p. 380.   [18] *Loc. cit.*, p. 387.

a reflective mind in an age even more ancient than Greek culture. This is one of the reasons why we speak of revelation as the source of their faith. Their own cultural maturity and intellectual penetration could not have brought about the reflection implied in their holy message; it was rather an illumination from above, a prophetic inspiration commanding them to obey the transcendent Lord, so obviously different from the gods of the surrounding people. In Greece human reflection and logical sagacity based upon intuition, anticipated revelation.

The psalmist speaks of the beauty of holiness; to the Greeks, beauty was itself holy. The holiness of beauty was the root out of which their speculative systems arose. Plato, reflecting upon this root, was the first to realize that this valuation is the mark of speculation. I shall later try to show that this reflection was the origin of Plato's doctrine of Ideas. The exalted tone characterizing the speech of Diotima in the *Symposium,* exhibits the enthusiasm that generated the doctrine. Plato here betrays his own deepest feelings and the very motive leading to the creation of his guiding concept: the realm of Ideas. We are permitted to accompany his ascent from the lower regions, where beauty unfolds, up to the highest and purest, where beauty itself reigns in all its sublimity, majesty, and sovereignty. It would be hazardous to imagine the way he arrived at this intuition; for an intuition it is, that is to say, something that cannot be strictly demonstrated, precisely because it is the principle, the ultimate reason, the premise of all demonstrations. But with a great amount of certainty we can say that the idea of absolute beauty summarized the very substance of Greek civilization, and the dynamics of the entire adventure of speculation.

" Beauty, true, simple, and divine " is described by Diotima as the zenith of thought and life, " beauty, pure, and clear, and unalloyed, not clogged with the pollutions of mortality and all the colors and vanities of human life." [19] It is the Divine itself which is conceived here in a logical method, conceived by speculative contemplation taking the place of mythological imagination.

[19] *Symposium,* pp. 211 ff.

III

THE RISE OF COSMOLOGY

GREEK speculation was cosmological throughout, but the first period, from the beginning to the epoch of the Sophists, was cosmological in a particular sense. It did not only center in the concept of the cosmos; it started with the contemplation of the visible universe, and slowly ascended to the discovery of the Invisible, without entirely transcending the visible universe. The visible universe remained, even to Heraclitus and Parmenides, the model and archetype of the cosmos, although both were aware of the invisible factor within that universe.

Only the Sophists turned away from the contemplation of the world to reflect on man. Socrates consummated the new and " heretical " movement. But even in the new period the conviction that the cosmos was the all-embracing reality to which everything belongs, including gods and men, was not abandoned. It gathered new strength and gained momentum in the speculation of Plato. Plato, however, no longer naïve in his cosmological contemplation, established his doctrine of the Idea on the basis of the Socratic ethics and thereby created a system in which the Invisible was of greater reality than the visible world. The Idea of the Beautiful and of the Good (not yet rigorously distinguished) [1] was of greater truth than any perceptible beautiful object of the visible world, existing in space and time.

Greek speculation was thoroughly cosmological: it never transcended the idea of an all-embracing whole, even though Plato and Aristotle no longer thought of it as merely visible. Only in its final period did the visible universe again come to the fore. A certain

[1] The Greek word *kalokagathos* unifies both the *kalon* (i.e., the beautiful) and the *agathon* (i.e., the good).

73

similarity between the first and the third period can, therefore, be apprehended. If one adopts the dialectical scheme of Hegel, one might say that the third period brought back the position of the first, but on a higher level, enriched, and deepened by the insight of the second period. I shall discuss this point in detail later on. The Hegelian scheme of thesis, antithesis, and synthesis can often be used with great profit, if one does not force material into a dialectical triad when to do so leads to artificiality or falsification. I do not doubt that there is a bit of truth, perhaps more than a modicum, in the triadic method. In the case of Greek philosophy this truth is evident; even non-Hegelians have divided the history of ancient philosophy into three main parts: pre-Socratic, classical, and postclassical. And this division agrees perfectly with the facts.

When we apply the category of the aesthetic to the entire development of Greek speculation, degrees or shades of aesthetic naïveté in the three periods must be differentiated. Socrates was the first to reflect upon the central importance of ethics. He deliberately abandoned cosmological speculation and radically transcended the aesthetic horizon of the Greek mind. When compared with thinkers influenced by Socrates, the pre-Socratics were naïvely and one-sidedly aesthetic in outlook and attitude. This influence was of course strongest in Plato, Socrates' personal pupil and friend. Through the mediation of Plato, Aristotle was only indirectly under the moral authority of Socrates. He was, therefore, again more typically Greek in his preponderantly theoretical or contemplative attitude. On the level attained by classical speculation, the philosophers of the final period returned to the cosmological trend of the first, but ascribed primacy to ethical and religious considerations.

In the first period the cosmocentric spirit was unbroken, but even in it stages of development are to be distinguished. In the most naïve stage, the visible universe was in the foreground (so-called Milesian school); subsequently the Pythagoreans, Heraclitus, and Parmenides discovered the Invisible; and finally, on the *niveau* of the first stage, a definite synthesis between the first and second stages was accomplished, a synthesis achieved by emphasizing the visible cosmos as the true object of cosmological contemplation bearing invisible elements within itself. Empedocles, Anaxagoras, and Democritus, the outstanding figures of the third stage, are more " physically " minded than Parmenides, Heraclitus, and the Pythagoreans. Thus the characteristically Hellenic feature came to the fore again and again and obtained ascendancy after every deviation.

Cosmology in the strictly philosophical sense began with the Milesian school. As far as we know, Thales was the first to think about the unity and the first cause of the universe in terms of scientific speculation. But in a broader sense cosmological philosophy can be traced back to Homer and Hesiod. In Homer and Hesiod, cosmology was not separated from theology; it had a theological meaning and comprised also a philosophy of man. A poet thinks in images, metaphors, similes, and not in concepts; consequently the different issues of the philosophical sciences were not yet distinguished. As a matter of fact, this lack of differentiation is relatively true also of the first period of scientific speculation. And even Plato did not yet separate the various philosophical disciplines; such division had to wait for Aristotle.

Homer and Hesiod were not yet philosophers in the strict sense of Thales and his successors; nevertheless they contributed much to the rise of speculation. The gods of Homer and Hesiod were still mythical in the traditional fashion, but they began the process of spiritual enhancement so vigorously continued on the level of philosophical ethical analysis. The reproach heaped upon the Homeric gods by Xenophanes, Heraclitus, and Plato is justified: the purity of Homer's and Hesiod's representation of the divine did not meet the demands of the philosophers. In their poems the Olympians quarrel, scold, deceive, and are deceived. The poets made full use of their poetic license. However, Homer improved the standards of divinity, especially of Zeus.[2] In exalting Zeus over all the other gods and heroes, he initiated the trend leading to a purer monotheism and to an ennobled conception of holiness. Hesiod oscillated between the conception of an all-wise, farseeing, righteous, and just

---

[2] Jaeger, *Paideia,* I, p. 54: " The Zeus who presides over the heavenly council in the Odyssey personifies a high philosophical conception of the world-conscience. . . . The poet holds the supreme deity to be an omniscient power, far above all the thoughts and efforts of mortal men. . . . The divine will which governs the whole story . . . appears always omnipotent."

Zeus and of a Zeus " who made women to be an evil to mortal men with a nature to do evil," and " who craftily deceived his wife with cunning words." [3]

The "cosmos" of Hesiod is governed by Love (Aphrodite and Eros) and Justice (Dike). " Neither famine nor disaster ever haunt men who do true justice. . . . But for those who practice violence and cruel deeds farseeing Zeus ordains a punishment. . . . The virgin Dike, the daughter of Zeus, . . . sits beside her father and tells him of men's wicked heart." [4] Hesiod had a strong conviction that the industrious man will be rewarded and the idle will be punished in the end. But he also proved to be a typical Greek in making " right proportion " the " best in all things " [5] and " Harmonia the daughter of golden Aphrodite." He was a moralist tempered by his fundamentally aesthetic feelings. But what is most important in our context: Hesiod was the forerunner of the Milesian school, inasmuch as he put the question, What was in the beginning? His cosmology is a cosmogony and at the same time a theogony; he personified all the powers that rule the cosmos. " At the very first Chaos originated." [6] This answer shows, however, that he was not yet a philosopher in the strict sense; the deities or divine personages (following the first deity) are not generated by Chaos, but simply born later.[7] The question is philosophical; the answer is still in terms of an epic. Hesiod did not believe that all was created by, or is to be derived from, the first god: he did not yet think in terms of an ultimate and absolute origin or principle, as Thales and Anaximander did later. His Chaos is not yet an arche, a first cause or the like.

The cosmos of Hesiod was not merely the physical world, but also the world in which we as social beings, as individual workers, as human persons, have to toil and to strive — we who know moral values and depend upon the divine power. Likewise the cosmos of speculative philosophy was not only the visible world but also the world of values and decision, the world of human destiny and divine government. Thales was not a philosopher and a " wise " man be-

[3] *Theogony*, v. 600 and 889 f.

[4] *Works and Days*, v. 230, 238, 256 f.

[5] *Loc. cit.*, v. 694.

[6] *Theogony*, v. 116.

[7] Chaos means in Hesiod not a state of disorder, but of emptiness. Cf. Herman Fränkel (in the book quoted above), p. 142.

cause he was an astronomer and a scientist, but because he was seeking for the ultimate origin of all things and the ultimate meaning of human existence. His cosmos was therefore both visible and invisible. The visible aspect was, however, in the foreground of his speculative intuition, as is indicated by his choice of Water as the supreme cause. This water-principle was more than a beginning of chemistry or molecular physics; it had a metaphysical dignity and power presuming to supersede the very gods. And yet it was a metaphor, taken from the visible world; a material substance thought of as supreme.

To avoid misunderstanding and misinterpretation the term "material" and the term "nature" used in connection with the Milesian school ought to be defined carefully. The nineteenth century was inclined to misunderstand and to misinterpret the ancient epoch of thought in the direction of modern scientism or naturalism. Even a Hegelian like the famous author of the *History of Greek Philosophy*,[8] Eduard Zeller, says (in his short manual) of the pre-Socratic thinkers: "Their philosophy is rightly called 'natural philosophy' after the chief object of their inquiries."[9] In agreement with a mythical conception of nature, Thales thought of all natural objects as animated. But this alone does not yet fully characterize his concept of nature. To arrive at a correct interpretation of the system and principles of the pre-Socratics, their aesthetic and naïve ideas of the cosmos must be remembered. The term *physis* is much wider than our term "nature." It not only designates physical nature, but includes the essence of all things in its connotation. It is a metaphysical term, not a physical one. And since pre-Socratic metaphysics is cosmological and cosmogonic, the term "nature" had a cosmocentric meaning. Its connotation not only includes the world of animated natural objects (e.g., trees, mountains, oceans, and so on), but also comprehends the inner world of human feelings, passions, actions, and intentions.

The literal explication of the Greek term *physis* ought not to put us in mind of the natural sciences or the nature they investigate. Its literal translation is better approximated by such phases as "the nature or essence " of man, of the state, of history, of all things. The

[8] *The Philosophy of the Greeks in Its Historical Development.*
[9] *Outlines of the History of Greek Philosophy*, 13th ed., p. 25.

Greeks very nearly thought of *physis* as we think of " essence " —
the true being of phenomenal things. When its essence unfolds or
grows, an object becomes what its " nature " indicates. *Physis* is derived from *phyein* (to grow). *Physis* is the cosmos as it develops its
original being. Aristotle thought out the implications of this half-
organic, half-aesthetic conception in his system of change. At the
beginning of Greek speculation these implications were merely implied, not yet explicit. The meaning of *physis* as the metaphysical
being of all that is, was first made conscious by the Eleatics, whose
books are supposed to have had the title *On Nature,* and in the case
of one of them (Melissus), *On Nature or on Being,* a title identify-
ing the terms underlying physics and ontology.[10] Even Plato still
spoke of nature in the sense of true being.[11]

The merely scientific interpretation (the term " scientific " understood in the modern sense) of early Greek philosophy is, however,
not merely the error of modern naturalism and scientism. It has
a much older origin. It goes back to the very oldest account of the
history of philosophy, to the first book of Aristotle's *Metaphysics.*
Aristotle's discussion of the philosophic views of his predecessors
has been regarded as the most authoritative source of the history
of ancient thought. It has been constantly repeated and was not
thoroughly criticized and questioned until the present.[12] And yet it
is evident that Aristotle's discussion was never intended to be a historical report; it has no historical truth in the precise sense. It is
neither complete, exact, nor in agreement with the facts. Aristotle
admits that his purpose is not historical but merely systematic: " To
go over their views [i.e., those of his predecessors] will be of profit
to the present inquiry, for we shall either find another kind of cause
or be more convinced of the correctness of those which we now maintain." [13] What he actually found in the ancient system was not " another cause," but rather the confirmation that his own concepts of
the supreme principles were right and correct. He went through the

[10] This meaning echoes in the title of the work of Johannes Scotus Erigena, *De
divisione naturae,* where nature also points to Being as such.

[11] For instance, *Republic,* p. 597, where *" en tē physei"* means "in the realm of
the Ideas."

[12] Compare H. Cherniss, *Aristotle's Criticism of Pre-Socratic Philosophy,* 1935.
Also the books of W. Jaeger.

[13] *Metaphysics,* pp. 938^{c}4 f.

systems of his predecessors only to attain such confirmation. And such could readily be found because Aristotle looked at them all through the medium of his own philosophy. His whole discussion serves exclusively to prepare for the exhibition of his own scheme. He would only show that the views of the older thinkers were one-sided or defective since the categories of his own metaphysics were still unknown. And only the latter could solve the problems that were insoluble on the premises of his forerunners.

In the first book of his *Metaphysics,* Aristotle substitutes his own concept of " cause " for the arche of the pre-Socratics. And since he distinguishes four kinds of causes, he subordinates the supreme cause of the early writers to one type of his own. Of his four types (the formal, the final, the efficient, and the material cause), Aristotle identifies the material cause with the arche of the ancients. The ancients, with the exception of Empedocles and Anaxagoras, did not know any of the other three types of cause. Empedocles' concept of strife and friendship "vaguely" introduced a kind of efficient or moving causality. And Anaxagoras was the first to speak of reason and purpose; but even Anaxagoras appealed to reason only as a *deus ex machina,* when he could not give any other explanation of the necessity of an event or effect.[14] Empedocles had an inkling of efficient causation and Anaxagoras of final causation, but both were too immersed in the presupposition that the material cause alone matters to discover any other type of causality.

Aristotle's whole argument is not convincing. The pre-Socratics did not yet distinguish the four causes of Aristotle; they did not yet conceive of causality in the sense of Aristotle. And, therefore, they did not yet have any comprehension of what Aristotle calls " material." Moreover, they did not yet distinguish between physics and metaphysics. And their usage of the term *physis* did not yet denote a physical principle in the sense of Aristotelian terminology. But, if such terminology is to be used, it denotes rather a metaphysical principle (our own terminology is still influenced by the distinction of Aristotle).[15] To say the least, Aristotle's inclusion of all the pre-Socratics under the title " physiologists " is misleading. Unfortunately

[14] *Metaphysics*, p. 985^a.
[15] The word " metaphysics " is not his, but is derived from the order of his books as arranged by the editors of his works.

all later historians followed suit. The label " natural philosophers," or some similar title, is, therefore, nearly always used in histories of philosophy, not only to designate the philosophy of Thales, Anaximenes, Hippasos, Metapontinos, and others, but also to describe the philosophy of Heraclitus and Parmenides. Of course, in a sense, the former group sought their first principle in water, air, fire, or the like, and, if the modern usage of the term be avoided, they were " materialists." But Heraclitus and Parmenides obviously transcended the horizon of any kind of naturalism.

The historical inaccuracy of Aristotle's statement can also be proved in another manner. Aristotle's discussion omits mention of Anaximander, even though Anaximander is not unknown to him. Elsewhere Aristotle quotes his principle and analyzes it.[16] Why, then, did he omit Anaximander from the review of his predecessors? Because Anaximander's first principle, the apeiron, i.e., the Infinite, did not at all fit in the schematic summary of previous principles, as given in the first book of Aristotle's *Metaphysics*. Aristotle employs his own division of elements successively to ascribe one of them to each philosopher: water to Thales, air to Anaximenes (and Diogenes), fire to Heraclitus (and Hippasos). To fit into his scheme Anaximander should have taught that earth is the supreme ground of the universe; unfortunately he did not. Therefore, he could not be mentioned in this series. As far as we know, Empedocles was the first to add earth as a fourth principle. From Empedocles (and Plato) Aristotle took over the doctrine of the four elements (to which he added a fifth, the so-called quint-essence of the scholastics).

And what about Parmenides? Apparently he also did not fit into the Aristotelian construction of pre-Socratic doctrines. He had no material " cause " and evidently was not a " physiologist," even in the sense of the earliest thinkers or in the sense of Empedocles, Anaxagoras, and Democritus. Parmenides and Pythagoras could not easily be registered as " materialists " or representatives of a supreme material arche. What, then, did Aristotle do? He mentions the Pythagorean number principle under the heading of " matter," [17] but he obviously feels uncomfortable with Parmenides, whose " One " or " Being " he could by no means interpret as a material principle.

[16] *Physics*, pp. 187ᵃ, 21; 203ᵇ, 13.   [17] *Metaphysics*, p. 986ᵇ.

Therefore, of Parmenides and Xenophanes, he only says, "The discussion of them is in no way appropriate to our present investigation of causes" (he was certainly right), and of Xenophanes, he "gave no clear statement, nor does he seem to have grasped the nature of either of these causes, but with reference to the whole material universe he says the One is the god." [18] But did Xenophanes really refer to the "material" universe, even in the Aristotelian sense of this term? Would he have denounced with so deep a detestation the material statues of the gods only in order to substitute for them a material "cause"? Why did he proclaim that "the god sets in motion the All without any toil, by the power of his mind alone"? Rather does this not remarkably anticipate the theology of Aristotle himself? To use the language of Aristotle, does it not point to the "formal" and the "final" cause rather than to the "material" one?

Though no longer personified, even the "Water" of Thales was not a material cause; it was still a half-mythological concept, like the "Earth" of Hesiod. It had some kinship to the Homeric "Ocean." A century later Empedocles used mythological names for the four elements. And even a Church Father can say, "Our thought catches a glimpse of the divine nature as of some immense ocean." [19] Is it possible or even probable that Thales, who, as Aristotle reports, insists that "all things are replete with gods (or demons)," could have been a "materialist" in the Aristotelian sense? [20]

Caution must be exercised in using Aristotle's discussion in the *Metaphysics* as a historical source. His interpretation of the pre-Socratic thinkers is, to say the least, very one-sided. What remains of his report is the fact that all those thinkers were naïvely cosmocentric in their general outlook and that the cosmos, as they understood it, was mainly or primarily the world of the senses, especially the world our eyes can see. Nevertheless, the pre-Socratics inaugurated analytical dissection of the cosmos by distinguishing its diversity from the supreme ground out of which the variety of objects arise. Such is particularly clear in the case of the "Infinite" of Anaximander.

Anaximander took a cardinally new step when, in his comprehension of the ultimate source out of which everything visible and ma-

[18] *Loc. cit.*

[19] Gregory of Nyssa, *Against Eunomius*, Book I, ch. 26.

[20] *De anima*, A. 5, p. 411, a.

terial emerges, he abstracted from everything visible and material. Thales still clung to a physical substance, although conceptually transformed into an abstract, metaphysical principle of the cosmos; but Anaximander's arche was no longer such a substance. We can only guess what Anaximander really meant, but we know he climbed higher than his predecessors on the ladder of abstraction. Some interpreters believe that he abstracted from all the " qualities " of an object and thereby arrived at the concept of an object without any definite qualities — an indefinite object. This does not seem very plausible, since the Greek term " *apeiron* " does not suggest the indefinite but the infinite. And Anaximander apparently argued that the Absolute must be infinite, because it would otherwise exhaust itself and could not generate endlessly. He pointed thus to a peculiar property of the Absolute: it has to be inexhaustible or indestructible. This property alone mattered; it classified the supreme cause of all things as supreme.

By means of abstraction Anaximander approached the concept of the supreme as being invisible. Whereas Thales had selected and exalted a special substance to the rank of the Absolute, Anaximander reflected on the essence of the Absolute and recognized its essence as the basis of its rank. Whether Anaximander still thought of the idea of the Infinite, in spite of its rank and dignity, as of a sensuous substance, yet without sensuous qualities, is hard to say. Some later commentators do ascribe such a view to Anaximander, since he believed that the Infinite first generates the moist and then earth, air, and fire. Such a primitive physics seems to presuppose an equally primitive concept of the original force. But in any case we have to admire the capacity of abstraction and reflection in this second figure of the history of philosophy, a capacity never to be surpassed. Even if Anaximander still thought of an elementary object, the concept of the Infinite touches a feature of the Absolute that can never again be dismissed: its contrast to all finite, exhaustible, destructible things. Anaximander thereby initiated the fundamental distinction between the Absolute and the relative, and touched upon the mystery of the divine more energetically than Thales.

It may be doubted that Thales spoke of the god as " the mind of the cosmos " [21] (although a reason for this record must have existed),

[21] Fr. 23.

but there is better reason to believe that Anaximander identified the Infinite with the divine. Aristotle, who ignores Anaximander in the *Metaphysics,* mentions him when he discusses the concept of the Infinite in the *Physics.* He then says that Anaximander defined the Infinite as divine because it is " immortal and imperishable." Anaximander or his school asserted the Infinite " to encompass all things and to steer all things." [22] This doctrine, Aristotle argues, rests upon the reflection that completion shuts out termination. The Infinite is conceived of as being the " complete," i.e., the totality of all things. All things taken singly are confined each to its own limits; taken together, they cannot be confined any more but are infinite. To Aristotle the infinite is, however, only a potential magnitude which can never be actualized by thought and which therefore does not exist actually.

The critical consideration of Aristotle is a kind of guarantee that Anaximander or " his school" (Anaximenes?) argued the way he reports, since Aristotle would not have invented an argument with which he does not agree. To use Plato's term, to Anaximander the Infinite was not a potential, but, on the contrary, the most actual, the " really real." For this reason alone it assumed the rank of the divine — the origin and the unity of all that is. From the perspective of the relation between revelation and speculation it is of great significance that Anaximander, though on the level of cosmotheism or pantheism, thus approached the Biblical conception of the Supreme Being. He anticipated what the Bible and Christian theology mean by the Infinite, namely, what is in contradistinction to all other things, because such are finite; or in Biblical language, because such are created, whereas the Infinite alone is not created, but the Creator. In this respect, Anaximander was definitely less Greek than Aristotle, to whom the Infinite is the formless, and therefore the potential, the lowest in the hierarchy of things and beings. From such a point of view it is comprehensible that Anaximander appeared to be a " materialist " in the eyes of Aristotle; to Aristotle the merely potential was merely material.

We have touched upon a difficult problem; the problem of the Infinite is met at the many crossroads of history; we must try to disentangle its complicated web. Anaximander lived (610–545) in a

[22] *Physics,* p. 203^{b}.

time that witnessed the rise of Ionian speculation and tremendous upheavals in the realm of religious faith. Orphic cults from the barbarian north invaded the Greek cities, especially Attica and Magna Graecia (the Italian colonies); such were adopted by the Greeks and somewhat Hellenized in the Dionysian mystery cult. Was Anaximander perhaps influenced by this or some similar religious movement antagonistic to the Olympian gods, their " Apollonian " hilarity, poetic frivolity, and beautiful forms, exhibited by the sculptors? Was he, therefore, inclined to announce the colorless and shapeless Infinite as the supreme divinity? We do not know. We can only guess that some secret animosity against the stone and wood gods of the artists and against the mythical fables was at work in his mind, as it was in all subsequent Greek speculation. But while most turned toward the clarity and lucidity of strictly circumscribed concepts, so that the Absolute thereby conceived appeared in the light of a supreme " Logos " (Heraclitus), a supreme " Existent " (Parmenides), a supreme " Idea " (Plato), or a " Pure Form " (Aristotle), Anaximander conceived of it as being infinite, and consequently as not to be fully comprehended.

This incomprehensibility was of course not explicitly expressed by Anaximander. But we possess a fragment — the oldest known fragment of Greek philosophy — which seems to suggest that the infinite had a religious flavor with Anaximander, perhaps not unconnected with the antiartistic, anti-Apollonian Dionysian cult, and the Orphic conceptions of an ascetic life, denouncing Hellenic naïveté, and the enjoyment of a sensual spirituality. Nietzsche was the first to suggest an interpretation of the origin of tragedy from the Dionysian spirit. He was also the first to suggest that the pre-Socratics were under the sway of this tragic feeling.[23] But Nietzsche is not very competent here, since he saw everything in that period of his life through the medium of Schopenhauer's pessimistic metaphysics. Whether or not the Infinite of Anaximander had something to do with " the bacchanalian revel " remains a question. But in any case, it seems to point to the mystery of the divine in a mystical fashion, thereby implying that all things finite are generated and swallowed up by the underlying Absolute, alone persevering and exempt from the transitoriness

[23] In his posthumous essay *Philosophy During the Tragic Age of the Greeks,* written in 1873.

characteristic of everything else. The contrast between the Absolute and the relative, between the Infinite and the finite includes that of the Eternal and the temporal; all finite things must perish, since they have originated in or are subject to time; the Infinite alone is not subject to time. It is rather the power of time itself, reigning over the temporal and the transient.

The fragment here mentioned deals with this subject matter. The somewhat enigmatic text runs thus: " Whence things originated, thither, according to necessity, they must return and perish; for they must pay penalty for their injustices according to the order of time." [24] Or, in a more literal way, " All things are going back through destruction, whence they had come through generation, according to what is due; for they suffer just punishment by repaying to each other the wrong in the succession of time." Like an old oracle inscribed on stone, these lines challenge the mind of the interpreter and raise as many, or even more, questions as they intend or presume to answer. They are as riddlesome as the problem of time, which itself has provoked so many penetrating theories, and yet has withstood them all in its abysmal profundity. But this much can at least be learned, namely, that Anaximander's concept of the Infinite had not a merely physical connotation, as the legend of the " physicists " would demand, but an eminently social, moral, spiritual significance — indeed, a religious implication. It speaks about items usually ascribed to the domain of religion, e.g., the eternal destiny of man because of his moral frailty, and the eternal justice of the world-governing power. But even this oracle has been interpreted in a merely physical fashion, as if only the language were imaginative, whereas its content is related to such things as water and the other elements. It is obvious that such an interpretation is extremely arbitrary and " unscientific."

Even if one grants that only the words are mythological, this would only support the assumption that they deal with the mysteries of religion. They imply that man, finite as he is, is also inevitably guilty, and that death is " the wages of sin," to speak in the language of Paul. The word " repay " leaves no doubt as to the moral character of that guilt. Anaximander evidently believed, like the Bible, in

[24] Translated by Maximilian A. Muegge in *Early Greek Philosophy,* by Friedrich Nietzsche.

a just world-order and in the providential consequence of wrong-doing. Anaximander's cosmos is not only the visible universe; it has a moral meaning inseparably connected with it. Anaximander did not yet separate the invisible from the visible, the moral from the physical, the sphere of justice from the sphere of temporal succession. And it is this original unity of spheres, subsequently to be broken up and never again so easily united, that makes him a typical representative of the age of naïveté, in spite of the reflective sound of his oracular utterances.

Anaximander engaged in reflection and analysis. He moved in the direction of an ethical cosmology, thus preparing the way for such philosophers as Heraclitus, Plato, and the Stoics. And yet his mind still worked within the framework of an unbroken aesthetic culture.

Perhaps Anaximander's statement may be compared with Plato's dictum that time is " the moving picture of eternity." If it is correct to interpret the Infinite by means of the infinity of time, Anaximander did not yet understand eternity, in its timeless or supertemporal meaning, but only in its moving picture aspect, succession of time moments. But the difference between Anaximander's conception of time and that of Plato is remarkable. Plato thought of time in terms of cyclical movement, while Anaximander does not seem to have shared in this (typically Greek) idea, but rather seems to have thought of time in a historical, or at least social, fashion, in analogy to the generations coming and going, or to the individuals being born and condemned to die, in the sequence of times. His concept of infinity has not the " idealistic " connotation it has in Plato, but it is bound up with the actual life of men who live in the cosmos and depend upon the cosmic order of time.

IV

ASCENT TO THE INVISIBLE

I n the second period of pre-Socratic philosophy a new step is taken toward the discovery of the Invisible as the essential factor within the cosmos. Inasmuch as the " Water " of Thales and the " Air " of Anaximenes were principles representing the Absolute or the Ultimate Ground of things, they were imperceptible and not visible in the ordinary sense. And the " Infinite " of Anaximander was invisible to a still greater degree since it had no equivalent in the world of ordinary objects. Nevertheless, such early thinkers had not yet reflected upon the contrast between the sensuous and the rational, the perceivable and the conceivable, the visible and the invisible. Only in the second period did this distinction gradually grow, and the supreme principle took on an outspokenly intellectual or rational character. Heraclitus and Parmenides despised the man who relies on his senses, instead of on thinking as the avenue to truth. The Pythagoreans, as mathematicians, were from the outset inclined to assume that the essence of things can be discovered only by scientific investigation and speculative contemplation and not by sense perception.

Pythagoras, a half-legendary personality of whom we know very little, was born in Samos and emigrated to South Italy, where he founded a religious order seemingly akin to later Christian monasteries. Its members had to obey rules governing their ascetic conduct and to live a life devoted to studies and reflection. Not enough is known of the content of their faith to warrant the assertion that it was influenced by the Orphic cult, but there are striking similarities. And in any case there was a strong impact of Eastern ideas upon the mind of the founder, since he believed in the transmigration of souls. The Pythagoreans held that the soul was of a higher rank and significance than the body; it was, therefore, of utmost importance to keep the soul pure and to discipline the body to reach that goal. A certain contrast between soul and body was apparently an article of their faith, as the distinction between the essence and the appearance of things was an article of their thought. The Pythagorean order conspicuously demonstrates the inner bond between religious and philosophic ardor, and the close relation between the ideals of life and the ultimate goal of knowledge. It confirms the identity of the Absolute in the spheres of faith and thought.

One of the marks of progress in the development of philosophy is the ever advancing distinction and division of previously undivided units. The number of its concepts is ever increasing. Hesiod's thought lacks conceptualization; Thales introduces the first concept (arche); the Pythagorean doctrine contains a whole set of contrasting concepts, beginning with that of the Infinite and the limited (*apeiron* and *peras*). Anaximander had introduced the Infinite as the Absolute; the Pythagoreans conceived of it as the opposite of the definite; the prototype of the definite was to them the number-principle. In fact, even today, this principle is still the best example of definition. Arithmetic is an exact science precisely because the number units are so well-defined that we can calculate all things with them and can absolutely rely upon the rules determining their relations. What can be less disputable than 2 times 2 is 4? Counting is the most elementary and the simplest of all the operations of thinking. Nowhere does the intellect triumph so obviously and so completely as in counting and calculating, operations which therefore lead with the greatest evidence to intellectual truth. All times and all thinkers considered the universal power of arithmetic as the best proof of the fact that the intellect rules the world. Cosmologists, theologians, idealists, materialists, pagans, and Church Fathers are here in agreement.

The arithmetical order seems to be the order of all things, or at least an order that can be applied to all things. Entities, whether on the earth or in the sky, inorganic or organic, beasts or men, stars or ideas, are all countable, and subject to the rules controlling the whole system of numbers and the operations of computation and calculation. The arithmetical order seems to be of universal validity and domain; surely, the day had to come when it would be proclaimed as the universal principle — as the principle of the whole universe, as the cosmic arche. This day came with the Pythagoreans, who thought number was the key to the understanding of everything. The cosmos consists of numerical relations: they are the real things, not the visible objects of sense perception. Number is the true essence of all things. The cosmos is made up of numbers; he who can decipher them knows its secret truth. I wonder why so many historians are bewildered when they have to explain or to expound the system of the Pythagoreans. Nothing seems to be easier — especially in our times, in an epoch that holds the mathematical sciences in the highest regard, believing them to be the magic wand that opens the closed doors of nature.

The Pythagoreans are the most modern of ancient philosophers; for the first time in history, they transformed mathematics into metaphysics, a practice repeated in the past and present by most modern philosophers. Is it not the current opinion today that mathematics is the universal science, explaining the movement of the stars as well as that of the atoms? Is it not generally acknowledged that all the technical wonders of our civilization and the horrible weapons, and future discoveries that may make it possible to leave the earth, are the product or future product of mathematics? No system, therefore, should have, and in fact has, more adherents (although ignorant of their membership) than that of the Pythagoreans. The modern adepts of this metaphysical community are, of course, no longer so consciously cosmoreligious as were the ancients. They are convinced that mathematics is the key to the knowledge of the world without realizing that their secret metaphysical faith was anticipated long ago.

The cosmos is today no longer the object of religious and philosophic admiration and adoration. It is no longer the cosmos of old; it is now " nature," the object of science, in the modern sense. Unlike their modern descendants, the Pythagoreans were not only mathematicians and scientists. To them the cosmos was a thing divine; it possessed this quality because of its sublime beauty. And this beauty was most clearly and most truly expressed by the mathematical regularity of the celestial movements, which, at the same time, were musical harmonies, for they had discovered that the latter were based upon numerical relations between sounds. It is not certain whether the Pythagoreans went so far as to assert that all things " are " at bottom (or in the last analysis) themselves numbers (as some sources

seem to imply) or whether in a manner akin to Plato, who taught
that all things " imitate " Ideas, they simply taught that everything
" imitates " number-relations.[1] This issue is, after all, not important.
In any case the substance of their doctrine is that mathematics has
a metaphysical, a cosmic, significance, and that there is musical harmony in the " spheres." Aristotle classified the Pythagorean doctrine,
with all other pre-Socratic philosophy, as materialism. By asserting
that with them number took the position of water or air in the early
Ionian schemes, Aristotle tended to interpret the Pythagorean doctrine as if it simply proposed number as another material principle.
Such an interpretation does not do justice to the development from
the Ionians to the rationalism of the Pythagoreans. Number is not a
" material cause." It is a rational entity, since it permits us to understand the order existing in the universe and to submit it to a calculus.
No doubt the Pythagoreans were fully aware of the momentous step
they took in thinking, by which the ascent to the invisible aspect of
the cosmos began.

What the Pythagoreans called harmony was both an aesthetic and
a metaphysical law. They originated the view that the cosmic order
can be investigated by mathematics on the level of a naïve and aesthetic outlook. The cosmic order is essentially intelligible, and, like
a work of art, it is enjoyable. The rational and the aesthetic both
originally and basically coincide. An analogy exists between number
and music in so far as both form an intermediate sphere between
the opposites of the world of sense and the world of thought, between physical things and intellectual concepts. Number is not so
sensuous as physical things, but it is also not so conceptual as the
product of thinking. And in an analogous way music is not so sensuous as noises we merely perceive without enjoying, but music is not
so rational as principles, notions, categories, or philosophic systems.
Both music and mathematics are in between such extremes, mediat-
ing them on a middle ground that binds together what is otherwise
separate. As beauty is " truth contemplated by the senses " (a definition of Schiller's), so mathematical truth is " beauty contemplated
by the intellect." In both cases truth and beauty are inwardly united,
even before any breach between the intellect and sense perception

[1] The latter view seems to be suggested by Aristotle in *Metaphysics*, I, ch. 6,
p. 987[b].

occurs. The Pythagoreans did not yet heal that break; it was not yet a matter of course, as in Christianity and modern times. Since the Greeks still lived in the " paradise of the mind," it was natural for them to suppose that the world of sense was intrinsically united with the world of thought. Speculation, therefore, was considered able, and was called upon, to define the visible cosmos in terms of thought.

This naïve assurance encouraged philosophers to interpret the cosmic order in terms of an intellectual order. The first step in that direction was the doctrine of the Pythagoreans, who, as Aristotle says, were the inventors of mathematics and the first to give this science its name.[2]

The term " Number " is ambiguous. It may mean the principle of number exalted by the Pythagoreans to the rank of the Absolute. But it may also mean the numbers that figure in a particular equation or in counting. This ambiguity points to the mediator-function of mathematics. Number, as a concept, belongs to the realm of the intellect; number, as figuring in counting, belongs to the realm of things counted or calculated. Number, in one sense, is something invisible, an element of intellectual order; in another sense, it is something that is manifest in the visible world which it represents in an intelligible language. This twofold relation makes number particularly able to function as the means for a metaphysical comprehension of the visible universe. The Pythagoreans used this double aspect without reflecting on it. In their view the universe was accordingly not so much visible as audible, and could therefore, like music, be interpreted arithmetically. It was a cosmic orchestra playing a cosmic symphony.

The Pythagoreans were also the first (as far as we can tell from the sources) to apply their principle to the conception of the human soul and human society. They probably believed that the soul, like the order of the cosmos, is the harmony of the body,[3] and the authority of civic laws is to be derived from that of the cosmos. They engaged in considerable political activity, and for some time represented a powerful group in the Italian Greek city-states. They were defeated by other groups and disappeared as an order, after flourishing for nearly a century. But their philosophy never died out com-

[2] Cf. Jaeger, *Paideia,* I, p. 162.
[3] Plato, therefore, takes pain to refute this theory in the *Phaedo.*

pletely. It exercised its influence on almost all succeeding systems, particularly on Plato, who can be called a disciple of the Pythagoreans whom he met in Italy. We must also assume that Socrates was well acquainted with the ethical trend of the order. Not only did Socrates emphasize the superiority of the soul over the body and the ascetic consequence of this doctrine, but he also practiced this ethical principle in his own life.

Heraclitus of Ephesus, the most fascinating figure of pre-Socratic philosophy, is also one of the most fascinating figures in the entire history of thought. His fragments appear to be deliberate aphoristic sentences, but they might have been passages of a great book which, according to an ancient — though probably false — tradition, had the title " On Nature." His fragments are like glittering gems, each most finely cut. They are provocative and paradoxical, so that even the ancients called Heraclitus " dark." Heraclitus soared higher than the Pythagoreans in the quest for the invisible. While the Pythagoreans dwelt upon the middle ground between the extremes of reason and the senses, of thought and perception, Heraclitus discovered the very nerve of thought. He was the first philosopher to realize that the thinking mind has to respect a norm or a law, the norm or law of both thought and universe. Of course, this thesis was already implied in the Pythagorean doctrine that number governs the universe. But it was implied only in this special and restricted form. Heraclitus made known the universality and abstract validity of the thesis as such. This was perhaps the most momentous insight in the entire history of philosophy. It was the first reflection upon the possibility of philosophical knowledge itself and upon its range and significance. It was the most fundamental formulation of cosmological metaphysics. Even if it should prove true that Thales had spoken of the mind of the world, this phrase was not yet expounded in its implications and full meaning. Only Heraclitus told the meaning of the fact that there is reason in the order of the cosmos and that our reason can grasp that cosmic reason. Whether the Greek word " *logos* " and the English word " reason " are identical, is questionable, and I will discuss later this very difficult problem of interpretation.

More than any of his precursors Heraclitus emphasized the unity of the cosmos and tried to demonstrate it in several ways. Thales had anticipated the thesis that there is only one cosmos; but only Heraclitus made explicit what that means and how it can be ascertained. Among the ultimate concepts of the Pythagoreans we find the contrast between unity and multiplicity, a contrast that controls and creates the whole number system. Heraclitus was not content to state that there is this basic contrast and that the world could not exist without it. Rather, he insisted that the unity of the world is superior to its multiplicity, that the cosmos is cosmos only by virtue of that ascendancy of unity and thought; it is possible only because the function of unity is victorious in the very activity of thinking. Oneness and sameness belong together, and both are at the root of things as well as of thinking. " This cosmos which is the same for all was not created . . ." — this is one of the monumental sentences that characterize his whole speculation.

Sameness has a double significance. The cosmos is the same for all; i.e., all that is exists in one and the same all-embracing cosmos, and only in that way does it exist. But in a second sense the cosmos is the same for all, i.e., for all beings who think about it: " Thinking is the same to all." [4] Both senses taken together were the basis of his Logos doctrine, which is much more important than his doctrine of the universal flux that is usually placed in the foreground. To prove that all exists in one and the same All, Heraclitus tried to show that even opposites are ultimately one and the same thing or that it is one and the same thing that underlies contrasting polarities. This was one of the ways in which he disclosed the superiority of the thinking mind. Vulgar perception is persuaded that day and night, life and death, young and old, winter and summer, war and peace, and so on, are irreconcilable opposites which prevent us from understanding the intrinsic identity of the cosmos. But when we are not deceived by the superficial impression which they make but penetrate into the inner structure of the cosmos by means of analysis and reflection, then we must recognize their essential unity within an identical ground. " If you do not apprehend me, but the logos, then you have to agree wisely that all is one." [5]

Untiringly and in many ways Heraclitus tried to inculcate this fundamental doctrine into his readers.

The thesis that all things are in a continuous state of flux is only

---

[4] Fr. 113; cf. Frs. 114 and 2.　　　　　　　[5] Fr. 50.

derived from the doctrine of unity and serves to underline and to corroborate it in a twofold way. Everything — this is one trend of thought — has to change, because it is one-sided and consequently it cannot persevere.[6] The dynamic fluidity of the world originates in its intrinsic unity and identity which does not tolerate the permanence of any special thing or state. It has to yield to another thing or state; only thus are manifested its oneness and identity with any other special thing or state. The other trend is directly concerned with the opposites and exhibits their intrinsic sameness. The first trend is predominantly physical and empirical; it simply points to the fact that nothing remains as it is; the rivers flow, the sun moves, even the observer is constantly changing. The second trend is cosmological, metaphysical, speculative and dialectical; it is more important and more characteristic of the system and method of Heraclitus. Its controlling idea implies that there could not be any concrete unity without a duality integrated by a domineering oneness and identity. In other words, the metaphysical unity of the cosmos is the unity that unifies and reconciles opposites.

There would not be any cosmic unity (and that implies that there would not be any cosmos at all) if there were not contrary polarities which are reconciled to each other in and by the cosmic whole. Only in this way does a cosmic harmony and not merely an abstract unity exist. Heraclitus was the first thinker to realize that the contrast between thinking and things, between concept and reality, between abstract unity and concrete multiplicity, can be overcome only through a dialectical method which, instead of shunning the paradoxical, uses it to display the fundamental fact that abstract thinking alone never reaches the *real,* never penetrates into the core of its structure. Abstract thinking leads to abstract contradictions, which pointing to the limitation of such thinking transcend it in the direction of that intuition of the truth without which speculation is neither possible nor effective. Only by such a method does the Logos of all things come to the fore. The Logos does not exhibit flux, as the central manifestation of the ground of all things, but it develops the unification of the opposite poles of the cosmos — the pulsation of cosmic life. In that sense fire is the best symbol of the cosmos, be-

[6] This insight was already intimated in the one fragment we possess of Anaximander.

cause it is, as Heraclitus expressively states, "ever alive" (*aeizōon*).[7]

The meaning of the identity of the opposites is further illustrated by the example of the bow which goes back into itself after having turned away from itself, and of the lyre which also achieves its unity by means of self-differentiation. "People do not understand how that which differs from itself yet agrees with itself; how it by turning back to itself joins itself like the bow and the lyre."[8] This profound insight did not unfold its truth until Nicholas of Cusa, at the end of the Christian epoch and the beginning of modern times, asserted that the Absolute is the "*coincidentia oppositorum.*" The cosmos is One by integrating its multiplicity into its unity or by absorbing its diversity into its sameness.

The unity of the cosmos is not static but dynamic; it is not merely unity — it is also a multiplicity, eternally returning into the fundamental unity. A tension exists but it is constantly resolved into the identity of its poles, just as the two ends of the bow, at the moment of the highest tension, bring about the integration releasing the arrow. In this dynamic movement is generated the harmony of the spheres spoken of by the Pythagoreans. This "hidden harmony is better than the overt one."[9] The cosmic harmony is hidden, because it is not so visible as the opposition or the contrast. It is not accessible to the senses; a glance at the secret core of the universe and its inner harmony is granted only to speculative intuition and contemplation. A continuous conflict or struggle exists, without which there would be no life. But conflict is not the last word. Reconciliation and harmony result from it and characterize the state of the whole; conflict and war characterize only the dynamics which bring about the final and ultimate result. "To the god all is beautiful and good and just; only men regard something as unjust and something as just."[10]

In this last quotation Heraclitus qualifies himself as the typical representative of the Greek mind and its aesthetic-religious tendency. The cosmos is both divine and beautiful; it is divine, because it is

---

[7] Fr. 30. In Fr. 67, Heraclitus says explicitly that the god (i.e., the cosmos) changes "like" fire, not that he "is" fire.

[8] Fr. 51.

[9] Fr. 54.

[10] Fr. 102.

beautiful, and beautiful because it is divine. Heraclitus, like Thales, Anaximander, and Pythagoras, is a cosmotheist and to a certain degree pantheist. The same basic intuition unfolds in all these thinkers, as also in the subsequent Eleatic school and further in Empedocles, Anaxagoras, and Democritus. It makes them companions serving the same cause. It is an intuition that develops to an ever greater degree presuppositions and consequences implicit in the Greek mind. For a historical moment it was partially abandoned by the Sophists, and Socrates, modified by Plato and Aristotle, only to return again in all its original vigor and religious fervor in the Stoic school.

The mainspring of all that Heraclitus says is undoubtedly his aesthetic but also metaphysical intuition of the cosmos. He makes only more explicit what the Pythagoreans had said about the musical harmony of the heavens, a harmony uniting within itself concord and discord. It is a harmony more beautiful because of its victory over the disharmonious. This idea had such an enormous attraction for all subsequent thinkers that even a Christian Father like Augustine (in many respects still a representative of ancient speculation) used this idea as an argument for the vindication of evil and sin in the world. Heraclitus was probably the first to recognize the possibility of such a theodicy, valid of course only against the background of a naïve, aesthetic culture like that of pagan antiquity, with its cosmocentric outlook and its cosmotheistic speculation.

It is true that this speculation has a strong affinity with Biblical revelation. In spite of the contrariety between the two there is a deep kinship. Greek speculation moved toward Biblical revelation, not only in its criticism of mythology, but also in its stress upon the oneness and spirituality of the divine; in its conviction that the god is good and just; in its emphasis upon the order that governs the world; and in its logos doctrine which eventually could be taken over by Christianity and, although profoundly enriched and transformed, could become one of the cornerstones of Christian dogmatics. Heraclitus was most creative and powerful in pointing to all these directions. Justin Martyr praises him as one in whom the spirit of Christ was working and in this respect ranks him side by side with Socrates.[11]

[11] *The First Apology of Justin*, XLVI.

Like Hesiod and Anaximander, Heraclitus believed in Dike (Justice) as a cosmic power. " The sun will not exceed its bounds, otherwise the Erinyes, the aids of Dike, would find him out." [12]

The word " Dike " shows that Heraclitus, like his predecessors, is still tinged by mythology, but it also illustrates that his metaphysical outlook tended toward an ethical interpretation of cosmic necessity. He had a keen sense of moral duty and civil obligations. " It is duty to follow the common [law]." [13] Morality is derived from cosmic order and not the reverse, at least in Heraclitus' own version: " All human laws feed upon the one divine [law]." [14] " The disposition of man is not based on insight [*gnōmē*], the divine is." [15] Heraclitus revered the moral perfection of the divine will as much as he admired and venerated the aesthetic harmony of the cosmos. He was deeply convinced that *gnōmē* (a word difficult to render in English, because it is something between reason and judgment) rules the world. " Wisdom consists alone in the conviction that *gnōmē* governs all in all." [16] Whether this supreme *gnōmē* is personal, whether the cosmos is divine, because logos is at the helm, and whether his god has any relation to the gods of the traditional religion, especially to Zeus, Heraclitus does not clearly say and probably did not clearly know, as the aphorism seems to betray: " The one wisdom supreme will and yet will not be called by the name of Zeus." [17] There are many questions that we should like to have had answered by Heraclitus which he could not have answered, because he never raised them and could never have raised them since they are the outcome of the whole development of thought and faith in later centuries.

The greatest and gravest among those questions concerns the nature and meaning of the " Logos." This word, like *gnōmē* (and in fact like most terms of Heraclitus), cannot be rendered accurately and precisely in English. All we can do is to state as carefully as possible what he himself might have understood by the term. The original meaning is " word " or " speech "; it is derived from the verb *legein* (to speak). Heraclitus probably did not reflect upon the difference between " word " and " thought," or if he did, then only in a vague way. He was conscious of the difference between his own words and the truth which he wanted to convey by them. He asks

[12] Fr. 94.   [14] Fr. 114.   [16] Fr. 41.
[13] Fr. 2.   [15] Fr. 78.   [17] Fr. 32.

his readers not to mistake these two things, but to turn to the truth alone, forgetting about him. When he speaks emphatically about the Logos, calling it the same for all and demanding universal respect for it, he certainly means the true word or concept, the word which expresses the supreme truth about the cosmos. "Everything happens according to this Logos." [18] One might therefore say that it connoted the eternal essence of all things; but we must add at once that Heraclitus did not use the word "essence" or any terms that could be rendered by essence. We are, therefore, not much wiser when we circumscribe "Logos" by "essence." Only Plato applied the term "essence" (*ousia*) in a terminological sense. In one fragment of Heraclitus *"physis"* nearly possesses the same dignity as "logos." "It is wisdom (*sophia*) to say the truth and to act according to *physis*." [19] Here wisdom unites theoretical (metaphysical) and practical (ethical) insight. The same has to be said about "Logos."

The upshot of all such considerations is the conclusion that Heraclitus was an intuitive thinker whose concepts were not yet as definite and defined as we should like them to be. His mind was not yet so schooled as the mind of later philosophers who stood on his shoulders. But something else is involved in his proverbial "darkness": Heraclitus felt that there is a mystery which the human mind cannot decipher, an incomprehensible and unfathomable element which human thought will never fully penetrate. Who would blame him for this feeling? Only a narrow-minded positivist who does not realize how much poorer and more remote his own thought is from ultimate truth than the speculation of this ancient seer. Moreover, Heraclitus philosophized in an age in which intuition took the place of religious imagination; the latter was no longer ethically and cognitively satisfying. Heraclitus tried to express something that only religious revelation can adequately set forth. His speculation had to anticipate the part of revelation, and of necessity this task naturally made it "dark."

In a sense we can understand him better than he understood himself, because we can understand the limits of speculation and because we know that it has to end precisely where revelation begins.

[18] Fr. 1.

[19] Fr. 112. This word anticipates the ethical imperative of the Stoics.

This does not imply that we should interpret his oracles in a Christian mood. They are definitely un-Christian or pre-Christian; their very darkness or vagueness rests upon this undeveloped stage. What Heraclitus wanted was at bottom impossible: to conceive by means of logical thought what cannot be thus known. The supreme lawgiver of the universe and of the human community, the supreme judge of our deeds, and the supreme providence of history cannot be known by means of conceptual speculation. No wonder Heraclitus was vague when he touched upon this supreme mystery. It is not surprising that he is silent when asked: Do you mean that the Logos is a personal intelligence and will? Do you mean that the cosmic god and the Logos are the same? Do you mean that the Logos is reason? That our thoughts about the Logos respond and correspond to the cosmic Logos? Such questions are unanswerable for reasons already stated.

What makes Heraclitus so attractive and fascinating is just the unity of his profound intuition and of his penetrating comprehension, of his pious reverence and of his proud analysis, of his mythological imagination and of his bright and audacious criticism, of his high flight into the divine and of his sincere humility in facing the divine mystery. All these traits taken together make him venerable and dear to us; they make him immortal in the history of human thought and speculation.

"Thinking (*phronein*) is the greatest power." [20] "The divine law (*nomos*) commands out of its own authority, it has boundless power, and it prevails." [21] "How can one hide from that which never perishes?" [22] One word seems to anticipate the thesis of Augustine and Anselm that one cannot know God without faith. [23]

APPENDIX

1. In an anthology of the Scottish novelist George MacDonald (1824–1905) edited by C. S. Lewis, No. 147 on p. 68 runs: "Endless must be our terror, until we come heart to heart with the fire-core of the universe, the

[20] Fr. 112.   [21] Fr. 114.   [22] Fr. 16.   [23] Fr. 86.

first and the last and the living One " — this might give a clue to the fire symbol of Heraclitus.

2. In the time of Heraclitus the word *"Logos"* probably did not yet mean reason as the faculty of reasoning. Even in Plato and Aristotle it did not mean this faculty, but something like " concept," i.e., the word in so far as it has a logical significance, and implies a definition. Recently Martin Heidegger has given a new interpretation to the word as used by Heraclitus. According to his opinion we should go back to the original meaning of the word *" legein,"* from which it is derived. In Homer, Heidegger insists, *" legein "* meant " to collect " (a connotation still preserved in the English word " collection "). Heraclitus wanted to express the collection or synthesis of the manifold of things within the one cosmos. (*Einführung in die Metaphysik,* 1953, pp. 96 ff.) Although Heidegger notices that Heraclitus did use the verb *legein* in the sense of speaking, still he asserts that Logos has preserved its original meaning and does not mean " word " or " speech," even less " reason " or " law," but " collection " (the Germans mostly translated *" Logos"* in Heraclitus by *" Weltgesetz ":* " law of the world " or " world-law "). It suggests, he argues, an original togetherness, the unity of opposites or Being as such. Heraclitus would consequently be the first ontological thinker preceding Parmenides.

This interpretation, though interesting, nevertheless seems as arbitrary and subjective as all interpretations of other thinkers by Heidegger.

First, the word *"Logos"* in Homer meant " word " or " speech " and not collection, although the verb *" legein "* connoted in Homer, not to " speak," but " to gather," " to pick up."

Secondly, in Heraclitus *" legein "* connotes " to speak," so that I cannot see why Heidegger goes back to Homer in order to find his explanation of the Heraclitean *" Logos."* It is beyond all doubt that Heraclitus in some of his fragments understands by *" Logos,"* " word " or " speech," since he says that one should " hear " the Logos.

In the third place, Heidegger wants to eliminate all subjective implications and to restrict the whole philosophy of Heraclitus to a doctrine about Being (in agreement with his own emphasis on ontology). Although I would agree that Heraclitus is certainly in no sense a subjectivistic thinker, but a cosmologist, like all the other pre-Socratic philosophers, I do not recognize any trace of ontology in his fragments.

And the fourth point: there is an undeniable connection between Logos and thought in Heraclitus. In two fragments Heraclitus replaces " Logos " by " gnōmē," derived from *gignōskein,* " to know." But logos itself has a cognitive function in his fragments, although it is true that it has also the dignity of an objective power governing the cosmos. It is therefore most akin to the word " arche," implying the first and supreme principle. But it is characteristic of Heraclitus in contrast with the Milesians that his principle has the two aspects of reality and thought (as we would say to-day). It suggests thought that is not restricted to man's thinking but has cosmic reality.

V

THE FOUNDATION OF ONTOLOGY

PARMENIDES, the disciple of Xenophanes, continued the work begun by Heraclitus, though in another direction and with a different emphasis. Like his predecessors, Parmenides turned toward
the invisible; however, he did not seek the supreme principle governing the world, as Number or Logos, but instead, searched for the true
concept of the cosmos itself or for the concept of the true cosmos.
He thereby discovered the concept of Being as such — the most abstract of all concepts and in a definite sense the true " arche " of the
invisible world, representing at the same time the sum total of all
that is. It is an enigmatic concept indeed, most abstract and empty,
and yet also most concrete and all-embracing.

Because of this double aspect Hegel made the concept of Being
the beginning of his logic, a logic which was at the same time a dialectical ontology and a speculative metaphysics. Hegel was conscious
of his indebtedness to Parmenides, with whom ontology originated.
Perhaps it would be more correct to translate the Greek word *einai*
by " to be "; at least this would be a more literal translation. But it
would be very cumbersome to use the infinitive all the time; I shall
therefore stick to the usual term " Being." And we shall see that
Parmenides did not ask primarily, " *What does it mean to be?* " but,
rather, " *What is ?* "

The latter question concerns reality in an absolute or ultimate
sense. It is not concerned with what " is " in so far as it simply appears (that is to say, in so far as it *is* not truly). One might say: To
the Milesians the cosmos was divine because it was the unfolding of
an arche, of a supreme principle; to the Pythagoreans the cosmos
was divine because it was governed by the rules of arithmetic and
music; to Heraclitus the cosmos was divine because it was steered

by the logos; to Parmenides the cosmos was divine in itself, but only if it was truly conceived. His predecessors abstracted one element from the multiplicity of things and entities and proclaimed it to be the root or the head of all the others. Parmenides abstracted the true cosmos or the cosmos as it is, if truly comprehended, from all things and entities as they appear to the senses, i.e., erroneously. Parmenides abstracted the true from the false cosmos. (He was the first to make this distinction central.) He thus transformed cosmology into ontology; he conceived of the cosmos in an ontological fashion: as that which alone truly *is*.

The opposition between Heraclitus and Parmenides is not the difference between a philosophy of flux and a philosophy of permanence; at least this difference is not the most important one. The central difference is that between the logos principle and the concept of Being. Parmenides was the most abstract, as well as the most radical, of the pre-Socratic thinkers. If we are able to know what truly or really *is,* then we know all that we can desire to know — we have the key to the universe in our hands. Parmenides was therefore rightly convinced that the answer to his question would lead to the fullest satisfaction; it would lead to the final goal of all investigation and inquiry. One can thus well understand that he was proud of having raised the most radical and the most central of all philosophical, and perhaps also of all theological, questions.[1] Since the problem is the most radical that can possibly be raised, it is not surprising that the solution of Parmenides is also the most radical and I might say the most speculative.

There is another reason why the contrast of flux and stability, important though it is, does not touch the most crucial difference between Heraclitus and Parmenides. Heraclitus' emphasis on the dynamic nature of the universe was only one aspect of his cosmos. Strife and opposition are not the final decisive feature of things, but rather their harmony and unity. Likewise flux is not the ultimate character of the cosmos; the latter is rather the never-changing eternal order which regulates the ever-changing scene of the temporal world.

Heraclitus went even farther by intimating that the opposition

[1] In our time Paul Tillich, philosopher and theologian, has stressed this problem again and insists that it is the fundamental problem both in philosophy and in theology.

between good and bad, between the just and the unjust, is restricted to the human perspective but nonexistent in the divine mind.[2] In so far as opposites are not reconciled to each other, the world of opposites is a world of appearance only. Heraclitus distinguished two views of the cosmos: one, divine, to be comprehended by the philosopher alone; the other, merely human, in the last analysis illusory or false. Man is childish in the eyes of deity.[3] It might be concluded that Heraclitus, like Parmenides, distinguished two aspects of the world: the aspect of flux, merely human and not ultimately true; and the aspect in the mind of the god, true and stable. Such a conclusion, however, is not explicitly stated by Heraclitus. His fragments do not permit any definite decision about the relation between the two aspects. The point is obscure. And it is just this obscure problem to which Parmenides turned. The main difference between the two great cosmological thinkers is that Parmenides sought to elucidate the issue involved in the problem and sought to clarify a complexity of questions unanswered and scarcely raised by Heraclitus.

Speculation opened a completely new vista with Parmenides. Reflection and analysis advanced immensely. Progress in the history of philosophy always takes this form. A new step is not marked so much by the refutation of a predecessor but by clarification of points previously obscure or vague. A new stage in the development of thought is characterized by a new horizon and a new set of questions.

Parmenides beheld and attacked a new task with the greatest lucidity and vigor. A new chapter in the history of philosophy begins with him. Previous systems appear mythological when compared with his rational penetration and methodical argumentation. The step to the system of Parmenides was almost as momentous as the step from Hesiod to Thales or from the Milesians to Heraclitus. Parmenides was the first philosopher to apply a method of thought and to prove his points methodically. Perhaps this judgment is not quite fair since we possess too few fragments of his precursors. But after all we can judge merely on the basis of the known fragments; it might not be accidental that we possess more coherent fragments of Parmenides than of any predecessor. Perhaps succeeding generations

[2] See above, p. 57.   [3] Cf. Fr. 79.

deemed them more worthy of being preserved.[4]

The arguments of Parmenides are so conclusive that they retain their strength up to the very moment. Present-day writers who treat a man like Parmenides as if he had been a childish or confused thinker do not understand the profundity and gravity of his arguments, because they themselves are shallow, even though they know much more of the details of the world and of the history of philosophy.

Parmenides, like all speculative philosophers, relied upon intuition. But he did not only assert that this intuition contained the truth. He did not only proclaim, " This is the arche of the world," as the Milesians had done. He did not write like Heraclitus in the aphoristic style of brilliant oracles. Rather, he worked upon his fundamental thesis to corroborate its truth and to make sure that it was the only possible one. What is his thesis? Parmenides insists that the true cosmos or the totality of all that is, is closed on all sides; that it is a perfect whole, a kind of sphere, a system.[5] It is the totality, precisely because it does not need and does not tolerate any addition or anything outside itself. All his predecessors had taken this insight for granted, without question, and without thinking out all its consequences. Parmenides did not take it for granted but showed that it is most shocking, if we take it in earnest and inquire into its implications.

Parmenides was in all probability aware of the gravity and novelty of his thesis and he was also aware of the intuition underlying his reflective argument. Therefore, he starts with a prelude, a solemn proem in which he narrates the origin of his philosophy. His whole doctrine, for all its methodical and rational content, is written in verse. This alone indicates that Parmenides was immersed in the spirit of a predominantly aesthetic culture; his intuition was akin to mythological imagination. It begins with the words: " The horses which bear me conducted me as far as desire may go, when they had brought me speeding along to the far-famed road of a divinity who herself bears onward through all things the man of understanding."[6]

[4] See however Herman Fränkel, *Dichtung und Philosophie des frühen Griechentums*, p. 453.

[5] Fr. 3: What is " is to me something coherent, for wherever I might begin, there I shall return eventually."

[6] Fr. 1, translated by Arthur Fairbanks in *The First Philosophers of Greece*.

He goes on to relate that he was driven through the gate, where the night separates the day, to Dike, the deity of Right and Justice, already known to Hesiod, Anaximander, and Heraclitus as a cosmic power. She welcomed him and taught him the truth. Throughout the poem it is not Parmenides, but Dike, who speaks and argues! This deity of Justice turns out to be an acute and penetrating philosopher who knows how to defend not only the cause of the innocent but also the ontological thesis and all the consequences to be derived from it!

From the wholeness and self-sufficiency of the Existent (I use this word for the translation of the Greek *ōn*, participle of the verb " to be," which signifies the totality of all that exists as one all-embracing unity), Parmenides derives by logical analysis the impossibility of change and of any movement whatsoever. If the absolute is rigorously thought of, without the deception caused by experience of the world of sense, it must be concluded that it cannot change. Change presupposes that the Existent is not at any moment complete and perfect, i.e., that it is not the Absolute. Change as such implies that two different stages or states of the Existent could equally well express its wholeness. If such were possible, neither stage would be absolute. Two absolute stages or states are as impossible as two Absolutes.[7] Change connotes that the Absolute can be absolute in two different forms or modes; but to be absolute means to be identical. Heraclitus had pointed to the continuous change of everything and everyone. Parmenides draws the consequence that the world of change cannot be the absolute world; it cannot be the true cosmos. Although we do not accurately know whether Parmenides was acquainted with the writings of Heraclitus (some scholars believe that he criticizes Heraclitus in one of the Fragments),[8] I assume he was. His argument is more advanced and it seems to presuppose the thesis of Heraclitus. Because Heraclitus is right that there is a general and ceaseless flux in our world, our world does not agree with the standard of absolute Being and of absolute truth. The finite things in our world are not the cosmos as a whole.

Parmenides seems to say that the truth found by Heraclitus con-

---

[7] This argument is akin to Spinoza's proof that there cannot be two substances.

[8] Fr. 4, verses 6 ff. See the critical discussion of this belief in W. Jaeger's *The Theology of the Early Greek Philosophers,* p. 101.

cerning the permanent instability of all things is so shocking because we rightly demand that the Existent be not unstable. The sun seems to lose its identity when it constantly changes; we cannot step twice into the same river. Things may lose their identity, but the cosmos does not. Consequently the cosmos does not change, even if everything within the cosmos is ever changing. Wholeness and Changelessness mutually demand each other. The river and the sun are not the cosmos, and no single thing or being can be the cosmos, precisely because they change. Change is possible only within the whole of all that exists; since the whole is not a single item, or since it does not exist within a greater whole (there is none, if we understand ourselves rightly in speaking of the absolute whole), it cannot change. As a whole it remains what it is, always, although its parts (if it has parts) may change.

Parmenides argues further that the whole cannot have parts. We cannot even say that it " always " remains what it is; the term " always " presupposes that there are parts of time in which the Existent exists. It cannot have those parts. If it had, it would be partitioned or divided and this is impossible. The absolute whole is absolute because it is not divided but is a whole — complete, and completely itself. Any crack, any split, any differentiation, would allow change and change would entail that the whole and the parts are not entirely and completely integrated and identical with the whole. And the same is valid with respect to parts of time in which the Absolute exists. If we understand by time the succession of moments, then the cosmos does not exist in time at all, but rather in one moment only.[9]

For the same reason the cosmos has no beginning and no end. It is neither in time nor does it have a purpose. As Heraclitus had already said, it " always was and is and will be." [10] It exists in an eternal Now (*nyn*). If it were created or generated, something else would exist that created or generated it. If it ceased to be, it would make room for something else. Both possibilities are excluded because the cosmos is the sum total of all that is. Parmenides lays great stress on adding that the cosmos also could not have come out of nothing or perish into nothingness, because nothing cannot vie with Being. If it could, Being would not be all-embracing; it would not be absolute. This argument is of particular importance because it hits the crucial

---

[9] Fr. 8, verse 5.   [10] Heraclitus, Fr. 30.

In the second place, he repeats his fundamental thesis when he emphasizes the impossibility that anything could exist outside or besides the Existent. Since this is impossible, thought also cannot exist outside the Existent but is identical with the Existent " in which," Parmenides says in an almost untranslatable phrase, " it is expressed." [14] He seems to hold that the concept of Being is immanent within that Being which is conceived. This is the first time in the history of philosophy that a thinker reflects upon the relation between thinking and being, i.e., upon the most ardently debated problem of epistemology. But Parmenides does not seem to be interested in the epistemological aspect of the problem. At least as far as we can learn from the unfortunately enigmatical and short statements that we possess, he was interested only in discarding any duality within being. Since he realized that thinking might establish such a duality, when it reflects upon its relation to being, he warned that this assumption would be a dangerous error. Thinking can hit the truth only when it is not in any way separated from its object, i.e., from the being which it is thinking. The ontological thesis of the absolute oneness, inner unity, and completeness of the Existent determined him to formulate the most consistent and fateful program of all future rationalism: the identity of thought and being.

Some interpreters have mitigated the character of the identity thesis by trying to avoid its radical harshness. J. Burnet, e.g., waters down the words of Parmenides which literally rendered are: " The same is to know and that on behalf of which thought is," [15] by letting Parmenides say: " You cannot find thought without something that is as to which it is uttered." But Parmenides expressly uses the shocking and unmistakable term " the same." And he uses the same term in the first phrase, where he literally says, " It is the same to know and to be." [16] In the translation of Burnet the thesis of Parmenides is adulterated into the harmless and trivial statement that thought always presupposes the existence of something to which it refers. But this is not at all the meaning of the term " identity." Parmenides was

[14] Fr. 8, verses 34 f.

[15] *Loc. cit.*

[16] Fr. 5. F. M. Cornford renders this sentence thus: " It is the same thing that can be thought and that can be " (*Plato and Parmenides*, 1939, p. 34). I doubt whether this translation is correct. Parmenides probably never distinguished " what is " from " what can be."

in full earnest when he asserted that there is no difference between that which is and that which is conceived by thought. It is not permissible to attenuate the boldness and radical nature of his challenging words simply because they sound inconceivable. Parmenides attacks a problem that Burnet does not even see.

If in the realm of speculation we trust thought as Parmenides did, are we not obliged to claim that our thought does not deviate in the least from the truth? And when the truth is concerned with the nature of being, are we not also obliged to insist that our thought of the Existent and the nature of the Existent itself are one and the same thing? This, and nothing else, is the substance of the "identity-thesis" formulated in all strictness and clarity by this first "rationalist."

Parmenides considered thought in a way parallel to perception, because he was aware of the underlying intuition that makes his speculation possible. Sense perception relies upon the certainty that its object and the impression of the object are one and the same object. I am sure that the paper on which I write and the paper that I perceive when writing down my words is one and the same paper. Likewise Parmenides felt sure that the Existent within his intuition and the Existent itself did not differ in the slightest respect. He calls the intuition "thought," which in Greek means intellection or intellectual contemplation (*noein, noēma*) and is not a mere reasoning or an operation that presupposes the existence of its object outside itself. It is rather a kind of intellectual perception which identifies the object grasped or seized by the mind and the object as it exists by itself. This identity is underlined by the narrative which tells that Parmenides had to receive the truth from the lips of the deity.[17]

The reflection upon the intricate relation between being and thinking was not for the sake of solving the epistemological problem but to protect and fortify the ontological thesis. Too confident in the ability of the mind to penetrate into the substance of being, Parmenides did not inquire into the possibility of such a penetration. He only wanted to avert the conclusion that the duality of being and thought brings about a duality in the essence of being. Such a duality was actually assumed by Aristotle, at least with respect to the things we perceive: the duality of form and matter. By proclaiming the

---

[17] Cf. the thesis of Berkeley: *Esse* is *percipi*.

identity of being and thinking, Parmenides attempted to get rid of all difficulties with one bold stroke. The tone of his phrases seems to indicate that he himself felt the paradoxical character of his thesis.

Parmenides was more sure of his assertion of the identity of the opposites because he regarded the duality of thinking and being as an evident symptom of the falsity of all philosophy based upon sense perception. Having formulated the thesis that thought and its object are the same, Parmenides reproaches those who trust daily experience: " Consequently all will be nothing but the name that mortals have stated, convinced that it is true: generation and destruction, being and nonbeing, motion and mutation." [18] The implication is: What I am saying is not merely a " name," but is the thing itself, and therefore thing and name are not to be distinguished in my thought and teaching but are absolutely the same. My thought is itself the thing at which I aim. This does not mean that the thing is nothing but thought; rather, it means that thought is nothing apart from the thing (i.e., from being). Parmenides is a speculative realist, not an idealist; his speculation is objectivistic (as that of all Greek thinkers), not subjectivistic.

If we again compare Heraclitus' and Parmenides' reflection upon the relation between thought and the real, they resembled each other inasmuch as all Greeks resembled each other. Both thought objectively even when they thought about their own thought. Heraclitus calls thought " Logos," a cosmic principle; Parmenides also insists that his thought is not only subjective and human — it is divine, the result of instruction received from the deity. But there is a momentous difference between the two great speculative thinkers. The Logos of Heraclitus is not the cosmos, but a cosmic element or constituent. The thought of Parmenides is directly one with the object of his thought, with the Existent being: with the being of the cosmos, as understood by thought. Parmenides was an ontological thinker; Heraclitus was not. Heraclitus did not yet reflect upon the ontological relation between Logos and cosmos; therefore, the epistemological relation between the two is also obscure. By virtue of his ontological attitude Parmenides reflected on the relation between thought

[18] Fr. 8, verses 38 f.

and being; their ontological identity also explains the epistemological function of thought, or the power of knowledge to grasp its object as it is in itself.

Parmenides could identify thought and being, however, only because he distinguished two kinds of knowledge — the true and the illusory — and two corresponding " worlds." This duality took the place of Heraclitus' duality of logos and cosmos. For his identity-thesis, Parmenides had to pay the price of the unresolved duality of the divine and the merely human approach to being. The identity-thesis warranted the ontological thesis of the oneness and unity of being (or the Existent) and justified a rationalistic approach. But it confronted Parmenides with the problem of the merely human approach; he did not give the slightest hint of its solution. Parmenides was satisfied to reject the second avenue as false and illusory. He failed to explain why and how such erroneous knowledge can arise. Moreover, Parmenides does not tell us how the common sense world of experience, the temporal world of change, generation, destruction, multiplicity, and incompleteness can be derived from the only true and real cosmos, in which such features are nonexistent. He does not even try to derive illusion from truth and difference from identity. If the true and real world alone truly and really exists, such an explanation and derivation should be capable of actualization by the only true knowledge. Because of this failure Parmenides is as naïve as his forerunners.

The whole speculative scheme of Parmenides rests upon his cosmological intuition, an outcome of the basically aesthetic and aestheticoreligious foundation of his philosophy. A comparison of his system on this point with the system of Heraclitus immediately discloses a remarkable difference. Heraclitus (as the Pythagoreans) thought of cosmic beauty in terms of music; Parmenides, as it were in terms of sculpture or architecture. Heraclitus (to use the terminology of Nietzsche) was a Dionysian thinker, even though he condemned bacchanalian revelry; Parmenides, on the other hand, was an Apollonian. His cosmos was stable and stationary; Heraclitus', fluid and dynamic. The cosmos of Parmenides stands in an imaginary space without moving in time; that of Heraclitus rises and expires like music. Heraclitus likens the life of the cosmos to an ever-licking flame; Parmenides likens it to a perfect globe.[19] The logos of Heraclitus may partly have originated from the musical rhythm, which in Greek is also called " Logos," meaning the firm form governing the ever-flowing stream of sounds.[20] The " thought " of Parmenides, on the other hand, is expressed in the entire architectural or sculptural structure of a work of art.

As the Logos of Heraclitus has its analogy in the Christian Logos, so the Existent of Parmenides has its analogy in the Biblical Creator-God. The Absolute of Parmenides resembles the majestic figure of the Old Testament in five respects: in its Oneness, Transcendence, Perfection, Eternity, and Sameness. The intuition of Parmenides, though fundamentally aesthetic, was nevertheless also religious; in that respect it paved the way for the Christian age. It is interesting to compare the arguments of Parmenides for the unchangeableness of Being with those of the Jewish Platonist Philo for the unchangeableness of God. Philo, a contemporary of Jesus, even called God the Existent (" ōn "), as did Parmenides. Philo argued, like Parmenides, that God must be One and cannot move or change, since he embraces all things and is not dependent upon anything outside himself.[21] The Greek Church Fathers also argued in a similar vein. " To suppose excess and defect in the infinite and unlimited is to the last degree unreasonable, for how can the idea of infinitude remain, if we posit increase and loss in it? "[22] Parmenides would not have called the Existent " infinite " and " unlimited," since his feeling was too typically Greek and aesthetic to permit the supreme to be without form or shape, but basically, as far as their concepts are concerned, the infinite God of Gregory and the One of Parmenides are the same absolute being. Of course their religious interpretation is not at all the same.

The religious difference comes to the fore when we reflect upon

[19] Fr. 8, verse 43. Notice that Parmenides does not assert that the Existent *is* a sphere, but is " *like* the mass of a well-rounded sphere." The legend of his " materialism " is easily supported by the carelessness of reading his words; even so learned and conscientious a scholar as A. E. Taylor quotes this passage falsely (*Socrates*, p. 57. 1953).

[20] Cf. W. Jaeger, *Paideia*, I, p. 126.

[21] *The Unchangeableness of God*, especially ch. 57 (Loeb edition, III, p. 39).

[22] Gregory of Nyssa, *Against Eunomius*, I, ch. 15. Gregory compares God with a circle (*loc. cit.*, ch. 42), as Parmenides compared the Existent with a sphere.

the relation between the Absolute and the relative or between God and world. Parmenides separated them so rigorously as to obliterate any bond between them, whereas the Biblical thinker joins them by conceiving God as the Creator, Sustainer, and Ruler of the world — a God who guides, warns, punishes, and redeems man. Parmenides contemplates the Existing. The Biblical thinker stands in an " existential " relation to God, a relation that prompts him in the first place to think of God as his Lord, to be obeyed, feared, and loved; a God who responds to the person in an equally personal way. Nevertheless, the same ultimate problem that Parmenides left unsolved confronts the Christian theologian: the problem of the origin of evil. Parmenides, it is true, did not think of evil in the moral sense; instead, he thought of error, illusion, fallacy, i.e., of the defects of knowledge. This again characterizes the difference between the representative of a predominantly contemplative, theoretical, intuitive culture and that of a predominantly active, existential, and ethical faith. But there is a common denominator in the problem of the " second path " and of the origin of evil: both cases contain the difficulty of combining the absolute perfection of the ultimate with the deficiency of man. Parmenides did not attempt to solve this problem. The Bible solves it by the story of the original Fall. Parmenides traced the imperfection of human knowledge and of the world in which man has to live to the failure of the human mind to avoid illusion; the Bible makes man's failure to withstand temptation responsible. Augustine tried to combine both these views.

I will close this chapter with a quotation from Plato who, able to read and to study the whole poem of Parmenides, learned intensely from him. In the *Theaetetus,* Socrates says: " I have a kind of reverence, not so much for Melissus and the others who say that ' all is one and at rest,' as for the great leader himself, Parmenides, venerable and awful, as in Homeric language he may be called, him I should be ashamed to approach in a spirit unworthy of him. I met him when he was an old man, and I was a mere youth, and he appeared to me to have a glorious depth of mind. And I am afraid that we may not understand his words, and may be still farther from understanding his meaning." [23]

[23] Pp. 183 f.

What shall we say when Plato, himself "venerable and awful," was afraid of not understanding his great predecessor and teacher? We must be on our guard not to become so shameless as to believe that we can understand him, and to feel superior to him, as so many modern critics do.

VI

FROM DOGMATISM TO SKEPTICISM

THE first period of Greek philosophy reached its zenith in Heraclitus and Parmenides. The ascent to the Invisible was accomplished. Their speculative systems established the science now called metaphysics. Both had little regard and respect for the world of sense, for the physical universe, for things finite and temporal. Heraclitus, however, was at least convinced that the metaphysical principle finds its confirmation and illustration in the experience of daily life; whereas Parmenides discarded experience as illusory and deceptive. The successors of these two heroes in the first period no longer had their stature and originality. They were no longer so intensely and exclusively directed toward the knowledge of the Absolute. They were more interested in the visible world and did not care to distinguish the absolute and the relative, the eternal and the temporal, the divine and the human so rigorously and methodically as Heraclitus, and especially Parmenides, had done. In that sense they were less critical than Heraclitus and Parmenides had been; they were more " dogmatic." Of course the labor of their predecessors was not in vain. They did not simply forget the problem and the insight of Heraclitus and Parmenides. They continued their work but on a less inspired level of thought.[1] Only Plato again resumed the ascent to the Invisible, from a new point of view.

Empedocles, Anaxagoras, and the atomists Leucippus and Democritus are metaphysicians like Heraclitus and Parmenides. But they are also physicists; their metaphysics is thoroughly tinged by their

[1] In a sense all pre-Socratic or pre-Platonic thinkers can be called " dogmatic " because none of them reflected upon the intricate difficulties of the relation between knowledge and its object. And in another sense all pre-Kantian thinkers did not reflect upon those difficulties either.

physical outlook, and, in turn, their physics is tinged by their meta-physical vision. Physics and metaphysics cannot be completely sepa-rated in Greek philosophy. This statement even holds with respect to Aristotle, who wrote separate books on physics and metaphysics. Em-pedocles, Anaxagoras, and the atomists, however, have no metaphysi-cal outlook distinct from their physical outlook. Their cosmos is the visible universe, even though their thought is metaphysical. They can more legitimately be called metaphysical physicists or natural phi-losophers than any of the earlier thinkers. If the term " physiologists " or " physicists," often applied to all pre-Socratics, has the meaning of " metaphysical physicists," it is most valid with respect to this last group of pre-Socratic thinkers. I suppose Aristotle was induced to apply the term " physiologists " to the whole first period of Greek philosophy because he was temporally closer to this last group. Seem-ingly, he generalized the impression they had made upon him, when compared with Socrates and Plato.

There is a development within this last group. Empedocles was more closely attached to Heraclitus and Parmenides than were his successors. Like Heraclitus and Parmenides, Empedocles still had the air of a divine messenger who reveals the mysterious depth of the deity. But his deity was more thoroughly and narrowly identified with the physical world than the cosmos of Heraclitus and Parmen-ides.[2] Anaxagoras and the atomists continued in this direction. The whole group displayed a tendency to materialism.[3] The word " na-ture " (*physis*) now took on the peculiar meaning of the sensuous world today connected with it, when we speak of physics or the natural sciences in the modern sense. From Empedocles, through Anaxagoras, to Democritus, this latter trend was increased steadily, whereas the specifically metaphysical trend steadily decreased.

The thinkers of this period were also less original than their fore-runners. They were still original, if compared with the syncretists and eclectics of the final period of Greek philosophy, but they them-selves can be called syncretists or eclectics, if compared with the great figures who preceded them. In various ways they strove to combine

[2] Cf. Frs. 28, 29, 30, 31.

[3] Whereas Parmenides spoke of the cosmos as being like a sphere, Empedocles calls it outright " a sphere " and at the same time " the god."

the incompatible principles of Heraclitus and Parmenides. Such incompatibility is most striking, if Heraclitus is interpreted in terms of *flux* and Parmenides in terms of *stability*. Probably these terms have become identified with Heraclitus and Parmenides because their successors toiled to unite flux and stability in the physical universe.

Each in his own way assumed that something in the universe is changeable and something is not. These two features are compatible, if all processes of change are interpreted to be changing relations between unchangeable elements, conceived either as " roots " (Empedocles), " seeds " (Anaxagoras), or " atoms " (Democritus). By such a ruse, both Heraclitus and Parmenides seemed to receive credit for discovering the truth, and, at the same time, they seemed to be reconciled to each other. To explain the derivation of the vast variety of apparent things from the first principles, things were conceived of as a mixture or composition of the basic elements. The deeper issues of the systems of the founders were no longer appreciated and understood. The new systems became dogmatic so that they finally provoked skepticism, relativism, and subjectivism, in the period of the Sophists. Perhaps this reaction indicates that the systems were no longer worthy of continuation. The reaction itself released new forces which came to the fore in Socrates and through him in Plato.

Such a judgment may sound harsh and even pretentious, if it be recalled that modern science learned much from the later systems. For Empedocles, Anaxagoras, and the Atomists are much closer to the spirit of modern times than are the austere, stern, scientifically barren, paradoxical, and one-sided principles of their ancestors. But if their greater kinship with the spirit of modern science be extolled, do not forget that modern science should not be made the measure and standard of philosophic truth. The more strictly scientific the modern mind is, the more science prevails in matters metaphysical, the less is it truly philosophic. For philosophy is forever bound up with issues that cannot be answered by the exact methods of the sciences, methods that in their own field are most admirable.

Ancient philosophy is the rival of ancient religion. In spite of their vast difference in outlook and interest, all the Greeks agreed on this point. And even in modern times the great physicists are not called philosophers in the pure and proper sense, if they are only physicists. Only those scientists who ventured to build up systems vying with Greek metaphysics, like Descartes or Leibniz, are truly philosophers.

The metaphysical physicists were genuine philosophers and not merely physicists or positivists in the modern sense. By seeking the truth about the structure and process of nature, they sought the meaning of the world and life, of man and god. They observed the material substances, their properties and their processes, only in order to arrive at an understanding of the universe at large. While preferring to investigate the external world, they did not confine themselves to the investigation of single facts but speculated about the nature and process of the whole as a whole. Like all Greek philosophers, they were cosmologists; their physical world was a cosmos and not merely nature, i.e., it was a well-ordered, indeed a beautifully ordered, divine whole. Obliged to explain the principle constituting the whole as a whole, imaginative language and mythological reminiscence were legitimately employed. By fulfilling their task they substituted a speculative religion for traditional religion and thus in their own way prepared the path for the new religion that was to replace the old by revelation instead of speculation. Let us now study the cosmotheistic view of Empedocles, Anaxagoras, and the Atomists, omitting all features of merely physical significance.

Empedocles is the most mythological and Democritus the most scientific in the group. Empedocles' intuition of the cosmos and its life is akin to that of Heraclitus. The whole is constantly moved by contrary inner forces called " strife " and " friendship," or " hate " and " love." Empedocles' different pronouncements at various places make it hard to decide whether such expressions are symbolic or whether he believed in a universal or cosmic soul, living in all things. Even when he seems to speak plainly, it is never quite certain whether or not he is still speaking metaphorically. Empedocles' universe is as thoroughly symbolical as that of a medieval philosopher like Hugo of Saint Victor; everything physical has a spiritual meaning; everything spiritual has a physical embodiment. If a work of art conjoins two opposites, the physical and the spiritual, in one and the same imaginative unity, then the world of Empedocles, like that of his predecessors, is analogous to a work of art. The physical feature, however, seems to prevail in his quasi-aesthetic picture. Empedocles says that "all things have understanding and participate in mind." [4] Does he suggest here that understanding and mind are self-dependent powers, or at least powers that are not merely physical or material but intellectual or spiritual? Such must remain doubtful; in another place he asserts that mind in man is "blood which surrounds the heart." [5]

Empedocles' solemn words, which otherwise may remind us of the sacramental poem of Parmenides, do not ring so convincingly as when uttered by the older prophet-philosopher. Too much is imitation in the language of Empedocles, when, like Parmenides, he invokes the gods: "From lips that are holy cause a pure stream to flow." [6] Even so, these words manifest the religious mood of the author and the attempt to arouse the impression of a speculative and at the same time religious revelation.

But what was original and intuitive has now become imitative and dogmatic, bordering on the rhetorical. When Empedocles boasts that he surpasses the measure of mortal men,[7] that the disciple who hears his words hears the voice of the deity,[8] and exclaims, "Friends, I know that the words which I utter contain truth," [9] one cannot help having the uncomfortable feeling that this style is not really authentic. His doctrine that strife and friendship successively move the cosmos is, however, an ingenuous enlargement of the system of Heraclitus. Empedocles borrows from Heraclitus the idea that war is the father of all things, correcting and supplementing it by the idea that friendship unites all things. In a way Empedocles is on this point even more Heraclitean than Heraclitus himself, since he upholds the doctrine of the universal polarities even with respect to the principle of strife and its counterpart. Empedocles thus corrects the one-sidedness of Heraclitus, who made strife alone the dominating power. But Empedocles did not recognize that Heraclitus was more profound in letting the opposition between contrasting things or powers dominate the temporal world. Heraclitus sought harmony between them solely in the view of the god and in that of the philosopher, who, in his speculative vision, acquires a divine perspective. Empedocles no longer contradistinguished the temporal and the

---

[4] Fr. 110, verse 10.
[5] Fr. 105.
[6] Fr. 4, verse 16, tr. by A. Fairbanks

[7] Frs. 112, 113.
[8] Fr. 23.
[9] Fr. 114.

eternal; his metaphysics was physical, through and through.

Nevertheless, the contrast between love and hate is more emphatically pronounced in Empedocles than in Heraclitus, an emphasis not only original, but also true of the world in which we live. Hesiod's story of the golden age, which transformed and deteriorated in four succeeding stages, was an early mythological attempt at a philosophy of history. Empedocles is less pessimistic. The age of hate replaces the age of love, but is itself again replaced by a new age of love. But this cyclical conception is not genuinely historical; it originates in the observation of the rhythmical process in the visible cosmos. It is therefore in full agreement with the basically aesthetic and detached contemplation of the Greek mind. It expresses the impersonal and impassionate attitude assumed by an uninvolved spectator of the movement of the sun and the stars. And yet it might be also true of history; in addition to development and freedom, history displays repetition. Some epochs look more peaceful and friendly than others. There seems to be a perpetual change of periods dominated by constructive and associative work, and periods characterized by enmity, tension, and rage.

By thinking of the cosmic process in terms of friendship and strife, Empedocles transcended a narrow naturalism and approached an ethical and religious cosmology. Although his principle serves to explain the natural process of composition and decomposition, the words " strife " and " friendship " betray a meaning surpassing the existence of mere facts regulated by causality. This meaning would hold even if these words were employed only in a metaphorical or mythological sense. They do not express a law in the sense of modern science, but they express a cosmological order. The cyclical turn of cosmic forces signifies an aesthetic balance permitting the spectator (cf. the Pythagorean conception of the harmony of the spheres) to enjoy the cosmic spectacle. Empedocles surely felt a meaning in that spectacle analogous to the meaning of human life and destiny, i.e., a religious meaning. Although the cyclical rhythm points to an ascendancy of the aesthetic over the ethical (wherefore Nietzsche loved this cyclical conception), love and hate are of ethical origin. Empedocles transplanted their ethical significance into his cosmological speculation.

The contrast between the polarities in the doctrine of Empedocles can be compared with, and was perhaps even derived from, the Heraclitean scheme. But it also has an affinity to the two ways of Parmenides, since the latter mirror the fundamental contrast between truth and falsity, analogous to that of good and evil, admittedly connected with Empedocles' opposition of friendship and strife. This analogy is not the only indication of the close relation between Empedocles and Parmenides. Like Parmenides, Empedocles insists that nothing ever originates or perishes in a radical and absolute sense;[10] the All is solid, without empty space, so that nothing can ever enter it;[11] it is a perfect sphere, enjoying absolute solitude.[12] But the meaning of these Parmenidean doctrines is changed. Empedocles' description concerns only one stage in the cyclical development of the All, the stage in which love prevails. Empedocles, moreover, seems to think of the All in terms of space and matter; Parmenides used spatial and material concepts only in a metaphorical sense. Empedocles repeated the words of Parmenides without filling them with the same speculative content; in his language the words of Parmenides have therefore a dogmatic sound without a real inner life.

The main difference between Pythagoras, Heraclitus, and Parmenides, on the one hand, and Empedocles, on the other, concerns the relation between the absolute and the relative, the eternal and the temporal. Strictly speaking, there is no absolute and no eternal at all in Empedocles. The All itself is ever changing and subject to time. The Number of the Pythagoreans, the Logos of Heraclitus, and the Existent of Parmenides do not change and are not subject to time. By this most momentous modification Empedocles prepared the way for the relativistic and subjectivistic attitude of the Sophists. Empedocles was the first to conjure up the spirit of the nihilistic revolution.

Logos and Being are missing in his system. If Empedocles had reflected upon his own thought and upon the idea of the eternal cosmos, he would have discovered that his own doctrine contained these two spiritual powers in disguise. The absence of such reflection makes

---

[10] Fr. 11.

[11] Frs. 14, 17.

[12] Frs. 27 and 28. According to W. Jaeger, the word here rendered by "solitude" means rather "rest" (*The Theology of the Early Greek Philosophers*, p. 141).

his system one-sided and deficient when compared with those of his greater predecessors. The worm of degeneration was already at work. The Logos idea and the concept of Being exalted the systems of Heraclitus and Parmenides above the level of temporal change, death, corruption, and hate; but the system of Empedocles remained in the fetters of a continuous change, in which neither love nor hate are ultimately victorious. There is no ultimate in the world of Empedocles; nothing is truly absolute and truly eternal. There is no true god in his thought, although in one passage he speaks of the god with great reverence and devotion.[13] But perhaps even this utterance was only an echo of words previously spoken by Xenophanes.[14]

Empedocles still echoed the classical period of constructive and spiritual speculation, but the latter had already become eclectic. His successors advanced in the same direction, thereby evoking the revenge of skepticism. Anaxagoras was even more physically minded than Empedocles. The philosopher's exclusive task was to observe the visible world; his theories serve to explain his observations. Nevertheless, Anaxagoras was still a speculative cosmologist and not merely an empirical scientist. Aristotle even praises him as an epoch-making metaphysician because he introduced the idea of a world-mind (*nous*) into his scheme, thereby abandoning the school of the materialists and determinists by pointing to purpose and reason in the universe. Aristotle's praise, however, greatly exaggerates the role of Anaxagoras in the development of thought. In the first place, Aristotle did not rightly appraise the contribution of Heraclitus and Parmenides. And, secondly, the cosmic mind of Anaxagoras was not more spiritual than the human intelligence of Empedocles. Anaxagoras continued to interpret all things on the basis of a physical metaphysics; his idea of mind served this same purpose. Sextus Empiricus even called him "the most physical" among the early thinkers.[15] Socrates, as Plato's *Phaedo* states, was so repelled by the doctrine that he learned from Archelaus, a disciple and the successor of Anaxagoras, that he gave up all interest in cosmological speculation

[13] See above p. 68. In one passage he calls gods both strife and love. Cf. Fr. 59.
[14] It is interesting that Empedocles, in spite of his presumptuous claim to divinity, accuses and condemns himself in his poem on *Purifications* as "a fugitive from the gods and a wanderer, at the mercy of raging strife" (Fr. 115; tr. by Fairbanks).
[15] VII, 90.

and turned to the study of man alone.[16]

Anaxagoras can be called the first empiricist among the cosmological thinkers. When asked to what end he was born he answered, "For the contemplation of sun and moon and sky." [17] Also characteristic of his sober, empirical mind is his declaration that the whole firmament is made of stones,[18] by which, in an age believing in the divine nature of the sun and the stars, Anaxagoras anticipated modern science. The empirical tendency of his intellect and his theory can also be recognized in his thesis that not one substance only, as the oldest Ionians had assumed, is at the bottom of the universe. There are as many different properties of things as we experience. Anaxagoras thus abandoned the idea of an arche and turned to the opinion of daily life. Empedocles had already taken the initiative by substituting four elements for the one substance. For the sake of common sense experience, Empedocles had in principle sacrificed the idea that one substance represents the absolute. But his philosophy was still motivated at least by the speculative desire to assume that four substances were absolutes, while the vast multiplicity of appearances was only composed out of these fundamental elements. Anaxagoras categorically denied such an assumption by replacing the absolute substance by an indefinite number of particles, merely parts of things as we experience them. He thereby destroyed the whole speculative undertaking and moved in the direction of an empirical science of nature.

But in spite of this empirical and scientific tendency counteracting the speculative trend of the founders and fathers of philosophy, Anaxagoras was not simply a scientist. His astronomical observations may have been valuable, but, like Empedocles, he was still a cosmologist and therefore has a place in the history of philosophy. Although Anaxagoras' concept of mind has a naturalistic undertone, two fragments disclose its truly metaphysical function and dignity. The first insists that in contrast to all other things the mind is not composed of qualitative particles, but is, as the second fragment states, "infinite

[16] *Phaedo*, p. 98: "What expectations I had formed, and how grievously was I disappointed! As I proceeded I found my philosopher altogether forsaking mind or any other principle of order, but having recourse to air, and ether, and water, and other eccentricities."

[17] *Diogenes Laërtius*, II, 10.

[18] *Loc. cit.*, II, 12.

and sovereign and not mixed with anything, but exists separated from them and by itself alone. . . . It is the finest and purest of all things and it owns an absolute knowledge of everything and the greatest power. Mind rules over everything . . ."[19] Mind has set all things in order and is the prime mover of all things. Anaxagoras' repetition lends emphasis to his thesis: " Nothing is separated . . . from another, except mind."

In spite of its quasi-physical language, this theory undoubtedly has a speculative significance. It even has an evident kinship with the theological theory of Aristotle who, for this reason, was perhaps so impressed (unless directly influenced) by Anaxagoras. The expression " infinite " reminds one of Anaximander, although its meaning is disputed and obscure. But, most of all, the sovereign power which Anaxagoras ascribes to the world-mind seems to indicate clearly its uniquely cosmic function. This mind gives the world process a certain direction. A state of chaos existed at the beginning. Mind brought about cosmic order and unity; this pursuit is not yet finished, since there is still much disunity in the world. At first glance it would seem that Anaxagoras assigned to the mind of the world a teleological power, if not a will and a purpose. But a careful examination makes such an interpretation questionable. For the power of the mind is apparently not essentially different from the power of a mechanical causality; it does not direct but simply pushes blindly. Anaxagoras speaks nowhere of purpose and will; he only says that the mind owns " an absolute knowledge."[20] Of course this expression is in keeping with the general Greek trend favoring knowledge as the highest value, exceeding will and action. Aristotle in this respect is also a disciple of Anaxagoras. His own concept of the supreme god selects knowledge or intuition as the characteristic divine feature. And the direction of the cosmic process is not brought about by the will and purpose of the god, but by the desire of the world to reach out to the perfection of the divine. No wonder that Aristotle praises Anaxagoras' conception of the teleological power of the cosmic mind.

It is astounding that Aristotle did not realize how much more tele-

---

[19] Frs. 11 and 12.

[20] The Greek word used is *gnōmē* which is akin to *gignōskein* (" to know "), but which also means " insight " or " judgment."

ological was the conception of Heraclitus. Even the few extant fragments clearly show that Heraclitus conceived of the Logos as directing the actions of man and not only as knowing what happens in the
world.[21] If our sources are trustworthy, Heraclitus, not Anaxagoras,
was the most ethical and teleological of the earlier thinkers. According to Heraclitus, the cosmos is strictly governed by divine justice;
the good triumphs eternally in the mind of the god. Parmenides less
explicitly conceived of his cosmos as ethically governed. And yet the
perfection ascribed to the Existent is not merely physical but is primarily spiritual; this spirituality includes aesthetic and ethical perfection. When compared with the relative and temporal, the invisible
is victorious and absolute in the Pythagoreans, Heraclitus, and Parmenides. In Anaxagoras such an absolute power of the good and the
beautiful is excluded by the temporal character of the universe. The
latter is always imperfect, though in the course of time it tends to
become more united and less chaotic. In this most conspicuous and
most momentous respect the older philosophers are infinitely nearer
to the Biblical faith than Empedocles and Anaxagoras.

In the Atomists decline is even more pronounced. From the perspective of the history of the natural sciences the Atomists are the
most important school. From the perspective of the history of philosophy they are the least outstanding and remarkable. The half
legendary Leucippus and his better known disciple Democritus are
indeed the founders of modern scientific theories concerning the constitution of matter. Their theories are of historical interest for chemistry and physics, but for the questions of Being and Logos, of God
and man, such theories are of little if any import. The Atomists lead
the history of the natural sciences, because they applied the Pythagorean idea of the prevalence of number to the realm in which this
prevalence is indeed decisive. Their theory of the composition of
material substances made history because it paved the way for the
mathematical understanding of nature. Their own ideas, to be sure,
were still somewhat speculative, lacking the experimental impulse
of modern science. But they did think of material substances solely
in terms of numerical and geometrical factors: size, shape, and posi-

---

[21] Frs. 2 and 115.

tion of indivisible particles — moving in empty space and continuously changing their composition and decomposition without changing themselves. Their concepts were consistently mechanistic, even with respect to the soul and its perception of the material world.

The scope of their problems, however, indicates that they were not only scientists but philosophers. In addition to their atomistic theory they developed an ethical system, a philosophy of history and of culture, and an epistemology. But their main metaphysical concepts were concerned with the material world. Their views in other fields were determined by this central interest. Like Empedocles and Anaxagoras, the Atomists sought for a syncretistic unification of Heraclitus (flux) and Parmenides (stable being); but, at bottom, the Atomists did not retain the metaphysical intuition of either. They did not speculate about the unity of opposites, nor did they resume the motives that prompted Parmenides to found ontology. The Atomists offered no solution to ultimate problems because they themselves never envisaged such problems. The perspective of the relation between speculation and revelation therefore encounters an " empty space " when it examines the Atomists. By not recognizing the real issues of life, the world, and divinity, the Atomists were as blind as the necessity controlling their world. Empedocles and Anaxagoras had considerably narrowed down the horizon of philosophy; the Atomists curtailed it even more, hardly answering any metaphysical question, a costly price to pay for the accuracy and mathematical exactitude now made the measure and norm of truth and knowledge. The more one-sidedly our view is restricted to the investigation of the world of sense, the more the scope of the cosmos is extenuated and the significance of speculation depreciated.

No wonder that after Democritus speculative enthusiasm abated for a while. Atomism and skepticism are intrinsically connected with each other. Metaphysical interest already abdicated in the philosophy of Democritus. The slightly veiled presence of skepticism is about to break forth. Atomistic philosophy marked the bankruptcy of the cosmological approach to the ultimate. Without a new approach speculation was doomed to vanish from the earth. The new path taken by the Sophists appears to have radically abandoned cosmology and to be solely interested in the problems of humanity.

The Atomists contributed much to the gradually increasing realization that philosophy is definitely not science, in the narrow sense; philosophy answers questions raised by religion in a manner different from religion, on the plane of speculative abstraction, analysis, and reflection. The Atomists prepared the way for the separation of philosophy and science which took place in modern times. Physics and astronomy were never radically separated from philosophy in ancient times; mathematics alone had an independent development. The union between the natural sciences and philosophy once more came to the fore in Aristotle, thereby creating the richest and broadest system of antiquity, a system that characteristically denied a strictly mathematical theory of nature and rejected Atomism.

It is more than symbolical that Protagoras, the champion of the Sophists, was a fellow citizen, a close friend, and a disciple of Democritus. The Sophistic movement was the immediate consequence of the agony that metaphysics suffered with the Atomists. The degeneration of metaphysics reached its apex with the Sophistic movement. Dismay and a lack of courage and confidence, necessary to produce new speculation, were not only the result of a shift from great metaphysical creativity to a syncretistic uninspired dogmatism. They were also caused by the shocking host of schools and systems, each claiming an exclusive monopoly to the whole truth.

The adventurers and discoverers had had their day; nothing new seemed to remain. The turn to physics and to accurate observation of the empirical world, the turn to what we would today call " positivism," was the result of speculative disenchantment and disappointment. If so many possibilities exist of enunciating the nature of the Absolute and of defining the essence of all things, which of all these various showpieces deserved the greatest trust? Or is there none that really grants any security and any certainty? Is it perhaps impossible to discover the absolute and ultimate truth? Is this truth so hidden from the human mind that only one security and certainty can be offered, namely, the insight into the relativity of all speculative human insights? Must man eventually abandon all hope of ever being able to establish a system disclosing the final truth concerning the nature of things, the cosmos, and the deity?

Such questions must have arisen in the minds of thinking men. Arising out of such a situation, the Sophistic movement met such needs and doubts halfway. The Sophists did not pretend to know what is true in the last analysis. On the contrary, they admitted that they did not know the Absolute and that no one can ever know it. Skepticism appeared on the scene for the first time in the history of thought. It seemed under the circumstances to be the only logical conclusion. It was a very serious conclusion — not only the result of a momentary plight, but a conclusion of lasting significance. It is after all true that man's mind is not able to penetrate into the inner core of being; there is a barrier to even the most courageous and most sagacious intellect. Skepticism is an eternal element in thought, not simply because man is easily discouraged when he faces a tremendous task. The task is too heavy indeed. Adventure and ingenuity are too easily deceived into believing that the mind has found a bridge over the abyss and has sighted the promised land. The promised land is not promised; it is forbidden already in the book of Genesis. Man fell because the serpent promised to teach him what God alone knows, and thus he would become like God.

By their own failure to reach the end of their speculative investigation of the mind of God, the Greeks now experienced the wisdom of this Biblical story. The Sophist was the devil laughing in the background, making the best of their calamity. Unaffected by the tragedy, the Sophist enjoyed the breakdown of a heroic gigantic effort. Bankruptcy was his triumph. Analogous movements are apparent at the close of ancient and again at the end of medieval speculation, and once more after the great metaphysical systems of the seventeenth and after those of the early nineteenth century. Each time the mind of man fully exerted itself to overthrow the sphinx, only to admit the poverty of the human intelligence when the speculative intoxication is passed. Philosophy eternally wavers between the Scylla of overconfidence and the Charybdis of complete resignation, between dogmatism and skepticism. A Socrates seldom arises, and when he does, he finds no friend in the common man.

The common man, disinclined to share the lofty flight into the unknown and ultimately unknowable, is the eternal adherent of the skeptic. The Sophists won the cause by fraternizing with the common people and offering them their cheap commodities. Their greatest mission did not lie in their teaching or preaching; unbeknown to themselves, they prepared the way for Socrates, their own consummator and conqueror. This paradox originates in a feature not yet mentioned: the Sophistic discovery of the riddle of man. Heraclitus had already envisaged this riddle: " The boundaries of the soul you can never find out, even though you might walk every road; so deep is her ' logos.' " [22] " I inquired into myself " [23] is an expression that might have a hundred meanings but might have foreshadowed the imperative inscribed on the door of the oracle at Delphi, the imperative chosen by Socrates as his life's maxim: " Know thyself! " [24] Greek philosophy, in the third stage of its first period, turned to man as its proper and central problem. The discovery of this problem is of the utmost historical interest. As long as the cosmos preoccupied and consumed all philosophical inquiry, man was regarded only as a small particle in the visible universe. Of course his significance, as the knowing mind, as the doer of cosmic law, was recognized by Heraclitus and Parmenides. But even so man was of secondary rank when compared with the cosmos, and the deity governing, or embodying itself within, the cosmos. Only when the question of knowledge was no longer answered in the affirmative was the nature of man and the quest for the bounds of his knowledge moved into the foreground of philosophical inquiry.

The ascendancy of this new focus point, however, should not be exaggerated and overrated. The Sophists denied man the knowledge of the nature of things, but they continued to believe in the cosmos and in cosmic truth. They doubted merely whether man can ever know ultimate truth, but they did not doubt that it was the ideal goal to know it. Unlike the moderns, the Sophists did not make man's mind or consciousness the creator of things. They did not imagine that man could ever be understood as the source of knowledge and truth. They did not go so far as to deny that man belongs to the world in which he lives and that his knowledge depends upon the organs that unite him with that world. The opposite is the case. Man can only know anything at all inasmuch as he does belong to the world; his knowledge depends upon the organs uniting him to it. It is for this reason that all knowledge is relative and subjective. The Sophists took for granted the naïve view of world and of man, even though their attention centered on man. They did not revolutionize the common Greek outlook. The Sophists substituted epistemological reflection for cosmological speculation, but they did not

[22] Fr. 45.   [23] Fr. 101.   [24] *Charmides*, p. 164; *Phaedrus*, p. 230.

change the primacy of theoretical contemplation.

Protagoras' insistence that things are as they appear to anyone [25] would simply restrict our knowledge of things to the knowledge of their appearance. Protagoras was not so bold as to reduce reality to appearance, as did Locke, Hume, and Kant. The Sophists did not anticipate modern subjectivism and skepticism. Nevertheless, they were revolutionary in denying the naïve presupposition of the metaphysicians and in focusing attention on epistemology, ethics, the philosophy of language, the state, society, history, culture, and religion. But the more outspoken their skepticism and relativism, the more manifest becomes the impossibility of their attitude.

Sense perception might be relative, as even Plato maintained, but relativism must have some limits. Thought and speech lose all meaning if such limits are not acknowledged. Here the mission of Socrates arose. If I deny ultimately the difference between truth and falsity, my thought is frustrated before I start to think. As Socrates points out in the Platonic dialogue *Euthydemus*,[26] I then commit "logical suicide." My speech and assertions are then merely play, deception, and self-deception. All serious discussion is absurd. All sincerity and righteousness is self-deception; all life a fraud and a lie. By going to such an extreme the Sophists became the advocates of injustice and illusion; they destroyed sincere communication, not only in the realm of philosophical discourse, but in the courthouse, the market place, and the public meeting.[27] Philosophy took on in that critical moment of history a most actual and practical significance. The spiritual and moral destiny of the nation was in the balance. Philosophy once more shook the religious foundations. In that dangerous moment Socrates came forth.

[25] Plato, *Cratylus*, p. 386.   [26] P. 286.   [27] *Gorgias*, p. 454.

VII

SOCRATES

REGARDED as strange even by his fellow men at Athens,[1] Socrates is the strangest figure in the entire history of philosophy. He is peculiar not only among the philosophers of all times and of all nations but as a human being. In the picture Plato has sketched Socrates appears to be the model man, worthy to be imitated by everyone, and yet inimitable. He was a typical Greek, a typical Athenian, and yet the most untypical of all the Greeks. He was a frank and stout defender of reason, and yet a profoundly religious man, with a touch of mystical feeling. He was a thinker without any theory or doctrine; a teacher without pretending he could teach; he was a prophet, but one does not know of what god. Endowed with a good sense of humor, Socrates was in deadly earnest whenever he talked. The most modest of men, he dared to criticize everyone. And in the hour of his trial Socrates displayed the proudest and most unimaginable boldness. His secret voice deterred him from becoming a politician,[2] and yet he said: " I am the only, or almost the only, living Athenian who practices the true art of politics; I am the only politician of my time." [3]

Such a series of contradictory features could be prolonged indefinitely. By recording his conversation and behavior in the varying situations described in his dialogues, Plato probably chose the only possible way to describe the unique and mysterious Socrates. Without the figure of Socrates, Plato's dialogues would not be more attractive than many other philosophical discourses. But Socrates makes them unique, uniquely alive, and fascinating. They immediately

---

[1] " What an incomprehensible being you are, Socrates! " *Phaedrus,* 230.
[2] *Apology,* p. 31.
[3] *Gorgias,* p. 521.

put us in mind of the gospel stories. Justin Martyr, the first Greek-Christian philosopher and one-time disciple of Socrates, was even moved to compare Christ with Socrates (identified with Plato). Socrates is portrayed as having condemned the poetical myth of the Greeks. He " exhorted men to become acquainted with the god who was to them unknown, by means of the investigation of reason." [4] Socrates was a Greek anticipation and counterpart of Jesus Christ. But one has to remember that such a Greek Christ was no Christ at all. Nevertheless, the human features of the two personalities can be compared without blasphemy. And the conversations between Jesus and his disciples can be compared with the conversations between Socrates and the young men he examined, educated, and illuminated by his superior wisdom, ardent devotion, matchless sincerity, unstinted courage, great humility, and mild humanity.

Such a comparison is not without danger; it must be restricted carefully. The difference between the Son of God and the Athenian who " seemed to be like a prophet, newly inspired " [5] is so enormous that it makes any comparison easily absurd and ridiculous. But that the comparison could nevertheless come to mind shows the extraordinary and unique stature of Socrates. What is even more important, it shows the close kinship between speculation and revelation, between philosophy and prophecy, between the cause of both, existing in spite of the vast gulf between the methods, the origin, and the spirit of the two approaches to the Absolute. It shows that philosophy cannot deny the outstanding value of the personality even in its seemingly impersonal and detached contemplation. It shows that the ultimate truth cannot be reached by any man without the effort of the whole man — his thinking mind, his striving will, and his feeling imagination. The weight of the personality is stressed by Plato's portrait of his beloved teacher and friend, more than it could have been stressed by any logical demonstration alone. Socrates repeatedly emphasizes that it is the impersonal truth that alone matters and at which he alone aims. He cares nothing for his own opinion; his own sole concern is with the knowledge of the truth.

[4] *The Second Apology of Justin for the Christians. Addressed to the Roman Senate.*

[5] *Cratylus,* p. 396.

And yet, Socrates' own personality is of the utmost importance; it means more than any of his utterances, detached from the total impression of his figure.

The contradictory quality and strangeness of Socrates is matched only by the interpretation given to him as a philosopher by various historians and scholars.[6] All agree that he is a remarkable thinker, perhaps the most remarkable that ever lived, and yet opinions of his greatness are widely different. At times one even has the feeling that the epithet " great," although freely attributed, is not fully justified by the record. And on other occasions one senses that a historian does not quite know why he calls Socrates " great." This strange fact can best be understood if we remember that Socrates was a philosopher without a philosophy, if by " philosophy " we mean a system of thought or a set of doctrines. Socrates never developed a cosmology, ontology, epistemology, philosophy of religion, and system of logic, or a theory of the state. And it is even doubtful that he taught ethics in the strict sense. Some would think of him as being only another Sophist of a queer and singular sort; others would have us believe that he was the author of the doctrine of the Ideas and the founder of logic. Some even doubt if we know anything about him or whether the portrait depicted by Plato has any historical truth. Some assume that he is great only because he happened to be the teacher of Plato and was glorified by his really great disciple. And others suggest that his reputation rests upon the *cause célèbre* which made him appear as the martyr of philosophy.

The wide variety of views and opinions about Socrates only confirms what I have said. He is as great as everyone concedes because he is a thinker and a prophet. By his very existence and personality he illustrates that philosophy and religion are inwardly bound together. The philosopher who searches more than he finds is most akin to a man chosen by God to reveal the truth. Socrates is great because he is neither a skeptic nor a dogmatist. The very individuality of Socrates was a living demonstration of the paradox that when philosophy abandons any claim to knowledge of the Absolute, without falling into the pitfall of skepticism, it ascends to its greatest heights.

[6] A good survey and critique of the historical sources is delivered by A. E. Taylor in his little book *Socrates*. I confine my discussion to the figure depicted by Plato.

Socrates was a philosopher who understood that the task of philosophy is to seek the truth without ever holding it fast. He was, therefore, always attractive to those who, desiring to know the truth, felt that the truth is too high to be enmeshed in any system or any set of doctrines. The truth can only be the permanent goal of striving and the ideal of acting. Socrates did not only teach this insight; he proved it by his life. His life became his philosophy; the latter could not be divorced from his conduct and attitudes.

Plato describes Socrates through the mask of a young man who says: "When I hear a man discoursing of virtue or of any sort of wisdom, who is a true man and worthy of his theme, I am delighted beyond measure and I compare the man and his words and note the harmony and their inner agreement. And such a one I deem to be the true musician . . . for he has in his own life a harmony of words and deeds." [7] Socrates probably felt that philosophy, as he understood it, could not be expressed in a system of thought apart from a living personality. Therefore, he never wrote a line, gave public lectures, or composed any treatise or discourse. His exclusive medium of self-expression was the living word, the occasional conversation, his famous interrogation. Seemingly without any definite plan or intention, he engaged his fellow citizen in questions which led deeper and deeper into the heart of the problem of life, its meaning, goal, and value. Socrates did not pretend to know the answers but repeatedly admitted his ignorance. He realized the over-all importance of his questions; he was convinced that no one living would not agree with his emphasis. The most human and most worthy obligation, is, therefore, to seek an answer, a search that may mean a lifelong adventure. Man has no choice but to seek, even if an answer cannot be found. As man must live, he must philosophize. To philosophize is the human way of living; it distinguishes man from the beast.

Philosophizing is inseparably bound to man's special nature. Man loses his humanity if as a beast he lives only for his own preservation. Humanity involves obligations. It requires the fulfillment of duties. Man can live in a worthy or in an unworthy manner, a distinction that he ought to know. Man ought, therefore, to inquire into the nature of virtue, happiness, and wisdom, three intrinsically connected

[7] *Laches,* p. 188.

items. Only he who knows what virtue is can strive after it; and only he who strives after it can become happy. The art of living is based upon such knowledge, knowledge that Socrates calls wisdom. Wisdom is therefore the highest goal of life and of philosophy. " Philosophy " literally means the pursuit of wisdom. In this sense every human being is or should be a philosopher; only thus he can discharge the basic obligation of life and become a man in the true sense. Such knowledge is infinitely more important and necessary than all other scientific or speculative knowledge. Man need not know the reason why the sun moves around the earth or why and how nature proceeds as it does. But he must know what he has to do to live a worthy life and to gain the happiness inevitably conditioned by the fulfillment of this fundamental obligation.

Socrates did not prove such basic convictions. He took them for granted, as earlier thinkers had assumed that the cosmos is the true object of speculation, whose core could and ought to be penetrated by the human mind. Socrates, not without the example of the Sophists, but in a quite different fashion and spirit, turned away from all cosmological speculation to the inner investigation of the human self. Socrates opened an absolutely new horizon. The greatest wonder is not the outer world, nor even the invisible power governing it. The greatest marvel is the soul of man. Cosmic beauty is as nothing when compared to the beauty of the inner man. If any access is to be had to the deepest ground of existence, it is to be found in the inward part of man himself, in the center from whence springs the ability to control and govern one's own life. In that inner center man encounters the deity; here is the source of all virtue, devotion, loyalty, courage, justice, veracity, and moderation. It is here that wisdom has its roots. Why should the human mind roam abroad and investigate stars and stones, when the most central, the most vital truth — the truth about you — dwells so near? If man can find out anything worthy to be known, it is here within himself. And this truth should be easier to discover than the truth about the cosmos at large; it is so near — indeed, it is identical with our very self.

One may say: If this is the upshot of the Socratic philosophy, then it was not so much a philosophy as a religious awakening; Socrates was not so much a thinker as a preacher; not a scientifically minded man but a spiritual and ethical educator; a missionary, a prophet, or the like. Undoubtedly Socrates was all this, and yet, at the same time, he was a profound thinker who laid bare a truth no philosopher can dare to ignore. He was unquestionably right in pointing to a previously neglected realm of inquiry, a realm at least as important as any chosen by previous thinkers of the first period as their sole or central object. Socrates is so untypical, his method, emphasis, and discussion so baffling and startling, that it is impossible to label him. To Greek speculation he brought an element completely alien to it, an element that might be called revelatory, in the sense of the Bible. But Socrates introduced it in the style and on the level of Greek thinking, in a language the Athenians could well understand and take to heart. And even then they felt the strangeness and feared the impact of this new wisdom. Socrates, the powerful debater, the ironical jester, the inexorable searcher, outwitted the wittiest of his fellow countrymen.

This overmodest and unambitious fighter was the most dangerous of men when opposed. Without directly refuting the argument of his opponent, Socrates' questions made the latter feel that he was wrong, or at least that his pretension to know the truth was unwarranted. Socrates forced his adversaries to recognize their inner weakness in character and intelligence, a method that made him the victor in argument but also embittered those who were defeated and compromised. The Athenian pharisees therefore grew in number and power, until they finally won the outer ascendancy and caused his execution. But Socrates was not dead after his death; he outlived all his enemies.

The strong personal and spiritual effect upon his disciples can be appraised by the words of Alcibiades spoken at the banquet at which Socrates and others talked about the nature of Eros. After Alcibiades had compared Socrates with one of the busts of Silenus, outwardly repulsive but when opened in the middle found to contain images of gods, he goes on to say: "When we hear any other speaker, even a very good one, he produces absolutely no effect upon us, or not much, whereas the mere fragments of you and your words, even at second hand, and however imperfectly repeated, amaze and possess the souls of every man, woman, and child who come within hearing of them. . . . My heart leaps within me more than that of any Corybantian reveler, and my eyes rain tears when I hear them. . . . I have heard Pericles and other great orators, and I thought that they spoke well, but I never had any similar feeling; my soul was not stirred by them, nor was I angry at the thought of my own slavish state. But this Marsyas has often brought me to such a pass that I have felt as if I could hardly endure the life which I am leading. . . . He makes me confess that I ought not to live as I do, neglecting the wants of my own soul. . . . He is the only person who ever made me ashamed. . . . For I know that I cannot answer him or say that I ought not to do as he bids." [8] Notice how often Alcibiades uses the word " soul," which was probably not often used by him. This hard-boiled warrior gets soft and mild and feels contrition when Socrates speaks.

The charm of Socrates produced a moral change, a kind of conversion, a deep inward revolution of the whole personality — not merely an intellectual experience or improvement. It was a religious effect, though not generated by the usual religious means. This was the secret of his power over men. Philosophy as understood by him was a new life, a renewal of the heart as well as an instruction of the mind. If the much used and much abused term " existential " implies that philosophy is not a matter of abstract thinking only, but that it should always be rooted in the inward soul, reforming and purging the latter, then Socrates was an existential thinker. Perhaps he was even the most existential thinker of all time! Kierkegaard's emphasis upon this point is certainly right.[9] He calls the attitude of Socrates " passion of inwardness in existing " and an " analogue to faith," definitions hitting the heart of Socrates' philosophy and individual character and conduct.

The scope of Hellenic existence was immensely enlarged by, and even totally transcended, in Socrates. Socrates applied means of discussion and methods of thought well in line with the theoretical nature of the Greek, e.g., his love of debate, gift of logical reasoning, predilection for contemplation and reflection. And yet the spirit animating his conversation was no longer Greek. His hearers probably felt that strange inwardness and that passionate faith and were as much transported as they were frightened when he addressed them.

[8] *Symposium,* pp. 215 f.
[9] Cf. especially *Philosophical Fragments* and *Concluding Unscientific Postscript.*

Socrates discovered a new dimension of the human soul and a new approach to the mystery of existence. The words "soul" and "existence" took on a new significance and meaning when he uttered them. Even the very word "cosmos" could not retain its previous connotation; it had to cope with a new dimension. And it was Plato who drew the consequence of this insight. In the mind of Plato, cosmology, the study of which he resumed, profited from the discovery of Socrates; it was resuscitated in the spirit of Socrates. The new dimension is the dimension of the Biblical conceptions of man and God. Of course Socrates did not know anything about the revelation of the Biblical Creator and Lawgiver; nevertheless, his soul groped and longed for it. Kierkegaard is perfectly right in this respect, and Nietzsche also instinctively felt that in Socrates a new element, less typically Greek than the pre-Socratics, had been introduced into the historical drama of thought. The Athenian court that indicted Socrates was certainly moved by political intrigues; nevertheless, the judges were not completely wrong when they scented something totally revolutionary in the Socratic conversations, something adverse to their national traditions and their mythological consciousness. Socrates did not "introduce a new deity" into that consciousness. And yet he did reform the religious feelings in the direction of an overthrow of the Olympian gods and of polytheism in general. His contribution to this religious earthquake was probably greater than the critique by Heraclitus and Xenophanes had been.

Socrates discovered the dimension of the moral conscience, a dimension unknown to the Greeks, at least in the sense of an inner tribunal of the individual self — so central in the Christian consciousness. The Greek language had no special word to designate the moral conscience. The "demon" of which Socrates often spoke only warned him not to do something; it did not command him to do anything positive. And yet the warning was the voice of his conscience. The warning voice of conscience is, in our own experience, louder and more distinct than the commanding voice. The Bible refers to the original conscience as it appeared in Eve, as a warning not to eat from the tree. The voice of conscience was intimately and intrinsically connected with the new dimension of the soul as discovered by Socrates. It was the most manifest experience of that new inwardness which characterized his personality and conversation. This conversation was first of all an inward conversation of the soul with the soul, of the self with the self. " I am . . . seeking to convince myself; to convince my hearers is a secondary matter with me. . . . I would ask you to be thinking of the truth and not of Socrates." [10] The last word reminds one of a similar utterance of Heraclitus. [11]

There was a depth in the soul of Socrates more akin to the depth of revelation than to that of speculation and cosmic intuition. Socrates was even afraid of his own wisdom. " I have long been wondering at my own wisdom: I cannot trust myself. And I think that I ought to stop and ask myself: What am I saying? For there is nothing worse than self-deception." [12] Only an extremely conscientious person could have spoken such words, betraying not only the fear of erring but also that dimension of moral inwardness so characteristic of Socrates. Socrates was wont to talk with himself before he talked with others, for he had discovered that (to use the words of Augustine) the truth is within the soul. When the soul is alone with herself, she is closer to the truth than at any other time. When the soul speaks with herself, nothing entices her to deceive herself; it is then quietly examining herself and the truth. This inward room of the self (self-conversation is the very lifeblood of the human self) is the room of truth, where the soul is at home. " When the soul descries herself in herself, she passes there into the realm of the pure and the eternal . . . and as long as she is allowed to stay within herself, she ceases to err. . . . Is this not the state of the soul that we call wisdom ? " [13]

These last words are taken from the dialogue *Phaedo,* a dialogue that is perhaps one of the most revealing concerning the inner position of Socrates, his faith, and his soul. But, on the other hand, the *Phaedo* contains doctrinal discussions that in my judgment belong to Plato alone. It is, of course, extremely difficult to judge. To a certain degree, what is purely Socratic and what is Platonic will always remain a matter of subjective feeling. I will presently say a few more words on this matter. But the sentence quoted seems to me to

[10] *Phaedo,* p. 91.
[11] Fr. 50; see above, p. 93. Cf. also Fr. 113: "Thinking is common to all," and the words of Socrates, "The discovery of the truth is a common good" (*Gorgias,* p. 505).
[12] *Cratylus,* p. 428.
[13] *Phaedo,* p. 79; cf. *loc. cit.,* 65.

be a sterling expression of Socrates himself. The very essence of all he had to say is that inner conversation is the purest source of veracity and truth — two things never to be separated in the mind and philosophy of Socrates. Here the new dimension of existence was most conspicuously discovered. Man is that being that can talk with itself, and therefore is a " self." And because man is a self, he can seek for truth and can find it. And because man can talk with himself, he has a conscience and is a moral being; he is a moral being first and a being that knows other things second. And only because he can talk with himself can he talk with other people and philosophize and seek the truth with them. Living investigation, and " midwifery," prompting him to help others to bring forth their own ideas; humility, in learning even from those who were much less wise than he; constant preparedness to admit that he did not know anything for sure, but was a mere seeker for the truth like everyone else, generated the method of Socrates. His method was an outcome of the primacy of conscience or, in the words of Kant, " the primacy of moral reason." Indeed, in his own way, Socrates anticipated this central position of Kant.

The conversation of the soul with itself [14] is at the very heart, not only of the Socratic conversation but also of the Platonic dialogue, its historical sequel. Plato knew no method more suitable than that of Socrates to represent his own philosophy. Therefore, Plato imitated the living conversation of his teacher, thereby creating a new style, the philosophical dialogue. But what was a matter of immediate existence with Socrates became an artifice in the hand of Plato. Whereas Socrates philosophized wherever he stood or walked, whenever he found someone willing to answer his questions, Plato in contrast used the form of conversation only to develop his own more or less closed system of thought. We shall later see that it is this remarkable difference that distinguished the entire approach and thought of the two men. We must be grateful, however, to Plato, the great master of writing, for, like the gospel writers, Plato saved what would otherwise have been lost forever.

Socrates' stress upon the purity of the soul was perhaps an inheritance of the Orphic religion or of the Pythagoreans who had

[14] *Theaetetus*, p. 189.

come to Athens. In any case it has a religious tenor or undertone. One can even speak of a "religion of the soul" in Socrates. In Homer soul and body are one unity; the soul of the deceased is only a shadow of what it has been in life. If separated from the body, the soul of the dead man leads a sad and poor existence. Socrates, in contrast, thought of the soul as the real substance of the personality; the body is only a hindrance or even the coffin of the soul. Death signifies a deliverance from the fetters of the body, the entrance into a state in which the soul is absolutely free. If the soul is kept pure in life, it will enjoy the life beyond. Socrates even anticipated the Biblical idea of a last judgment; the task of keeping the soul undefiled in this life is, therefore, of utmost importance. "I am persuaded of the truth of these things and I consider how I shall present my soul whole and undefiled before the judge in that day. Renouncing the honors at which the world aims, I desire only to know the truth and to live as well as I can, and when I die, to die as well as I can. . . . I exhort you also to take part in the great combat which is the combat of life, and greater than every other earthly combat." [15] Such a conception of life is certainly not Greek in the classical sense. It is the expression of another spiritual atmosphere, a breeze of which had entered mysteriously into the soul of this strange Athenian philosopher.

Socrates thus paved the path toward a new religion which eventually was to conquer Greece and all Europe. Socrates' attitude toward his own soul was at the same time an attitude toward the divine. It created the possibility of comprehending the deity in a new way. The soul was for him most closely connected with the divine sphere. "The soul most resembles the divine." [16] From this conviction he concluded that the soul is immortal, even if he did not give the elaborate logical proofs ascribed to him by Plato in the *Phaedo*. To Socrates immortality meant a most intimate alliance with "the good and wise god," as he calls Hades in that dialogue. "The real philosopher has, therefore, reason to be of good cheer when about to die. . . . No one who has not studied philosophy [that means, who has not loved wisdom and sought for it] and who is not entirely pure at the time of his departure is allowed to enter the company of the gods, but the lover of knowledge [*philomathēs*]." [17] How high a con-

[15] *Gorgias*, p. 526.   [16] *Phaedo*, p. 80.   [17] *Phaedo*, p. 65.

cept of a philosopher and of philosophy! How religious a view! In the *Symposium* the philosopher is called a " friend of God." For " the gods have care of anyone whose desire is to become just and to be like God." [18] In no other man did Greek philosophy fulfill so perfectly its mission of preparing for the gospel.

Such is even more evident if we examine what might be called the " doctrine " of Socrates. (It is not really a doctrine; it is rather a kind of ethical wisdom like that taught in the Bible, especially by Jesus himself.) First of all, Socrates believed that virtue can be taught. But we know already what kind of teacher he was and what kind of teaching it is that is afforded by virtue. There is no " intellectualism " in such conceptions; it is true, however, that he conceived of knowledge in an exalted fashion and that logical thinking was more weighty and indeed more creative in him than it was in the Biblical prophet. The word *" phronēsis "* which Socrates mostly applies to his thinking, does not mean intuition (*noēsis*) nor knowledge (*gnōsis*), nor scientific understanding (*epistēmē*); rather it implies ethical considerations, a kind of moral pondering in which purpose, prudence, thoughtfulness are factors. In that sense Socrates can say: " All true virtue is the companion of phronesis." [19] It is this he would teach. And in this way virtue and knowledge are united and virtue is the result of thinking. Of course, Socrates also refuted the Sophistic thesis that there is no distinction between good and evil, and thereby he created the philosophical science called " ethics." But he created it in the form of an applied conviction. According to Socrates, there is no ethics if a man is not ethical in his heart, will, and conduct. Ethics is not a merely theoretical science that can be learned by merely logical demonstration. Conviction is as necessary for ethics as intuition is necessary for speculation.

Secondly, Socrates was convinced that " no one does wrong voluntarily, but all do wrong against their will." [20] In the same context he says: " It is not in human nature to prefer evil to good." This " doctrine " has always been cited in order to illustrate the optimistic and intellectualistic nature of his ethics. He seemingly teaches here that moral wrongdoing is the outcome of error, not of an evil will, and that the will never wills evil, but always the good. However, we

---

[18] *Republic*, X, p. 613.   [19] *Phaedo*, p. 69.   [20] *Gorgias*, p. 509.

must carefully examine his words. Is it not correct that no one wills evil for the sake of evil, but rather for the sake of some advantage, pleasure, or disaffection? Is it not true that the murderer does not murder because he wills evil, but because he wills the money or the wife or the position of his victim? And is it not the same with respect to all evil-doing? The wicked and the vicious perform their deeds because they want something that promises pleasure — not because they want to do the bad. Only the devil wants the bad for the sake of the bad. But the devil is a figure of religious faith and imagination, not a human being. Consequently, is not Socrates simply expressing the correct experience in the field of moral motivations and actions? Indeed, he is in full agreement with Paul: "I do not do the good I want, but the evil I do not want is what I do" (Rom. 7:18–25). Both Socrates and Paul are of the opinion that evil is not the result of a deliberate will.

There is, to be sure, a limit to the agreement between the Athenian philosopher and the apostle. Paul would say that evil is motivated by desire, passion, impulse, interest, but not by the deliberate will. Socrates would say that it is brought about, not by the deliberate will but by lack of wisdom, ethical insight (knowledge), clear thinking, and philosophy. To that degree Socrates may be called an ethical intellectualist. Indeed, he is still a Greek in spite of, or rather because of, his religious conviction, which was after all the conviction of an Athenian. Socrates joined insight and will and made the latter dependent upon the former. Therefore, he held that the will can be educated, if insight is trained by thinking. Saint Paul, in contrast, believes that the disposition of the heart, the seat of faith, governs the will and human action. Paul would therefore conclude that man can be educated best if he is taught the right faith. Unfortunately, an extended discussion of this difference would destroy the continuity of this volume.

But I might add that the difference between Socrates and Paul, apparent though it is, loses its severity somewhat when we remember that in Socrates the heart and the mind were much more united than we commonly assume. Thought cannot be severed from faith. It is this that makes his whole philosophical approach religious. The famous equation between goodness and happiness — the third of his doctrines — has to be understood in the light of his faith. Kant was wrong when he criticized this equation on the ground that it is not warranted by experience, cannot be demonstrated a priori, and united conceptually. Kant held goodness and happiness to be different in origin and nature. Such may be the case, but in Socrates it was faith that enabled him to believe that the good man would always be happy because of his goodness, and that only the good man can be truly happy.

Of course Socrates knew that fate can deprive the good man of his possessions and loved ones. His emphatic insistence on the thesis that the wise man is both good and happy was possible because he understood happiness not as being dependent upon any external conditions, such as wealth, health, honor, or repute; it is something absolutely inward: an inner harmony of the soul with itself and with the conduct of the entire person in life. In other words, by happiness Socrates understood a state of the soul dependent upon goodness and wisdom. It was for this reason that he felt so sure that his thesis was right. The Greek word for happiness (*eudaimonia*) has a religious quality that points to the relation between piety and well-being.[21] Socrates was convinced on the ground of his "religion of the soul" that this relation existed. Since the soul itself is divine the gods bless it, if it keeps its original and intrinsic purity and integrity. This ethicoreligious faith was the real source of his "doctrine" concerning the unity of moral goodness and moral or spiritual happiness — a doctrine shared by Biblical faith. One of the fundamental convictions implied in the latter is that "the Spirit himself intercedes for us with sighs too deep for words" (Rom. 8:28).

The just man is happy, according to the creed of Socrates, because justice and righteousness are themselves the greatest goods and are safe in the man who practices them. Therefore "it is better to suffer evil than to do evil . . . for doing injustice is the greatest of evils."[22] The word "evil" connotes, in the language of Socrates, both wrongdoing and misery. These two are basically the same, even though most people do not recognize this identity because they think of misery only in terms of worldly pains and bereavements, instead of understanding it in terms of spiritual sufferings. Jesus told the disciples they would undergo severe persecution and tribulation, but neverthe-

[21] "*Eudaimonia*" is defined by Aristotle as an activity in accordance with virtue.
[22] *Gorgias*, pp. 469, 475, 489.

less be blessed. Likewise Socrates says to his disciple Callicles: " I tell you that to be boxed on the ears wrongfully is not the worst evil that can befall a man, nor to have my purse and my body cut open; but that to smite me and slay me wrongfully is far more disgraceful and evil to the doer of the wrong than to me who am the sufferer." [23] And Socrates is in complete agreement with the spirit of Jesus, when he advises, " Never mind, if someone despises you as a fool and insults you but let him strike you and do ye be of good cheer," [24] or when he insists while imprisoned and condemned to death, " We must not do injustice, nor must we do evil to anyone whatever evil we may have suffered from him." [25] It is difficult indeed not to see and hear the inner kinship between words like these and the substance of the preaching of Jesus. But modern times always stressed the " intellectualism " of Socrates and the diversity of his faith and Biblical faith.

The truth is that Socrates is the most religious philosopher of antiquity, the most Christian figure in the pre-Christian pagan world. It is this kinship that makes him great. No wonder that the Athenians did not like him and eventually put him to death. One has only to read the *Apology,* probably the most loyal record about him [26] (Plato was himself present), to be impressed by the audacious sincerity and the ironical sagacity covering up the inner humility and devotion of this strangest and greatest of all the Athenians. Whether or not Socrates uttered exactly the words recorded by Plato does not matter so much. Undoubtedly they render the spirit of Socrates and his mood in this fateful hour, just as the gospel stories have preserved the substance of the spirit of Jesus and his behavior in the trial he underwent.

Only a heart of stone would not be stirred and moved when it reads how this wisest of the Greeks had to defend his divine mission against the petty men who judged him. Undaunted and certain that he was in the hand of a higher power than the Athenian court, Socrates tried to explain the meaning of his discussions and the purpose of his educational work, knowing that he was speaking to men too preoccupied with political passions and ambitions to understand his philosophic and religious ardor and activity, too much governed by

[23] *Gorgias,* p. 508.
[24] *Op. cit.,* p. 527.
[25] *Crito,* p. 49.
[26] Jaeger, *Paideia,* II, p. 37.

judicial chicanery and even malice to appraise quietly and generously his character and cause. It is a sad story leading to a sad end. And yet the reader feels so deeply the great issues for which Socrates stood, and the divine solemnity of his attitude, that he is not depressed but only elated and lifted up. A tragic event for the Athenian nation but an event that was " beyond tragedy " for mankind!

Socrates was certain that his work and obedience to the god who had sent him to the Athenians was not in vain, even though his person was doomed in the earthly sense, and his effort frustrated, if measured by temporal standards. The eternal significance of his task could not be judged or settled by any earthly court or political and juridical authority. This grave hour meant only one thing to him: to behave as worthily as he had lived, to be worthy of the inner vocation which he had been obliged to perform. " If now when the god orders me to fulfill the philosophic mission of searching into myself and other men, I were to desert my post through fear of death, or any other fear, that would be awkward indeed, and I might justly be arraigned in court for denying the existence of the gods." [27]

Socrates was sure that he was given to Athens by a divine power; his conception of the divine was religious in a more profound sense than was the conception of the judges, and of Athens and Hellas in its entirety. His faith was the deepest source of his philosophy and the source of his personality. In the moment of danger and trial this faith granted to him the courage and the spiritual freedom to speak as Plato tells us he did. His faith was no longer a pagan faith; neither mythological nor cosmological, it was an " analogy " to the Christian faith. Socrates was so lonely and alone because no one shared or could share in his faith. It was his personal charm and *charisma*.

The god whom Socrates obeyed and served had not yet been revealed to his nation. His religious mission could therefore not be understood. Accordingly Socrates could only be a short interlude between the pre- and the post-Socratics, between the first period of Greek philosophy, with its half-mythological cosmology, and the second period, in which Plato and Aristotle built their classical systems. Although profoundly influenced by Socrates, Plato was by no means a Socratic thinker; nor were the so-called Socratic schools, the Megarian, the Cynic, and the Cyrenaic, genuinely Socratic. A Socratic

[27] *Apology,* p. 29.

philosophy was essentially impossible because of the peculiar nature of Socrates. What he had taught was so personal that it could not be continued when Socrates himself was no more, except in the fashion in which Plato did continue it. Socrates remained the lonely and strange figure he had been in life, inspiring everyone who heard about him, but without a successor. A Socratic period between the pre- and the post-Socratic periods does not exist.

This leads me back to the question concerning the relation between Socrates and Plato and the portion of Plato's philosophy that has to be traced back to Socrates. I personally am convinced that Socrates had no share in that philosophy. Socrates did not discover and teach the ontology of the Idea or the doctrine of recollection as the source of knowledge. Socrates did not develop any strictly logical theory (theory of logic) or even an ethical or political philosophy, as developed by Plato. I know how difficult it is to defend this opinion, on the basis of the documents we possess, against those who aver that Socrates had a greater or smaller part in all the doctrinal elements of Plato's system. But if the picture that I have sketched of the personality of Socrates is to the point, Socrates did not invent and propagate such doctrines.[28] If this picture is correct, we cannot assume that the man who strictly denied that he had any definite theory or metaphysics would have generated it nevertheless; this would undo the earnestness of his frequent remarks, agreeing so well with the whole impression of his attitude. Socrates was too tied up with the concrete situations of life to bring forth the abstract thoughts of Plato. He was too much of a prophetic nature to have speculated about the origin of knowledge or the reality of Ideas.

In the *Apology,* presenting the most lively and the most historical portrait, Socrates denies explicitly and emphatically that he ever had taught any definite knowledge in the field of natural or of moral philosophy. " The truth is that I have no knowledge of the kind." [29] Why should Socrates in the hour of trial, facing his death, have concealed that he did have a certain knowledge, not in the realm of physics, but in that of metaphysics? If he had really developed such

[28] I cannot agree with the majority of scholars who believe that Socrates is the initiator of Plato's metaphysics, as even so learned and profound a scholar as A. E. Taylor does.

[29] P. 20.

a doctrine as that of the Ideas or any other strictly theoretical, epistemological, or logical principles, why did he not say so? Why should
Plato have deliberately concealed such a fact, if it was a fact, in his
rendering of the speech of Socrates? Would Plato conceal it in order
to make his own contribution to philosophy appear more original?
Such a motive would not well agree with the character of the great
founder of theoretical idealism and the great admirer of Socrates!
Plato, moreover, in his later dialogues, did put his own theories into
the mouth of Socrates. Would Plato have concealed the fact of their
foundation by Socrates in the *Apology* and yet ascribe such to him in
all the other so-called Socratic dialogues? The truth is that Socrates
did not found the idealistic metaphysics or any other philosophical
doctrine of Plato. Partly from gratitude and partly for artistic reasons, Plato generously introduced Socrates as a speaker defending
Plato's own theories and principles. Socrates would not have been
the seeker par excellence; the " gadfly of the Athenians," as he calls
himself in the *Apology;* the " true musician," in whom words and
deeds were in perfect harmony; the philosopher-prophet; in short, he
would not have been Socrates, if he had set forth the theory of the
Ideas, or any other theory.

Socrates was not a Sophist but he resembled the Sophists in a way
that Plato did not. If he had been the author of Plato's theories, he
would not have resembled them. He would not have been confused
with the Sophists in the past or even today. Full justice is not done to
Socrates or to Plato if, by distortion, Socrates is portrayed in the
rightful role of Plato, as the classical systematician, and not as a peculiar Sophist. Socrates and Plato cannot exist in one and the same
person. And we should not try to conceive of such an imaginary person, for such would be neither the one nor the other, because he
would need to combine the nature of both. I take it that even Kierkegaard erred in assuming that Socrates was the author of the thesis
that we know the truth by way of recollection. This idea presupposes
a theory of pre-existence which Socrates never propagated. He never
propagated any theory of immortality but was content with a faith
in immortality of a sort. In the *Apology* he bluntly admits that he
has no knowledge about man's destiny after death, as he has no
knowledge of any scientific kind.

It is true that Socrates by the severity and acuteness of his thinking indirectly promoted the origin of logic, epistemology, and ontology; that he prompted Plato and others to think methodically about these matters. But he himself was only the stimulating power in this development, not the author of theories.

One might go so far as to surmise that unless he rejected it outright, Socrates would at least have doubted the doctrine of the Ideas, had he lived long enough to become acquainted with it. Socrates would probably have preserved his " skeptical " attitude in opposition to this new type of speculation, although he might have admired its inventor as much as Plato admired his teacher.

The glory and charm of Socrates is that he was, and yet was not, a " philosopher," in the sense in which the history of philosophy uses that word. And he also was and was not a prophet, in the Biblical sense. Between these contrary figures Socrates was an inspired thinker, an arguing and debating seeker. He was perfectly and exclusively human, and yet a man of God. Unless we assume that God inspired and commanded Socrates to prepare for the coming of his Son, on the level and in the language of Greek philosophy, Socrates demonstrated, by his personality and conduct, that the human mind has resources enabling it to approach, by its own effort, the truth revealed in the Bible. If the duality and unity of the thinker and seeker in Socrates points to the wide range of human possibilities, one might conclude that he was the most human of all men, since he embraced this vast scope within himself. This might be why all historians agree that he is the greatest figure in the history of philosophy, and yet have difficulties in registering him under any definite historical title or genus.

VIII

THE COSMOS OF THE IDEAS

A. THE HERITAGE

SOCRATES had renounced cosmology. He could not and did not go back to it, to create a new cosmology, even on a new level. Plato was the heir not only of Socrates but also of the pre-Socratics. Plato was free to renew the old attempts now that he had learned from Socrates how to rise to the Invisible, supported by the inwardness and the moral insight of his great teacher. Plato was the heir of the whole pre-Socratic period, but especially of its middle (classical) epoch, in which Pythagoras, Heraclitus, and the Eleatics had built their towering systems. Plato was not affected by the metaphysical weariness of the late fifth century or by its resulting skepticism. The ardent faith of Socrates, his penetrating search for truth, his radical criticism, his unbreakable courage, and his victorious sincerity inspired the younger man and kindled the flame of an indefatigable inquiry into the mystery of being. The older thinkers had spoken about the mind of the world; the very word " mind " assumed a new depth after Socrates had lived and revealed his own mind. What does it mean that the cosmos is governed by mind? What does it mean that there is knowledge in things, as Heraclitus had intimated, when he spoke of the cosmic Logos? What is the relation between the Existent of Parmenides and the world in which we live each day?

Plato could dare to answer such great questions after Socrates had taught that the key to the mystery of the world is in the soul, or is even the soul itself. It was the religion of the soul that encouraged new investigations and awoke the hope of solving the unsolved riddles of the older philosophers. Therefore, the earlier dialogues deal so intensively with this religion. I shall not discuss the thorny question of the temporal succession of the dialogues. In general I agree with the picture of Plato's development given by Werner Jaeger in the second volume of his work *Paideia*. Jaeger defends the thesis that the dialogues written before the *Republic* were but steps leading up to the latter, the greatest of all dialogues.[1] In the course of many years Plato slowly developed his own theses and doctrines. After first writing fairly historical reports on Socrates, Plato began to intermingle his own views with those of Socrates. He continued to make Socrates the central speaker in his dialogues, until gradually this figure began to fade out and become not much more than a name behind which Plato himself stood. The dialogue *Phaedo* was a critical point in this development. The author of the Fourth Gospel preserved the original traits of Jesus and even reported original sayings not to be found elsewhere. And yet John depicted Jesus in the light of a new time and a new spirit. Likewise, Plato in the *Phaedo* transformed the original Socrates while retaining many features. Plato added much to the picture drawn by the earlier dialogues, but he profoundly changed the portrait of his beloved friend by making him the author of his own theory of knowledge and ontology of Ideas.[2]

Perhaps the *Phaedo* gives us the key to the origin of Plato's doctrines, because it shows how Plato concluded, from the original message and mission of Socrates, far-reaching consequences that had never entered the mind of Socrates himself. Indeed, there is a close connection between the prophetico-ethical convictions of Socrates and the discovery of the cosmos of Ideas by Plato. These Ideas are no longer so objectively conceived as the Number of the Pythagoreans, the Logos of Heraclitus, or the Existent of Parmenides. Although Plato's Ideas are not concepts in the human mind, they enter the human mind and make its knowledge possible. No doubt Heraclitus had first found the Logos in himself. But Heraclitus had not speculated on the relation between the cosmic Logos and the human mind or soul, but had thought objectively of the universal Logos. Plato, the disciple of Socrates, had learned that the knowledge of the self is more important than any other knowledge. The direc-

[1] See there also the discussion of the literature on the relation between Socrates and Plato.

[2] Cf. the new commentary on Plato by Herm. Gauss, 1952 ff.

tion toward the inner room of the self had become a guiding value to him. It was natural to him to put the question, How can we use that knowledge for the purpose of knowing the ultimate?

Perhaps Socrates had asked, "What is the nature of courage, self-control, justice?" and so on, and had thereby entered the road that eventually led to the theory of the Idea. Jaeger's thesis that Plato from the beginning aimed at the philosophic understanding of the state and at the definition of the true and ideal state is very plausible.[3] It is indeed striking that the earlier discussions are resumed and continued in the *Republic*. Plato's interest in the political sphere of life was certainly one of the dynamics in his life and thought. The tragic issue of the Peloponnesian War and the political disturbances and disorders that followed must naturally have agitated the thinking mind. The discussions of Socrates had centered around the question, What is the best form of life? His deep patriotism and concern for the welfare of his fellow men had prompted Plato to insist that Socrates was the best politician at Athens, although he never engaged in actual politics. We must not forget that religion and the state were most closely bound together in pagan nations. The gods were always the gods of a particular people, country, or city. The very name "Athens" is derived from the deity Athena, or vice versa. But because of his inwardness and conscience Socrates called the difference between the state and religion to the attention of the philosopher. Plato tried to bring together again the outer and the inner realm.

Plato thought it possible to construe by means of speculative thought the ideal of the "most beautiful state," in which the ideal of man, as Socrates personally had represented it, would become the model of the community of citizens, governed by wisdom and self-control. All Plato's thoughts were devoted to this political ideal. But since Socrates was an ethical politician, the state, as devised by Plato, also had to be ethically construed. It had to be also, and even in the first place, a state in which the absolute and divine truth, represented by the philosopher-governor, was the real foundation and the real goal — a sacred state — for the philosopher as conceived by Socrates is the friend of God, the administrator of divine wisdom and insight. The ideal state and the ideal community were supposed

---

[3] Julius Stenzel had already gone far in that direction in his profound book, *Plato der Erzieher*. 1929.

to fulfill the divine mission of Socrates, so grossly misunderstood by his accusers and judges. Plato's ideal state ought to make good the crime committed by the real state. Socrates had told the judges who had condemned him, " If you think that by killing men you can prevent someone from censuring your evil lives, you are mistaken." [4] Plato took over the office of censureship. Socrates had also told the judges that his main intention had been to educate the youth for the state, " to look to the state before he looks to the interests of the state," [5] i.e., to the ideal before he looks to the real state; Plato carried through this command of his teacher.

As the disciples obeyed the last will of their Lord to go into the world and to teach all peoples, so Plato obeyed the last will of Socrates, as he understood it, i.e., by thinking out the ideal constitution and by going to Sicily and trying to establish the ideal state there.[6] But this ideal was not only a political scheme, if we take the word " political " in the modern sense. Seen from the perspective of the relation between speculation and revelation, it was at the same time a political and a religious ideal. To use the language of the New Testament, it was an attempt to bring about the Kingdom of God in the form of a state. Plato's " republic " even influenced the origin of the Church. The *Republic* was renewed in a Christian version when Augustine wrote his *City of God*. Since the idea of a Church was completely unknown to the Greeks, Plato could believe it possible to unite the Socratic ideal community with the constitution of an ideal state. And this state had of course to be a philosophic state joining academy, church, and state into one body politic. For this purpose the dialogue *Republic* was written, the first type of political utopia, but meant in all earnest.

In this state, philosophy was the real queen, whom all institutions and all laws had to obey. In the place of a revealed religion Plato put his philosophy; the contemplation of the Ideas had to assume the role of religious worship and the highest Idea the role of the divine. In his later dialogue the *Laws,* Plato expresses this basic

[4] *Apology,* p. 39.

[5] *Op. cit.,* p. 36.

[6] See Plato's Seventh Letter. Recently the authenticity of that letter has been doubted. Compare Bertha Stenzel's essay on the question, " Is Plato's Seventh Letter Spurious? " in *American Journal of Philosophy,* LXXIV, 4, 1953, pp. 383–397.

thought, his most vital concern throughout his life, in the following words: " He who has not contemplated the mind of all things, which as we have said exists in the stars, and gone through the previous training [philosophy and science], and seen the connection of music with these things, and harmonized them all with laws and institutions, is not able to give a reason for such things as have a reason. And he who is unable to acquire this in addition to the ordinary virtues of a citizen can hardly be a good ruler of a whole state." [7] In this comprehensive statement all the features of Plato's ideal state are gathered together in one sweeping summary: the philosophic and the religious, the artistic and the juridical, the ethical and the political. The original unity of all the cultural spheres is retained under the title " state." But it is not the political constitution, in the narrower modern sense, that holds them together; the philosophic faith of Socrates is the binding force that sanctifies the whole building and vivifies all its parts. It is the Kingdom of God in a Hellenic fashion.

To devise the foundations of this edifice Plato had to transform the personal and individual faith of Socrates into an objective and systematic creed. And to perform this task he had to combine the Socratic inheritance with that of the great system builders of the invisible realm: Pythagoras, Heraclitus, and Parmenides. The latter prevailed as a model of Plato's own system. Plato faced the same task faced by the " syncretist " philosophers of the last period before the Sophists. He discharged his obligation, not in the form of a physical metaphysics, ignoring the ascent to the invisible and reducing the cosmos to the visible universe, but by upholding the ascendancy of the " upper " sphere. Plato supplanted the Existent of Parmenides by the cosmos of the Ideas. Plato thus united ontological speculation with the religious revelation of Socrates, a union that brought about the most superb and sublime system of antiquity. Plato is, of course, no longer Socrates. By systematizing the religious emphasis of Socrates and by uniting it with the speculative metaphysics of the pre-Socratics, Plato had to sacrifice the personal charm inherent in the unwritten and living mission of the prophet-philosopher. Plato did preserve the faith of Socrates in his dialogues, but it was no longer

----

[7] *Laws,* XII, pp. 967 f.

quite the same; the ethical purity and humanity of Socrates was lost. But Plato gained instead the stature of the greatest speculative poet-philosopher that ever lived; he created the greatest philosophic monument of that original unity which characterizes the classical Greek culture.

The older systems were immensely enriched and refined by Plato's broad personal culture, his ingenuous imagination, his Socratic touch, and his political aspirations. He pursued and developed the intentions of their founders, so that Plato can be called a Parmenides who had gone through all the political, religious, and cultural experiences of the fifth and fourth centuries. Plato also improved considerably the logical method of his predecessors. And by combining the stern and strict principles of Parmenides with the wider horizon of Heraclitus, he was able to explain the world in terms of the cosmos of Ideas. Of course Plato gave up some of the most profound insights of Heraclitus, especially the concept of the Logos and the vision of the unity of the opposites — a vision that was never regained in Greek philosophy; it had to wait until Nicolaus Cusanus renewed it at the end of the Middle Ages. The reason for this neglect is probably the intervention of the Sophists, who laid too much stress on the impossibility of any speculative knowledge of the ever-changing world. To evade their skepticism Plato believed it necessary to renounce any attempt at a knowledge of the visible world, except in terms of the Ideas. He left this realm to " opinion," i.e., to that sort of relativistic and subjectivistic half-knowledge described by the Sophists as the only knowledge left open to man.

The religious faith of Socrates was coupled with the faith in the knowability of virtue and wisdom. Justice and courage and other virtues were regarded by Socrates as of divine origin, sanction, and power. Socrates could therefore not hold that they are merely human ideals; he had to believe in their absolute reality. Socrates could not accept the relativistic and subjectivistic Sophist view, which interpreted ethical concepts as mere social products, varying from individual to individual, from nation to nation, from period to period. Briefly, Socrates was convinced that virtues like self-control, veracity, temperance, or courage were of absolute validity; their practice, of absolute value. If that is true, What kind of reality and objectivity do they possess? Whether or not Socrates posed this unavoidable question, one cannot know with certainty. He was probably so intent on teaching such virtues, and on insisting upon their teachability, that he did not ask what reality they have apart from the power they own in life and in the breast of man. Socrates was not interested enough in theoretical matters to engage in epistemological and ontological problems. Plato was most eager to put and to solve them. Even so, it was the faith of Socrates in the moral kingdom that kindled the keen desire in the mind of Plato to inquire into the kind of existence that we have to ascribe to that kingdom and to the idea of virtue itself.

The conception of the realm of Ideas was the answer given by Plato to the epistemological and ontological question arising out of the ethical faith of Socrates. This realm played the role of the ideal and yet also served as real, ethical norms, governing human life. But being objectively real and of divine origin, this realm also took the part of the Existent, as Parmenides had analyzed and described it; in other words, it took the part of the cosmos itself, as understood in terms of speculative intuition and intellection. Since Plato, like Parmenides, was convinced that the Invisible is the Real and that only the eyes of the thinking mind can see what is really real, the cosmos of the Ideas, like the Existent of Parmenides, was manifest only to thought. The world of sense, of passage, of time had only a sec-ondary truth, never to be raised to the level of the Divine and the Eternal. The true cosmos is of ethical dignity. This conviction united the ethical faith of Socrates with the cosmological ideas of Hera-clitus and Parmenides. Both had also taught that Justice and Truth are always combined and that the god knows the truth and performs the good. " The gods have care of anyone whose desire is to become just and to be divine." [8] Divinity and moral goodness are not sepa-rable. Therefore, the realm of absolute reality has to be both ethical and cognitive, a guide for doing and an object of knowing. This tenet, uniting the faith of Socrates with the ambition of ontology, is at the root of Plato's ontology of the Ideas.

B. Ontology of the Ideas

Although the Platonic Ideas have their origin in the ethical faith of Socrates and have therefore an ethical emphasis from the begin-

[8] *Republic,* X, p. 613.

ning, they could not constitute the intelligible cosmos if they did not comprise the totality of being as did the Existent of Parmenides. This combination of an ethical connotation and an ontological range characterizes the peculiar Platonic metaphysics and causes much trouble to its interpretation. But Plato himself did not reflect upon these difficulties; one might say he was quite naïve in this respect. The real world, the intelligible or noetic cosmos as intuited by the philosopher was both a realm of ethical, and therefore also of religious, dignity and even of holiness, and a realm underlying all that exists and even signifying its real being and its ultimate truth. The ethical significance and the logical function were united intrinsically as the good and the true also were united in Plato's faith and in his contemplative speculation. In this way Plato saved the Socratic emphasis for Greek metaphysics or made them compatible with each other.

Plato, however, did not discount the world of sense and change to the same degree as Parmenides had done. He was, as it were, a little more Heraclitean in this respect than Parmenides had been. Although he did agree with Parmenides (and the Sophists) that there is no ultimate truth and no ultimate reality in things that we perceive by our eyes and touch with our hands, still there is a grain of truth in our perceptions. Plato granted to the world in which we live a certain participation in being and in truth; to the degree in which our perceptions take part in the Ideas, they are not completely illusory, but reflect reality, as a mirror reflects the objects, or a painting imitates the original. Consequently, we can have a second-class knowledge of things spatial and temporal, a knowledge corresponding to a second-class truth and reality. But full and genuine knowledge is possible only about such things as are not in space and time, and have an eternal and " supercelestial " existence. And this knowledge alone corresponds to the absolute Being. Second-class knowledge is not so objective and stable as is the knowledge of things eternal and divine; it is, rather, conditioned by circumstances which, as its objects, are ever-changing. In this modified way Plato renewed the ontology of Parmenides, but he conceded a certain degree of validity to the world of " illusion " and human subjectivity.

The unchanging and independent things Plato called " Ideas," a term indicating that his conception of being was influenced from the outset by epistemological considerations inherited from the Sophists and not yet familiar to Parmenides. Plato was in this respect nearer to the conception of the Logos, i.e., to Heraclitus. Indeed, what Heraclitus had called Logos was a first approximation of the realm of the Ideas. Why did Plato not take over the term "Logos" from Heraclitus? Probably because the period of physical metaphysics and skepticism had interrupted ontological speculation; it would have been impossible to go back that far. Furthermore, Plato rejected the aesthetic vision of the unity of opposites, coupled with the Logos speculation in the scheme of Heraclitus,[9] and did not conceive of the invisible order in such a monistic way as the term "Logos" seemed to suggest. Rather, in a pluralistic fashion Plato thought of a multiplicity of genera or types ruling over the individual particulars.[10] This last reason discloses the epistemological reflection guiding Plato in his conception of the invisible realm. This realm consists of entities that can be known in a general way, i.e., by general concepts or by the concepts of the genera which the mind envisages when it does not merely perceive single things, but conceives of what is typical and identical in a definite group of phenomena. This identical element is the really real and at the same time the truly knowable.

Plato's conception of the Ideas is more abstract than the Existent of Parmenides, since Parmenides still had the visible cosmos as a model, although he discarded sense perception. And yet Plato's Ideas are more concrete than the Existent of Parmenides, because Plato took into account the variety of generic phenomena, although he abstracted from their individual and particular detail. By this device Plato ingenuously created the instrument for the knowledge of the physical world without abandoning the ontology of the spiritual world discovered by Parmenides. Plato took seriously the dictum of Parmenides that the object of pure thought and thought are one and the same thing, or that the object purely thought is itself of the very

---

[9] Cf. *Symposium,* p. 187: "An agreement of disagreements while they disagree there cannot be; you cannot harmonize what disagrees." But this was exactly what Heraclitus asserted.

[10] According to W. Jaeger, the term "idea" (as also the term *"eidos"*) was transferred by Plato from medicine to the realm of ethical, and then to that of ontological, concepts. *Paideia,* III, p. 24.

stuff of thought: Idea. It is immaterial, thoughtlike, " ideal," and can be known only by pure thought or by a cognitive contemplation rigorously distinguished from all sense experience and subjective knowledge. Plato, like Parmenides, ascended to the invisible realm, soaring high over the events of daily occurrence. But Plato did not lose sight of everyday experience. Rather, he transcended it only to win a perspective from which he could again look down and comprehend what his physical eyes descried. In this new version of ontology, the intention of Parmenides came to a final fruition, and the physical metaphysics of the " syncretists " was surpassed, their motives not simply cast out but fulfilled on a higher level.

Plato was enabled to perform this task, not only because the " syncretists " had taught him to appraise the visible cosmos more seriously and the Sophists had taught him to reflect upon the conditions of knowledge, but also because his ethical perspective, taken over from Socrates, had opened his eyes to concepts of an absolute validity and of a religious authority and sanctity. From the realm of such concepts of virtue, Plato transferred the principle of objective reality to the realm of all concepts which determine the essence of things and make them what they are: trees, stones, animals, plants, natural or technical products, habits, laws, poets, philosophers, individuals, states, and so on. Everything is what it is because it is subordinated to a universal Idea, governing and permitting the mind to know what it is. The Idea of a tree or a stone deviates from the Idea of courage or justice, in that it does not control and inform the will and intellect, but, instead, determines trees and stones, as the genus logically determines the individual subordinated to it, and yet the same principle is at work in both cases. Plato thought of logical subordination as an analogue to ethical domination. He felt justified in transferring the ethical principle from the ethical to the logical and ontological realm. Plato was convinced of the ethical goodness of the entire cosmos and of the divine origin of the Ideas. All things are what they are because they serve an end which in the last analysis is ethical. All things " obey " the ultimate intentions invested in the visible universe.

While such fundamental convictions and insights underlay all the dialogues of Plato, they underwent a development which introduced some modifications in his doctrine. Within the context of this book

these alterations cannot be studied in detail; I must confine myself
to such points as are relevant from the perspective of the relation
between speculation and revelation. The earlier dialogues betray a
greater kinship with the religious attitude of Socrates than the later
ones, in which the logical and mathematical elements of Plato's
thinking were prevalent. Nevertheless, the Socratic principle never
entirely disappeared. The Idea never ceased to point to its origin: the
ethical ideal. Plato's speculation never disavowed its religious background. But the speculative religion of the cosmos gradually out-
grew the ethical religion of the soul and of inwardness. Plato became more and more a Greek in whom contemplation outshone the
active faith of Socrates, and the fervor of cognitive knowledge overshadowed the wisdom of metaphysical resignation. The Parmenides
in Plato defeated Socrates. And yet the conqueror was ever tinged
by the Socratic belief in moral goodness as the highest of all values.
The Idea of the Good itself is accordingly the consummate Idea; it
is the zenith in the realm of the Ideas.

The word "idea" itself manifests the predilection of contemplation, for it is derived from the verb *idein* ("to see"). It means something that can be seen with the eyes of the mind, an intellectual image
or vision. The soul as described by Socrates in the dialogue *Phaedrus* saw the Ideas in their supercelestial place, when before her birth
she followed the gods on their steep road to the top of the heavenly
vault, where they behold what is beyond the stars and the heavens.
"There abides the very being with which true knowledge is concerned: the colorless, formless, intangible essence, visible only to the
mind, the pilot of the soul. The divine intelligence, nurtured upon
mind and pure knowledge; and the intelligence of every soul, capable of receiving the food proper to it, rejoices at beholding the
Existent, and, once more gazing upon truth, is replenished." [11]
Knowledge is basically an intellectual intuition. There is no possibility of acquiring knowledge of the Real except by direct contemplation. Therefore the mind cannot attain to the knowledge of the
Ideas by any earthly experience or any earthly operation. It is rather
furnished with that knowledge at birth. All that man can do, to become aware of this gift, is to remember what the mind has beheld

[11] *Phaedrus*, p. 247.

before man was born. Remembrance of a mystical kind is the only way by which the unconscious possession of the heavenly gift can be made conscious and actual. And this is possible because the soul is divine and immortal and independent of the temporal process of being born. The soul belongs to eternity, and only because of this origin can it ascend at any time to the eternal realm. The philosopher, as the friend of the gods, remembers better than other men what his soul has seen and can therefore teach others how to mobilize the power of recollection, the basis of true knowledge. " The mind of the philosopher alone has wings therefore." [12]

This whole passage in the dialogue *Phaedrus* belongs to the most solemn and most revealing in Plato's writings. The spirit of Socrates is still present but it is transformed into the spirit of Plato. In its half-mythological wording it is akin to the style of the introduction to the poem of Parmenides. What was a direct experience of the philosopher has now become the narrative of the Platonic Socrates, an experience in the state of pre-existence. But these differences of metaphor cannot conceal the substantial similarity between the speculative visions of the two great ontological thinkers. Both agree that the Existent, the true object of true knowledge, can be appropriated by the mind alone. Such knowledge concerned with the eternal and unchanging essence of all that is, is in rank and in time prior to any other knowledge.

Plato does not always use the word " Idea " when he wants to signify this eternal reality. In fact he seldom uses it. Much more frequently he speaks about it in other phrases, i.e., by adding the words, " In itself," to the ideal content, e.g., " Beauty in itself," [13] or by simply adding, " Itself," e.g., " The beautiful itself," [14] or by merely saying, " What a thing is," [15] or what it is " in nature." [16] Often he speaks about it as that which unites a manifold of particulars or as the " essence " (*ousia*) of things. [17] Sometimes he calls it " pattern " (*paradeigma*), type, universal (*koinon*); and at times he would name it in a general way as that which " is," or, like Parmenides, the Existent (*to ōn*). These various expressions have slightly different meanings, but they all point to the same entity: to that something

---

[12] *Op. cit.*, p. 249.
[13] *Republic*, VI, p. 507.
[14] *Symposium*, p. 211.

[15] *Republic*, loc. cit.
[16] *Republic*, X, p. 597.
[17] *Phaedo*, p. 76.

which has an objective existence and is also the object of pure thought. It is at the same time essence and concept; it unites these contrasts. It is a concept that has the power and the function of the Existent or the really real.

The Latin authors translated the word "*ousia*" by "substance" (*substantia*) because of Aristotle's usage. This translation has caused a lot of confusion, since Aristotle gave a new interpretation to the term. The best English translation of the Platonic term "*ousia*" is in my opinion "essence," since it is derived from the Latin *esse* ("to be") as *ousia* is derived from *einai* ("to be"). Thus it retains its original connotation by implying that which in an emphatic sense "is" and which is related to something else that depends upon it, as upon its essence, and from which it derives its own being.

"Substance" and "essence" are closely connected. We often use these terms loosely without distinction (a habit that can be traced back to the Latin translations of Plato and Aristotle). However, there is a significant difference between substance and essence. An essence is to be predicated of the thing of which it is the essence; whereas, substance is the very thing of which the essence is predicated. A definite individual tree in my garden may be an oak; then its essence is to be an oak or it is by essence an oak; the individual tree is itself the substance of this essence; it is not an oak in general, but this individual oak which stands in my garden. Or in using the term "Idea" I would have to state: the individual oak in my garden is not the Idea "oak"; this Idea is the essence of my oak, but my oak is the substance which "participates" (as Plato says) in the Idea "oak," and is an oak only because it participates in the Idea, or because the Idea constitutes its essence. To confuse "substance" and "essence" is to confuse Aristotle and Plato. Such a confusion may be fatal to a correct understanding, since Idea is an entity that exists apart from the individual thing, in an ideal realm, whereas the term "substance" suggests that it exists in the individual thing and is even identical with its core. I will come back later to this distinction in the discussion of Aristotle.

To illustrate the kind of difficulties that arise if we do not carefully distinguish essence and substance, I will say a word about the famous Orthodox (Cappadocian) formula of the Holy Trinity, which uses the term "*ousia*" in saying that the three Persons have one *ousia*. This formula is mostly rendered by translating *ousia* into "substance" with "three persons and one substance." Gregory of Nyssa understood the term "*ousia*," however, in a Platonic fashion, i.e., as "essence." Therefore, the formula loses its paradoxical character. It simply says that the three Persons have the same essence, namely, "divinity." Gregory makes this very clear by comparing Father, Son, and Spirit with three human persons called Peter, James, and John, who "are the same viewed as being — each was a man — but in the characteristics of their respective personalities, they were not alike."[18] The Latin writers no longer understood this Platonic language; they translated the formula by using the term "substance," instead of "essence," in an Aristotelian fashion. They thereby arrived at the paradoxical statement: "Three persons and one substance." We shall subsequently see that this confusion began with Aristotle.

The Idea is the essence not only of substances like the individual tree in my garden but also of qualities, properties, attributes, collective entities, relations, processes, events, and so on. At the apex of all Ideas, Plato put the Good, which, however, was not strictly distinguished from the Beautiful. The Good is the essence of all essences, and therefore no longer itself an essence, but "far exceeds in dignity and power" all the essences.[19] It is as it were the Socratic summit of his whole system. By placing the Good at the top of the cosmos, Plato indicated that being and goodness are intrinsically united. There cannot be anything that has not a certain goodness within itself, the source of its generation and sustenance. Everything exists only inasmuch as it serves the universal good which it represents in its own way. The universal good is the end (*telos*) of the cosmic process, the end therefore of all special processes within the cosmos. As everything has its own end, it also has its own "virtue"; a word not only confined to the moral sphere, although it has a particular meaning if applied to human action and value. Everything has its value, inasmuch as it pursues and attains its own end. The essences of things and processes are therefore not merely logical genera or ontological existents. They are also "ethical" entities, if one is permitted to extend the connotation of this term. The ontological function arose from ethics and never lost this root. Plato's whole ontology is ethical inasmuch as it is teleological, since the cosmos is dominated

[18] *Against Eunomius*, I, 19. Cf. Basil, ep. 38.   [19] *Republic*, VI, p. 509.

by a universal end. Plato's teleology is universal. Whatever is is good solely because it exists and participates in the realm of the Ideas. And in so far as something is good it is also beautiful. The ethical, the aesthetic, the logical, and the ontological are not yet distinguished, or if distinguished they are basically united.[20]

In the dialogue *Philebus,* Plato discusses the manner in which the Ideas and the phenomena are united. (Plato raises this difficult question in many dialogues but is never quite satisfied with his answer.) He introduces the principle of "law and order" (*nomos* and *taxis*) as the bond between these opposite cosmic spheres.[21] Consequently, in addition to the ideal eternal realm and the actual temporal realm, there exists a third sphere, distinct from the ideal and the actual, but composed of both and therefore able to unite them in an act of synthesis. The problem was inherited by Aristotle, whose metaphysics offer a new and subtle solution. Plato never found a satisfactory solution; the one given in the *Philebus* is, however, the most elucidating and most adequately attained. Plato sought to reunite the two spheres separated by the vigor of Parmenides. The goal of reunification seemed the most desirable and indeed the most urgent. Throughout history this problem remained the hardest and the deepest of all the problems speculation had to face. It is this problem that finally compels the human mind to capitulate and to admit that its own resources cannot cope with the abysmal depth of the Ultimate or the Absolute.

This speculative problem is dissolved in Biblical revelation by the imaginative conception of the Creation. The world is completely dependent upon the mind and will of the Creator and yet the world possesses a certain independence and self-existence. It is interesting that Plato, feeling not only the urgency but also the obscurity of this great problem, invokes the help of god. Socrates asks: " What nature shall we ascribe to the third or compound kind? " He receives the answer: " You, I think, will have to tell me that." [22] Socrates replies:

---

[20] Plato can therefore discuss metaphysical, ethical, political, epistemological, and logical questions in the same context. Such is his actual practice in most of his dialogues.

[21] *Philebus,* p. 26.

[22] Note that in the later dialogues to which the *Philebus* belongs Socrates deviates from his method of putting questions which his disciple has to answer. He is implored by the disciple to set forth the answer himself. This change alone would suf-

" Rather, god will tell you, if there be any god who will listen to my prayers." [23] And in the place mentioned above where Plato introduces the third principle that would furnish the synthesis of the two opposite spheres by means of its own synthetic nature, he again appeals to the deity who " seeing the universal wantonness and wickedness of all things . . . devised the limit of law and order." Plato evidently was fully aware of the tremendous difficulty involved in the unification of the separated spheres; he was not at all certain that the human mind could overcome it. In the final solution of the *Timaeus* Plato took refuge in a myth in which a divine architect forms the universe, i.e., Plato anticipated Biblical revelation in his own style and on the level of speculation.

In the system of Plato (if we are allowed to speak of a system — Plato was intentionally unsystematic in all his dialogues), the Idea never ceased to transcend the scope of the visible world. This world is forever imperfect, while the Idea is the ideal measure and goal toward which physical and finite things are striving without ever reaching their goal. Whereas Aristotle modified the Platonic architecture in this central point, Plato never swerved from this basic position. The Idea does not pertain to the changeable and perishable objects of sense experience, but to thrones beyond them in " splendid isolation." Each Idea has, as it were, the dignity and majesty that in the system of Aristotle is ascribed solely to the supreme god. And like this god, the Idea does not work within the phenomena, but the phenomena only participate to a certain degree in the Idea. The degree of participation is analogous to the man who, striving for the Ideal, wins a certain degree of excellence without ever reaching the fullness of that perfection which the ideal represents. Just as there is no perfect justice or goodness within the human soul, there is no perfect tree, perfect straight line, or perfect beauty within the sense world.

The Idea is " in itself." It has the independence and sovereignty of the soul as long as the soul is not yet defiled and determined by its

fice to prove that the figure of Socrates was no longer meant to portray the historical Socrates. " Socrates " had become a mere figure in the drama of philosophic conversation, invented by Plato to develop his own views in the form of a living discussion which, however, has lost its original charm and poetic probability.

[23] *Op. cit.,* p. 25.

companion the body. Indeed, the phrase " in itself " was probably suggested by the Socratic emphasis laid upon the purity of the soul and upon that self-conversation in which the soul is protected against the diverting and corroding infection of the impressions and passions. But in an even deeper sense the expression " in itself " may point to the riddle of the self itself which is the source of self-identity and which is mirrored in the need to appeal to god as the source of the Ideas.[24]

C. Cosmotheology

To a certain degree Plato approached theism, since he developed conceptions of a world-soul and even of a world-creator. But the cosmological trend of his thought is strong enough to remind us that he was the successor of the early cosmotheists for whom the cosmos itself was, if not the god, at least a divine being. Inasmuch as Plato's conceptions retain the immanence of the divine mind or soul within the larger whole, or inasmuch as they suggest that the god and the visible world are related to each other as mind and body or as soul and body, the Ionian pantheism is not entirely abandoned but only transformed. It is typical of Plato, however, that he did not resolve the theological problem by dogmatically adopting any definite theology. Plato's thought exhibits the spontaneous freshness of his dialogues, beginning ever anew; his concepts and points of view undergo constant development. As Socrates never taught any definite theory, so Plato too remained alive to the ever new motives and incentives of thinking; he did not at all worry about the multiplicity or the diversity of his solutions. The dialogue form of his writings was eminently well fitted to such a continuous growth.

Plato aimed, nevertheless, at a systematical understanding of the cosmos as a whole. The cosmotheological problem grew in the course of his development and took on ever greater proportions. How can the realm of the Ideas and the realm of the temporal world of change form one whole? And what place has the divine being in this whole? Plato never finished his inquiry into these matters. He kept asking these questions and tried hard to answer them. One scheme is rather permanent in all his answers: the idea of hierarchy. As there

[24] Cf. *Republic*, X, p. 596.

is the hierarchy of the two spheres of existence, the absolute and the relative, the eternal and the temporal, the unchanging and the changing, so also there is a hierarchy in each of those spheres. The realm of the Ideas resembles a pyramid. The zenith of that pyramid is the Good in itself; the lowest stratum consists of those Ideas which are nearest to the sphere of the phenomena. This pyramid not only has a logical significance, in so far as the lowest Ideas correspond with the most special or particular notions, whereas the higher and highest Ideas correspond to the most abstract or general notions, but it also has ontological implications. The most abstract Ideas are the " highest " in the sense of representing the greatest reality and possessing the widest power, while the lower ones are restricted in both respects.

In the realm of the phenomena we also face a hierarchical fabric. The human soul is almost in the rank of the Ideas themselves, while the merely material objects are of the lowest rank. As the passage quoted above indicates, the world of change is forever imperfect and even " wicked." As the Ideas represent goodness, so the sphere of the phenomena is infiltrated by evil forces. The boundary between the two realms is therefore strict, in spite of the hierarchical nature of each. There is no gradual transition between them, even though the human soul can be uncorrupted and the material world can be beautiful. They are related to each other as Being and nonbeing, as Truth and error, as the Absolute to the relative, the Pure to the impure, and so on. However, in so far as the phenomena participate in the realm of the Ideas there is some truth, some purity, some being in the phenomena too, and the more as its upper stages are approached. Analogous differences exist in the ideal sphere; the good itself is purer and more real and true than all the other Ideas. This hierarchical structure of the cosmos at large compelled Plato to speculate throughout his philosophic development about the relation between the Ideas, and in his later period he considerably modified his earlier doctrine. The opposition between the two spheres was never abolished, but it was mitigated by the principle of mediation.

Whereas in the first period Plato had maintained that each Idea is a kind of island like the Existent of Parmenides, absolute and in itself, gradually he came to realize that there is a connection and interconnection between the Ideas, a subtle and complicated network of relations. And this insight prompted him to admit that even non-being and falsity participate in being.[25] There are Ideas that seem to contradict the high standard and rank of the ideal realm, while soul and mind on the other hand seem to hold as high a rank as the Ideas. The cosmos as a whole emerged; the ultimate problem arose, How can thought account for the dualism of the spheres, and especially of the Good and everything else that exists? Perhaps by the dualism of god and world? Aristotle, the most creative disciple of Plato, drew this conclusion, as we shall see.

Plato took another step of consequence for later speculation. If the good is the extreme on the side of the ideal realm, there should also be an extreme on the side of the phenomenal world. Parmenides had argued that nonbeing is this uttermost pole, thereby contrasting the truly real and the illusive world. Plato took up this suggestion in his own fashion, and therefore demanded that the pole of negativity should have a function in the cosmos, both in the material and in the ideal sphere. Whereas the good as such is absolutely positive, the other Ideas originate from this positive pole by a negation which restricts the purity and oneness of the highest Idea. What is the source of this original negativity? This supreme and most vexatious of all speculative questions was unavoidable and even most pressing. There must be an ultimate and, as it were, " pure " nonbeing which contaminates the whole range of the cosmos except its correlative of pure being.

The unmethodical method of the dialogues permitted Plato to give several answers to this torturous question. What Plato called "dialectic" was mainly provoked by the need to build up the system of all Ideas including those which lead from the ideal to the material sphere. As early as the *Republic,* Plato recognized that need and proposed its fulfillment. He spoke in a metaphorical fashion [26] of four stages of objects corresponding to four stages of knowledge: first, the Ideas which the intuitive mind thinks by means of the dialectical method; secondly, the mathematical objects which the scien-

[25] See especially *Sophistes,* p. 258.
[26] In the so-called simile of the line: *Republic,* VI, p. 511. Another simile, that of the cave, elaborates these distinctions (*Republic,* VII, p. 517). I cannot discuss the difficulties arising when one tries to give a detailed and accurate interpretation of this metaphor.

tific understanding grasps by means of discourse; thirdly, the phenomena which only assumption and opinion can discern; fourthly,
the impressions which are the objects of sensation and lead easily
to deception. These four realms can be interpreted as that of philosophic speculation, mathematical analysis, empirical description, and
finally unscientific opinion. In the second realm, only hypothetical
knowledge can be attained, because it does not ascend to the highest
stratum, the first principle of all knowledge. Philosophic speculation is that " sort of knowledge which reason (Logos) attains by
the power of dialectical thought, using the hypotheses, not as first
principles, but only as hypotheses, i.e., as steps and points of departure into a world that is above hypotheses, in order to soar beyond
them to the first principle (arche) of the whole, and clinging to this,
and then to that which depends on this by successive steps, reason
descends again . . . from Ideas through Ideas and in Ideas it ends." [27]

Such is the program of Plato's dialectics, which he held fast in all
his later dialogues and which he endeavored to carry out in ever
new attacks and by changing procedures. In the *Parmenides,* the
Sophist, the *Philebus,* and the *Statesman,* Plato tried hard to settle
the task he had set before himself, without ever reaching a final
solution. I cannot pursue these attempts; such a discussion would
require too much space and would not contribute new facets to the
problem of the relation between speculation and revelation. May it
suffice to say that Plato saw very clearly the tremendous difficulties
in deriving the vast variety of genera and species, as we find them
by experience, from the supreme Idea through the medium of dialectical deduction and reflection. Such difficulties were in complete
agreement with his religious awe and his basic (Socratic) feeling that
there is a divine mystery impregnable to dialectical penetration and
connected with the contrast between good and evil, mirrored in the
contrast of being and nonbeing.[28] Plato's failure to cope with this
ultimate problem in an ultimate way has therefore not a merely negative but also an eminently positive significance. It implies philosophic
resignation, but it also betrays a religious reverence and a mystical
reserve.

Plato never radically abandoned the national religion: philosophi-

[27] *Republic,* VI, p. 511.   [28] See Appendix to this chapter on Plato.

cal speculation never completely superseded the belief in the traditional gods. There was a kind of chapel in the Academy in which the gods were worshiped. Throughout his career Plato prayed. He could not have prayed to the Ideas, not even to the highest one. Like many of his contemporaries, Plato was in a religious plight. As the critique of Xenophanes, of Heraclitus, and of poets like Euripides, his critique also of the Homeric picture of the gods assailed the traditional religion. Greek religion was corroded by this assault, but there was no other religion to which Plato could turn. His private religious life and his public philosophizing were thus in a state of tension. It is a question as to which was stronger. In any case a reconciliation was needed. One possible solution was to formulate the essence of the divine by means of conceptual reflection. Another possible solution to the problem, apparently insoluble by logical means, was the invention of philosophic myth, representing the deity in more or less traditional garment — for the sole purpose, however, of reconciliation.

With apparent ease and without doubting their existence, Plato can speak of the traditional gods and their deeds. But with perfect candor he can also speculate about the philosophic god. How Plato reconciled and harmonized these approaches within his own soul, we do not know. His pure logical considerations issued in the Idea of the good. But nowhere does he directly identify the good and the god. He remained perfectly silent about their mutual relationship. This cannot be a casual omission on his part. Plato was aware that the speculative and the religious approach to the divine mystery were equally valid, each in its own right and on its own ground. He was aware that speculation could not create a new religion any more than the national religion could attain that truth desired by philosophic thought. Plato knew that the Idea of the good could not take the place of the gods, and that the gods could not vie with the logical and ethical purity of the good. Thus he kept his personal faith and worshiped the gods while his speculation groped for the truth which the thinking mind can envisage and comprehend.

Plato evidently wanted to conceive of the divine in conceiving of the good, but he felt that the very concept of the good contained a mystery inaccessible to the human mind. "To reach what is now in my thoughts would be an effort too great for me," Socrates says, facing the crucial problem which the Idea of the good is supposed to solve.[29] Then he goes on to remark that he would be willing to speak of "the child of the good," namely, the sun who is "the author of sight." In like manner the good is called the author of scientific truth and knowledge, and thus it "may be said to bring forth being and essence of all things known." [30] Only by way of such a comparison or by analogy can the mind touch upon the supreme being, its creative power, and its relation to truth and knowledge. Plato never went further. He never dared — as Aristotle did — to think out the divine mind, its activity, its life, and its perfection. He veiled rather than revealed what seemed beyond all comprehensibility, and what was consequently to be left to divine revelation. Since, however, such a revelation, in so far as Greek religion was concerned, was not forthcoming, Plato tried to use his imagination to fill the gap and devised the famous myth of the *Timaeus,* in which the cosmos is created by a divine "demiurge." But before I discuss the *Timaeus,* I shall refer to the *Phaedrus* and the *Laws,* where Plato also expresses theological views.

I mentioned above that, in the *Phaedrus,* Plato develops the theory of recollection by which we are enabled to remember the sight of the Ideas we enjoyed before birth. In the same context Plato speaks of the gods who "stand upon the outside of heaven, and the revolution of the spheres carries them round, and they behold the things beyond." [31] The narrative goes on to tell that the god abides in those things, "and in beholding them he is what he is. And he who employs aright these memories is ever being initiated into perfect mysteries and alone becomes truly perfect." [32] Here Plato replaces the current mysteries by mysteries of his own insight or intuition. And, what is more important to Plato's theological views, he defines the god as being what he is because or inasmuch as he "beholds" the Ideas. The Ideas are accordingly prior even to the god, and they confer divinity upon him.

Plato thus indirectly suggests a primacy of speculative intuition over the traditional faith in the gods. The gods, he seems to say, belong to the realm of individual beings, whereas the Ideas are superior to that realm, in so far as they are the universal precondition of every-

[29] *Republic,* VI, p. 506.
[30] *Loc. cit.*
[31] *Phaedrus,* p. 247.
[32] *Op. cit.,* p. 249.

thing that exists, be it in the visible world of the phenomena or even in the invisible world of the divine beings. The Ideas are the essences of both and therefore more real. Even divinity is an essence that can be ascribed to the god but precedes him in rank and dignity. The godlike man is what he is only because he beholds the Ideas. Such is the root of his divine glory. Moreover, the root of divine and human dignity and value is the same faculty. God and man (more accurately the human soul) are fundamentally alike, but the Ideas are higher than both. Primacy is ascribed to speculative ontology, which anticipates revelation; logic and epistemology are derivative and secondary.

The difference between man and god is that the god eternally abides by the Ideas; man only remembers their sight and is forever in danger of forgetting them.

There is no fixed theology in Plato.[33] In the *Laws*, Plato suggests quite another conception of the divine being. Here it is neither an Idea nor is it divine because it beholds the Ideas. The divine being is rather understood as the soul of the visible universe, animating and moving it.[34] This deification of the soul is an echo of the old speculation of the pre-Socratics and of the Socratic religion of the soul. But the cosmic soul of Plato has not the inwardness and personality of the Socratic conception; it has lost its ethical flavor, and even its cognitive contemplation. It has assumed instead a quasi-physical or biological function. As the body needs the instincts, impulses, impressions, and emotions of its soul to fulfill its vital needs and to withstand the dangers implied in organic life, so the soul of the world fulfills the needs of the physical cosmos and regulates its life. The existence of the gods, Plato argues in the *Laws*, is to be proved in the first place by the regularity of the movements of the sun and the moon and the stars.[35] It is the order of the physical universe that assures us that it has a divine soul. It is true that in this context Plato is struggling against the " physical " philosophers — he includes Empedocles, condemning explicitly the doctrine of this pre-Socratic thinker that the four elements are the sole foundation of the cosmos — as rigorously and as vigorously as ever; nevertheless, he himself goes far in their direction by asserting that the souls of the stars are

---

[33] Cf. Fr. Solmsen, *Plato's Theology*, 1942.
[34] *Laws*, X, p. 898.
[35] *Loc. cit.*, p. 886.

the true gods, and that they are moved and determined by the cosmic soul.[36]

The concept of the soul developed here by Plato (and later adopted by Aristotle) is no longer the concept we know from the conversations of Socrates. It is rather the concept of that physiological force which spontaneously moves the body and promotes its ends and aims. It is no longer the spiritual inner life of the human soul, in the center of the prophetic mind of Socrates. It is rather the mathematically ordered astronomical movement which Plato regards as divinely regulated and from which he infers the essence of the central cosmic soul. Great stress is laid upon the difference between the movements determined from without, and those determined from within the body by its soul. Spiritual inwardness is thus replaced by physical inwardness. The depth of Socratic spirituality is supplanted by a cosmotheological speculation established mainly on the basis of astronomy. " What is the definition of that which is named ' soul '? Can we conceive of any other than that which has been already given — the motion that can move itself? " [37] It is as if Plato had fallen back to the stage of the physical metaphysics which equates the cosmos with the visible universe.

But this impression has to be corrected. Plato still maintains the deeper concept of the soul inherited from Socrates. " Characters and manners and wishes and reasonings and true opinions and reflections and recollections are prior to length and breadth and depth and strength of bodies, if the soul is prior to the body . . . The soul is the cause of good and evil, base and honorable, just and unjust, and of all other opposites, if we suppose her to be the cause of all things . . ." [38]

Plato was torn between the cosmotheological and the ethicotheological, between the pre-Socratic and the Socratic, between a predominantly polytheistic or pagan and a predominantly monotheistic or " Biblical " position. Can we expect anything else in a Greek thinker who has been the disciple of Socrates but who has renewed the original Greek tendency toward cosmological speculation? Indeed, nothing else is to be expected. In Aristotle the originally Greek motivation grows even stronger and even more overshadows the system than in Plato.

[36] *Loc. cit.*, pp. 898 f.   [37] *Loc. cit.*, p. 896.   [38] *Loc. cit.*

There is another interesting remark in our passage. The " Athenian," who takes the place of Socrates in the *Laws,* raises the question whether there is only one soul of the world or two, i.e., the one good, the other evil. The "Athenian" concludes that there must be two, but that the good world-soul must be stronger because of the apparent order which controls the heavenly movements. " The soul directs all things in heaven, and earth, and sea by her movements." She is " herself a goddess, when truly receiving the divine mind she disciplines all things rightly to their happiness; but when she is the companion of folly, she does the very contrary of all this." " If we say that the whole path and movement of heaven, and of all that is therein, is by nature akin to the movement and revolution and calculation of the mind, and proceeds by kindred laws, then, as is plain, we must say that the best soul takes care of the world and guides it along the good path." [39] Plato here makes the world-soul dependent upon the world-mind. If the mind directs the soul, all goes well; if it fails to direct the soul, all goes wrong. The mind of man as well as that of the world is always good. But the soul is weak and can create disorder and evil in man as well as in the world, if the mind does not control her.

But what is this world-mind? " Of what nature is the movement of mind? To this question it is not easy to give an intelligent answer." [40] After this warning the Athenian nevertheless gives an answer. The movement of the mind is circular, while all other movements deviate more or less from the circular line. Since the sun moves around the earth in a circle, its movements are controlled by the world-mind. But, after we have been led to this astrotheological belief, Plato continues to argue that the astral gods are not indifferent to the destiny of man and are never unjust but rule the world with the utmost care and with perfect justice. If appearance contradicts this truth, it does so only because the gods are not interested in the " lighter and lesser concerns," [41] but with the whole. " The ruler of the universe has ordered all things with a view to the excellence and preservation of the whole, and each part, as far as may be, has an action and passion appropriate to it. Over these, down to the least fraction of them, ministers have been appointed to preside, who have

[39] *Loc. cit.,* p. 896 f.   [40] *Loc. cit.*   [41] *Loc. cit.,* p. 902.

wrought out their perfection with infinitesimal exactness. And one of these proportions of the universe is thine own, unhappy man, which, however little, contributes to the whole; and you do not seem to be aware that this and every other creation is for the sake of the whole . . . and that you are created for the sake of the whole, and not the whole for the sake of you." [42]

Such a faith combines both the scientific and aesthetic spirit of Greek culture with the ethicoreligious spirit of Socrates. But the first dominates in allowing an astrotheological speculation to protrude. The whole — that is, the visible universe in which you and I are infinitely little particles — is more important than the destiny of the individual soul. Plato's religious consolation is akin to that of the last ancient thinker, Boethius, who let philosophy itself advise man to contemplate the whole as a whole and thereby be lifted up over one's own petty and insignificant well-being or misery. The " lighter or lesser concerns " are the existentially most telling, personal, and individual circumstances under which a man lives. And if he is not permitted to believe that they are in the hands of God, he cannot be consoled religiously. In Plato the joy of contemplation outweighs the charity of the Biblical God.

On the other hand the laws introduced in his great book take care of the orphans in a way not surpassed by any Biblical prescription. " Men should have a fear of the gods above, who regard the loneliness of the orphans . . . The guardians of the law shall take charge of them year by year as of their own kindred." [43] But there is also a dictatorial tone in that philosophically administered state which reminds one of the most sinister aspects of the Roman inquisition or of the modern " totalitarian " state. The man who is impious shall be put to the test, and even if he " has a righteous nature, hates the wicked, and dislikes and refuses to do unjustice, and avoids unrighteous men, and loves the righteous, he shall be placed in a house of reformation and detained there for at least five years in isolated confinement, and if he does not recant after that period, he shall suffer capital punishment." [44] What would Socrates have said to such a law? Plato knew

[42] *Loc. cit.,* p. 903.

[43] *Laws,* XI, pp. 926 f. Or compare this other word: " Let every man honor with every sort of lawful honor his own parents " (*Loc. cit.,* p. 932).

[44] *Op. cit.,* X, p. 909.

why he did not make Socrates the speaker in this last book on the ideal state.

In the *Timaeus* — of all the dialogues the most influential in the Middle Ages — Plato finally undertook to depict in a philosophic myth the creation, or more accurately the formation, of the visible universe by the divine artist. To a greater extent than Aristotle who, like Heraclitus and Parmenides, denied creation, Plato remained near the truly religious conception of the relation between God and the world. The cosmos is a living being and, since it is made by a divine architect, it bears the features of a god. There is harmony and proportion and the spirit of friendship in its appearance. The cosmos never ages and never undergoes any disease. It is (using Biblical language) "very good." Reminding us of the Absolute of Parmenides and Empedocles, it is perfectly round like a sphere and revolves in the same place in a circle. In the center is located the world-soul which pervades and embraces the whole cosmos. The world-soul is the best of all things created.[45]

After creating the sun and the stars the divine demiurge addresses them in the following remarkable fashion: "Gods, children of gods, who are my works, and of whom I am the artificer and father, my creations are indissoluble, if so I will." [46] As in Biblical revelation the world depends in its existence and in its sustenance entirely on the personal will of the "Father." The creator-god gives instructions to the minor gods, as the Biblical Creator likewise ordains the light to shine and the animals to fill the sea and the earth and the air. The demiurge then creates the human soul, which is quite similar to the soul of the world, as man, according to the Bible, is created in the image of God. The human souls are distributed throughout the universe, each to a peculiar star to which it returns, if it has lived a pure life on earth.[47] Plato then describes the creation of the physical world in detail. But for our purpose it is not necessary to go any farther.

The whole scheme of Plato seems to disclose how strongly he was influenced by the Pythagorean doctrine that number rules the phenomenal world. Some scholars even believe that Plato had arrived at

[45] This idea anticipates the Arian heresy, which thought of the Logos as being created.

[46] *Timaeus*, p. 41.

[47] This scheme influenced Origen in his *De principiis*.

a stage in which he substituted number or at least the Ideas of numbers for the realm of Ideas. The *Timaeus,* although supporting such a hypothesis (which is furthermore strengthened by the critique of Plato or Platonists in the works of Aristotle), to a certain extent nevertheless maintains the old doctrine of the Ideas. The divine demiurge, Plato assures us through the mouth of *Timaeus,* " must have looked to that which is eternal; for the world is the fairest of creations and he is the best of authors." [48] Plato speaks of the patterns which the artificer had in mind in the same way that he had always spoken of the Ideas. The patterns are unchangeable; by copying them in the visible world, God makes everything as beautiful as possible. The perfection of the pure patterns cannot be attained in their copies, because opposed to it is the receptacle in which the patterns are remolded, conceived of as empty space, and the sensible material, filling the space and on which the types are imprinted.

It is characteristic of this whole scheme that the demiurge looks at the patterns but does not produce them. The patterns are presupposed, the demiurge is only the copyist. He is doubly restricted: by the independent existence of space and the material and by the independent existence of the patterns. Plato remained to the end a representative of the contemplative ontology, even while he went far in the direction of an active quasi-Biblical faith. Speculation takes the place of revelation; it is the source and ground of his philosophy.

Appendix

The very ultimate mystery concerning the relation between God and the world originates in the irreconcilable opposition between good and evil, or in Biblical language between God and Satan. The deepest reason why Parmenides was so emphatic in distinguishing being and nonbeing, and in discounting nonbeing, originated in the same cause. Parmenides, however, was not aware of this reason because the opposition between truth and error was in the foreground of his thought. Plato, influenced by the ethical pathos of Socrates, was fully aware of the supreme opposition

[48] *Timaeus,* p. 29.

which prompted him not to deviate from the separation of the two spheres. When Plato discussed the problem of the relation between Being and nonbeing or the One and the many, as he does in the *Parmenides,* he knew very well what was at stake. Plato basically agreed with the rigorous distinction of Parmenides, but he saw the ontological necessity of a mediation between the extremes. How highly he esteemed and admired Parmenides we have seen above.[49] Parmenides is the only philosopher of rank whose name he applied to a dialogue and whom he introduced as a speaker. In the dialogue that bears his name he honored Parmenides, moreover, by making him (fictitiously) the teacher of the young Socrates, who in all other dialogues is always superior to all other persons present.

The dialogue *Parmenides* has given rise, since the oldest times, to the most divergent interpretations.[50] Some interpreters have taken the position that Plato was not in earnest but wanted only to show what is the result when abstract thinking is made the measure of truth, and that only nonsense can come from such an attempt. Others have taken exactly the contrary position and have asserted that this dialogue is the most profound, the most important, and the most revealing of all. Hegel called the dialogue a dialectical masterpiece of the first rank. Other modern interpreters believe it to be a kind of training ground for unexperienced thinkers. The same variety of opinions can be found with respect to the place the *Parmenides* takes in the temporal succession of Plato's writings. Some would plead that it is one of the most mature and therefore one of the later dialogues; others consider it a rather early work, written when Plato still enjoyed arguing solely for the sake of argument.

The dialogue undoubtedly deals with the thesis of Parmenides that the Existent is pure being and that nonbeing has to be totally excluded from it because, as the historical Parmenides had taught, it leads only to fallacies and illusions. It is therefore a very serious matter with which the dialogue deals. I agree wholeheartedly with the valuable commentary of Cornford, who shows that there is no sophism, and no logical jokes, in the *Parmenides,* if one studies the details carefully. And I also agree with his opinion that Plato did not intend to write an exercise only but was in earnest when he examined the thesis of the historical Parmenides in all its consequences and demonstrated victoriously that this thesis is untenable.

However, when Cornford says, that he " could find not the faintest sign of any theological revelation," and that " the second part of the dialogue is an extremely subtle and masterly analysis, dealing with problems of the

---

[49] See p. 115.
[50] Cf. Francis Macdonald Cornford, *Plato and Parmenides,* 1939.

sort we call logical," I cannot agree with him so unreservedly. Of course there are no theological " revelations " in the piece. Theology can never " reveal " anything. Even as Christian theology, it does not reveal God, but only relies upon revelation. Plato's theology is based upon a speculative vision which has the function of revelation. I do not agree that the dialogue *Parmenides* has only " logical " matters as its object if one does not define " logic " (as Cornford does not) in the sense of Hegel's " logic," which in fact is his metaphysics, and which indeed deals with the problems of Plato's *Parmenides*. In contrast with Cornford, I hold that the dialogue treats the deepest metaphysical, not only logical, matters and that in this respect the Neoplatonic interpreters and their predecessors came nearer the truth than their opponents.

Plato goes through eight " hypotheses," i.e., propositions beginning with the word " if," and shows what the consequences would be, if the hypothesis were true. In this way he examines eight possible positions that thought can take when confronted with the problem of being. In each case he asks what will follow if the thesis is right that the Existent is One only. Plato himself was, as we know, convinced that the Existent is not simply One, but rather the manifold of the Ideas. Plato agreed with the historical Parmenides in upholding the distinction between the really real and the seemingly real, but he disagreed with him because he wanted to " save " the phenomena by means of their participation in the Ideas. The discussion in the dialogue confirms these agreements and differences. Plato starts from the hypothesis that the (Parmenidean) One exists, and proves that this assumption leads to an absolute nihilism. He then goes on to modify the first hypothesis so that the One and the many would be compatible with each other, and proves that this modification avoids the negative result of the first hypothesis and is consequently acceptable. Cornford speaks of ambiguities in the concept of the One and believes that the duality of the first and second hypotheses ensues from this ambiguity. This interpretation is not false, but it fails to stress the reason why Plato conceives of the One in an " ambiguous " fashion, i.e., that in the first hypothesis he refutes the historical Parmenides, while he develops his own concept in the second.

I cannot here enter a detailed analysis of the dialogue. I must refer to the book of Cornford and to a very concise but excellent interpretation, based on the opinion of Nicolai Hartmann but carried through in detail.[51] I agree with Dr. Chen basically, although I would utter one doubt.

[51] *Über Platons Dialog Parmenides,* von Chung-Hwan Chen. The German text was submitted to me by the author. An English translation was published by D. J. Allan in *The Classical Quarterly,* Vol. XXXVIII, Numbers 3 and 4, 1944.

Hartmann and Chen, unlike Cornford, hold that the dialogue is not merely a logical exercise but contains the most important metaphysical problem of the Ideas, which it solves in a new fashion approaching the views of the *Sophist,* and indicates how Plato conceived of the Ideas and their relation in the latest period of his development. According to this interpretation Plato had come to recognize that the Ideas have no self-dependent existence outside the things that " participate " in them; rather this " participation " has to be understood as a kind of community (*koinonia*) of the Ideas. Parmenides was wrong when he ontologically abstracted the Existent from the existing things; abstractions do not exist. But things cannot be understood without Ideas which compose them. When we start from the first hypothesis which takes the One in an abstract sense we cannot proceed beyond the tautology that the One is the One and even this proposition is not correct because it doubles the One and conjoins the two One's with an " is " thereby already composing Ideas instead of persisting in the one Idea of the One.

There remains, however, one great difficulty. If things in space and time that can be perceived by the senses are the only Existents, which kind of being has to be ascribed to the Ideas? And how can the composition of non-existing Ideas generate existing things? Certainly, the program of dialectical thinking as outlined in the *Republic* demanded that this thinking begins with and ends in Ideas, and that thereby the whole constitution of the world is derived from the supreme Idea by means of division and subdivision, as the dialogue *Sophist* exemplifies it. But did Plato really succeed in discharging this task? The *Parmenides* merely demonstrates that it is impossible and self-destructive to isolate the Ideas, and that only their community discloses their function and explains how and why opposite determinations are compatible with each other in existing things, so that even being and nonbeing, and all the other contrasts, can be united in things which exist. But in order to arrive at this result Plato had to transcend the horizon of Ideas; he had to assume that existence changes the character of the Ideas by adding an element which itself is not an Idea but something that holds Ideas together, even when they contradict each other. What is that element? And how are the Ideas related to that element? I do not think that Plato solved this problem in the *Parmenides,* as Chen seems to assert. Rather we meet here again that unsolved problem which characterizes Plato's whole philosophy, and which prompted Aristotle to transform it.[52]

[52] The unsatisfactory conclusion and the vast variety of interpretations originate from this failure.

IX

THE CONSUMMATION OF GREEK THOUGHT

A. General Character of the Philosophy of Aristotle

By pursuing the development from Thales through the pre-Socratic period to Socrates and Plato, one can collect all the aspects and problems of the Aristotelian system. Aristotle is the heir of them all. This does not mean that he administered this heritage in the spirit of his predecessors or that his own philosophy solved all the unsolved problems. Aristotle created a system of his own, in which the systems of his forerunners were not obliterated but preserved. Hegel has correctly observed that every great philosophy is as individual as is its author, who looks at the world and at life from a completely new point of view. In a way every philosophy is therefore a " thing-in-itself," circumscribed by the unique vision of its creator. In that sense neither Parmenides nor Heraclitus had any successor; their visions could not be improved or corrected by any other vision. They were what they were, mirrors of the Absolute reflected by the individual temper and character of a great personality. But this conception of the history of philosophy is not the only one possible. In fact, it is one-sided and therefore false when made the only valid one.

The romantic or aesthetic conception just outlined needs to be supplemented by the opposite perspective, according to which every system is the logical consequence of its predecessor. Each system continues where the previous ones did not succeed or were vague and obscure. Seen from this perspective, Aristotle was the legitimate consistent heir and administrator of all the thoughts uttered before him; not only did he persevere in the same direction but he also clarified past issues, elucidating what his predecessors had left in the dark. Indeed, one of the differences between Plato and Aristotle is simply the greater clarity, the more precise formulation and definition of concepts, the more specified and thereby illuminated possibilities and alternatives of thought. The scholastics called him " the philosopher " without any amplification, and Dante called him " the master of those who know." Aristotle deserves this title. There was never any thinker who could better express himself, and consider more exactly his own principles, or more carefully prepare and carry through his theories and doctrines. Compared to Aristotle, all Greek philosophers before and after him walked without light, without a sure purpose, without an energetic will, and without a precise method.

This impression is of course partly caused by the comparative number of his extant theoretical writings. But this fact is certainly not accidental. His works have been preserved because his immediate and later disciples and adherents recognized their immense value and therefore collected and edited them with the greatest care and respect. Philosophy in its strict, methodical, critical, and scientific sense begins with Aristotle. Some people would add that it also ended with him. It is true that he has no rival in this respect who surpassed him; very few equaled him. His system is a " system " in the full sense of this word. All his forerunners uttered opinions, wrote aphorisms, composed poems or dialogues; he alone and as the first philosopher wrote separate books on all the separate subjects of thought; he created the philosophical disciplines or sciences, as they still exist. He built up logic in all its branches and consummated them so that posterity could hardly add or change anything — a miraculous work. But his greatest, though also most problematic and obscure, book is the so-called *Metaphysics,* a book enigmatic in origin, in composition, in its subject matter, and in its intentions; it is probably the most influential philosophical book ever written, in spite of its difficulties and uncertainties.

Aristotle's philosophy is a system because it is a whole in which definite principles dominate and order thought, divide its parts, and bring about completion and perfection. It is a system because the world as depicted in this panorama is itself of a singular balance and roundness, a real cosmos, like the cosmos envisaged by Parmenides, but infinitely more intensified and detailed, embracing both the invisible and the visible, the finite and the infinite, the physical and the metaphysical, the ontological and the ethical, the human and the divine hemispheres. Plato had already looked at the whole of reality as a hierarchical order; likewise Aristotle, although in a more systematic style, thought of the cosmos as a huge structure, rising from the bottom to the top by means of steps. The higher levels rest upon the lower, and all of them make up a system of steady and stable development. There is change and movement in this system, but there is also eternal order and changeless form. In this grandiose fashion Aristotle unites the motives of all his forerunners and binds them together in one great vision.

This system represents the consummation of Greek speculation. Although a Platonist of a sort, Aristotle is more typically Greek than Plato because he is less Socratic. The basically Greek attitude, i.e., the primacy of contemplation, observation, theoretical intuition, was absolutely victorious in him. These features (in so far as they can be used as characteristics of Greek thought) were stronger in Aristotle than in Plato. Since the latter was still under the influence of Socrates, his speculation manifested the prophetic and ethical attitude of his great teacher. Aristotle was no longer influenced by the immediate impression of the personality of Socrates, but solely by the Greek tendency toward pure and absolute knowledge. Thus he can be regarded as the archetype of Greek classical thought.

Although he was not born in Athens, Aristotle had adopted the Athenian spiritual intellectualism during his long stay in Athens. He studied for twenty years in the Academy of Plato and returned later to Athens, where he opened his own school. His style of thinking and writing shows to the highest degree all the features of Athenian sagacity, versatility, plasticity, dialectical subtlety, agility, logical lucidity, penetration, and discernment. In Aristotle the aesthetic and theoretical spirit triumphed once more unreservedly and unbrokenly; it found its supreme philosophical expression. Although Aristotle, at least in his classical works, is less an artist than Plato, yet the artistic spirit of his nation was more powerfully alive in him and more formative in his central conceptions. While Plato was fundamentally ethical and political in his main predilection and emphasis, Aristotle was fundamentally a scientist. Theoretical contemplation was to him the most cherished and most highly regarded human activity, but in this contemplation artistic imagination and creativity were by no means excluded; they were rather themselves in operation. For the term "theory" did not mean to Aristotle what it means to us. It was an intuitive vision. Such a vision underlies his thinking and his system, as it had been operative before in the speculation of the pre-Socratics and in Plato.

The Aristotelian cosmos is, as it were, the work of an artist or rather (since there is no divine creator in his scheme) it is an architecture analogous to that formed by an artist. The material and the spiritual factors penetrate each other as they do in an artistic composition.[1] Form and content are one. Similar to that of the Pythagoreans, the cosmos of Aristotle contains a sort of harmony based upon its perfect unity, generated and guaranteed by the world-mind. This mind takes the place of the Heraclitean "Logos." There is, however, no coincidence of the opposites in the sense in which this principle dominated the philosophy of Heraclitus. In spite of order and harmony there is also imperfection and chance in the world, in contrast to the absolute perfection and necessity of the supreme mind. The cosmos of Aristotle is in this respect more akin to that of Parmenides, who also separated the imperfect world from the ideal Existent. But whereas this Existent was regarded as the only true reality by Parmenides, Aristotle, like Plato, "saved" the world of change and chance, to which he ascribed an even greater reality. Although separated from the perfect world-mind, the imperfect world is perfectly well ordered; its very imperfection is, as it were, in order. Things are as they ought to be. There is no realm of ideas and ideals outside them. They perfectly agree with their forms,[2] in spite of their imperfection. This might sound inconsistent. To understand this seeming contradiction it is necessary to study and to interpret the system of Aristotle more closely.

Aristotle abandoned Plato's ethical teleology without altogether abandoning teleology. He replaced ethical by biological and technical teleology (inclusive of artistic teleology not distinguished in principle from the technical). Nature does not strive after an unattain-

---

[1] It is characteristic that Aristotle uses most frequently artistic creativity as the model for all generation; he insists bluntly that "things formed by nature are in the same case as products of art. For the seed is productive in the same way as the things that work by art" (*Metaphysics*, 1034a).

[2] The term "form" should not be applied to Plato's Ideas. It corresponds only to the Aristotelian scheme in which the Idea is interpreted as a quasi-aesthetic form (*eidos, morphē*).

able ideal like Plato's Ideas, but rather after a reachable end that is normally attained. Unlike Plato, Aristotle was not an enthusiastic thinker but a sober and scientific observer who registered " what is " and who was content with this record.[3] He descended from a family in which the medical profession had been hereditary, and he himself had gone to Athens in order to study medicine. Throughout his life Aristotle never completely disavowed this inclination. His philosophy betrays it in many ways. As Kant's *Critique of Judgment* can illustrate, there is an inner affinity between the organism and the work of art, between biological and aesthetic teleology. In both cases, we judge in relation to the ends that organize the whole structure, be it of the living being or of the work of art. In both cases we face a whole which dominates its parts so that all the parts fit together in composing the life of the whole, be it the physical life of the animal or the spiritual life of the work. It is this common feature that determines the teleological thought in the system of Aristotle.

While Plato thought of the relation between Ideas and phenomena in ethical terms, Aristotle thought, instead, of the relation between forms and things in analogy to organic, technical, or artistic activity. Even in the realm of ethics itself, this analogy is predominant. Therefore his ethics is partly a technical advice as to how man can become happy, partly an aesthetic interpretation of virtue as the right proportion, between extremes of behavior. If a man keeps clear of those extremes, he applies the adequate means to attain the end of all human striving, namely, the greatest happiness possible. While Socrates and Plato were impelled by the spirit of moral, political, and spiritual reformation and education, Aristotle was eager to understand the existing political constitutions of states and to describe ethical life as it is, if a man chooses the right conduct for the ultimate goal.

It is characteristic of Aristotle's ethics that he mostly uses the term *kalon* (" beautiful ") to signify the morally good. He regards as the highest virtue and at the same time as the supreme happiness, not practical action, but theoretical contemplation; not ethical, but " dia-

---

[3] This is true at least with respect to the classical works of Aristotle. Werner Jaeger has shown that the young Aristotle, who was still enchanted and inspired by Plato, was himself enthusiastic.

noetical " virtue, i.e., the ability to grasp and to comprehend the truth. There is a striking analogy between the attitude of Aristotle and that of Hegel; both substituted for the primacy of " practical reason," as pronounced by their predecessors (Plato and Kant or Fichte), the primacy of " theoretical reason," although this term does not mean the same thing in Aristotle and Hegel. Kant and Fichte depicted the ideal state as Plato did; Hegel, like Aristotle, conceived of the best state not in order to revolutionize existing conditions but solely for the sake of understanding and comprehension. Nothing is more remote from Aristotle than a utopian conception, whereas Plato's *Republic* can be called the first utopia ever composed and the model of all similar subsequent attempts.

While Plato put the Good at the top of the hierarchy of Ideas, Aristotle believed truth to be the most excellent and prominent of all values. Kant was aware of his kinship with Plato in this respect. In a chapter of the *Critique of Pure Reason,*[4] he considers Plato as his predecessor, while Hegel, on the other hand, praised Aristotle because of his attitude toward knowledge, contemplation, and truth. Plato says, " The Good is the cause of knowledge and of truth . . . , it surpasses them in beauty." [5] Aristotle says: " Contemplation (*theōria*) is the most delightful and the best " of all things; [6] and, in his *Ethics,* " The activity of philosophic wisdom is admittedly the pleasantest of virtuous activities; at all events the pursuit of it is thought to offer pleasures marvelous for their purity and their enduringness." [7] Accordingly, he defines happiness in its perfection as the fruit and even the very essence of that contemplative activity at which the philosopher aims: " The activity of reason, which is contemplative, seems both to be superior in serious worth and to aim at no end beyond itself and to have its pleasure proper to itself. . . . It follows that this activity will be the complete happiness of man. . . ." [8] " Happiness by its very nature is therefore itself in the last analysis a form of contemplation." [9] This conviction expresses the

[4] *Transcendentale Dialektik,* I, i.
[5] *Republic,* VI, p. 509.
[6] *Metaphysics,* 1072b24.
[7] *Nicomachean Ethics,* X, ch. 7 (1177a24–27).
[8] *Loc. cit.,* pp. 1177b18–24.
[9] *Loc. cit.,* p. 1178b31.

innermost spirit of the Greek mind in the most succinct and superb formula.

Aristotle abandoned, more radically and resolutely than Plato, not only the exclusively ethical emphasis of Socrates but also the Socratic "agnosticism." Plato had already dared to comprehend the mystery of the divine in a manner that Socrates would never have dared; Aristotle went much farther. He gave up the mystical awe so characteristic of both Socrates and Plato and the reluctance to think out and to put down a definite theology. Thus he became the leader of all subsequent ventures in that field, the typical metaphysical theologian of all times. Plato was, in all places where he approached the "divine center" (to speak with W. Jaeger), very careful to underline the ultimate impossibility of knowing the nature of god. Aristotle, on the contrary, felt sure that philosophic analysis and penetration is able to reveal even the most secret things. His speculation therefore assumes the tone and attacks the task of religious revelation. By simplifying the manifold directions in which Plato had touched upon the supreme mystery and by reducing the theme of theological knowledge to only one firm position he gained in clarity and precision what he lost in religious awe and humility. He eliminated the Idea of the Good and its quasi-divine splendor. He also eradicated the Platonic world-soul in both its good and its evil manifestations. He replaced both by a world-mind that was supposed to retain the majesty and sovereignty of the Good and also to assume the function of the good world-soul. This was certainly a stroke of genius.

The Aristotelian god is more personal than both the Platonic world-soul and the Idea of the Good. He is as personal as the demiurge in the *Timaeus*. But he is not a creator or architect of the world; he is merely by implication its eternal mover. Only in obliterating the scheme of an actively creative demiurge could Aristotle supersede the mythical story of the *Timaeus* by a sternly theoretical analysis which tried to make his conception of the divine mind as logically plausible and persuasive as his other metaphysical doctrines. This whole theology could of course be accomplished only because Aristotle did not merely change the Platonic attempts at a knowledge of the divine, but also transformed the entire ontology of the Ideas. And this most important and fateful correction or alteration was brought about by the change in emphasis due to the fact that Aristotle was much more physically minded than Plato. The famous painting of Raphael in the Vatican, called *The School of Athens,* emphasizes this difference in the most graphic manner. Plato appears in this painting as an old man accompanied by the young Aristotle. Plato points to the ceiling and Aristotle to the floor. Indeed this was the fundamental difference between master and pupil.

While Plato combined Parmenides and Socrates, Aristotle, though standing on a Platonic foundation, nevertheless definitely returned to the physical metaphysics of Anaxagoras, whom he praises so greatly in his report of the earlier thinkers. Plato is the typical representative of a priori thinking: therefore, he stressed the innate ideas, the dialectical method, deduction by means of logical classification, the primacy of the abstract over the concrete or of the universals over the individuals, the transcendent reality of the Ideas, the importance of mathematics, and other features. Aristotle, on the contrary, did not believe in innate ideas but taught that ideas originate from experience; he did not employ deduction so much as Plato, but rather induction; he did not develop a theory of dialectical relation between ideas; in his scheme the individual and the concrete have a function much more fundamental than they have in Plato; he denied the reality of the Ideas, their transcendence and their divinity; he was not a mathematician but rather a biologist; he was, to sum it up, not so much a rationalist as Plato but, rather, an empirical scientist.

However, this contrast must not be overrated. It is the greatness of Aristotle that he was not at all one-sided. Compared to Plato, he was definitely an empirical scientist; nevertheless he did not neglect or disparage the role of intuition and reason in thinking. He did not cancel the universals but recognized their significance in thinking as well as in things. He was, to be sure, not a mathematician, and even fatefully undervalued the role mathematics has to play in physics and astronomy; nevertheless, he understood mathematics to a certain degree. In a word, Aristotle was not at all an empiricist like Locke or Hume; he saw very clearly the right of the rational and the deductive. He was, after all, a Platonist, a speculative thinker, the founder of the first metaphysical system.

The shift of interest and stress from Plato to Aristotle implied, however, a fundamental reorientation and reorganization of the whole cosmological structure. Biology assumed a metaphysical prominence and dignity never previously attached to it, not even by Empedocles, who was especially interested in the organic world. Of course, when we speak of biology today we mean something much more restricted than it meant to the Greeks in general and to Aristotle in particular. The word *bios* (" life ") had a wider range than organic life. It circumscribed the whole sphere of life, including the life of man, of the soul, of the mind, of the will, of historical life, and even the life of the gods or of the supreme god. Aristotle was therefore able to apply biological categories to existence in its entirety, and thus to ennoble biological thinking by exalting it to the rank of metaphysical speculation. This thinking could bind together the opposite spheres of nature and spirit, of animal and man, of instinct and causality, of necessity and freedom, of change and growth, of the organic and the artistic, of the human and the divine. Thus a wide span united many aspects that seem to be opposed to each other. Existence understood as life in this wide sense was made the common denominator of all that is and could be interpreted by a universal metaphysical theory. In this way Aristotle felt able to conceive of cosmic life by means of contemplative thought.

The central concept of this metaphysics is accordingly the concept of end (*telos*).[10] This concept includes both the end of an organic development or growth and the end of the deliberate will. It connotes both the end in time and the end of an action: it connotes the final cause of a natural process and the final purpose of the will, and so it is excellently well suited to a universal understanding of becoming. Unlike Plato's ontology of Ideas and Parmenides' Existent, Aristotle's metaphysics is a metaphysics of becoming and not of being. Aristotle has little in common with the Dionysian romanticism and universal dynamism of Heraclitus, and yet there is a kinship between them based upon the metaphysical stress upon becoming instead of being. And this same emphasis also conjoins Empedocles, Anaxagoras, and even Democritus to the main principle of Aris-

---

[10] The English word " end " renders much better the meaning of the Greek word *telos* than the German word *Zweck,* because " end " unites both purpose and final cause, while the word *Zweck* merely covers " purpose," i.e., the end of willing.

totle. For Aristotle was inclined to value the visible and physical cosmos, so utterly disparaged by Parmenides and at least unacceptable to Plato. From this perspective it is understandable why Aristotle taught the immanence of the Ideas rather than their transcendence, thereby deeply modifying Plato's entire outlook and the very concept of the Idea.

B. METAPHYSICAL PRINCIPLES

For many reasons it is very difficult to give a short account of Aristotle's metaphysical principles. The *Metaphysics* is, for all its explicit analysis and its great lucidity, nevertheless a book almost as obscure as the oracles of Heraclitus. It is first of all not a book composed by the author for the purpose of publication, but rather a collection of essays written in different periods of his philosophic development and gathered together after his death by the editors of his extant works. It is furthermore written in a very succinct style, as if it were a draft for his lectures or notes which he or his students jotted down. It is consequently not well organized and very uneven in its methodical perfection, its ultimate intentions, and its emphasis upon this or that detail. It is also difficult because of the obscurity of the matter with which it deals and because of the profundity and subtlety of the discussion.

There is still another difficulty in presenting Aristotle's *Metaphysics*. Since there is no book of greater and wider influence upon the subsequent development of scientific metaphysics, the interpretation of this book has undergone a vast variety of different or even opposite viewpoints. It is almost incredible that Aristotle has been equally praised by thinkers otherwise completely different in outlook, creed, and perspective. Pagan antiquity and medieval scholasticism, Arabic and Western philosophers, Church Fathers and Renaissance Aristotelians, Leibniz and Hegel, Dante and Goethe have sung the praises of Aristotle. Pantheists, Catholic and Protestant theists, Thomists, Scotists, naturalists, deists, idealists, and existentialists have extolled " the " philosopher. In short, Aristotle has appealed to almost every kind of thinker.

It is evident that such an enormous scope of interpretation must have its cause in an equally enormous many-sidedness and variegation of principles. Aristotle is probably the most multiform and the most variously interpreted of all thinkers. Indeed, there is hardly any aspect of the universe, visible or invisible, that was not seen by him and that was not disposed of in proper order. His method of elaborate distinctions and divisions enabled him to take into consideration even opposite views of the same fact or datum without meeting contradictions or allowing such paradoxes as Heraclitus indulged in. Although he categorically denied that there are any ultimate contradictions in existence, and therefore did not permit any contradictions in thought, nevertheless he united polarities by means of his method of distinction, and this unification is even the very heart and core of his metaphysical thought. Aristotle has his own manner of taking into account the coincidence of opposites discovered by Heraclitus.

Consequently, his metaphysical principles are in themselves polar. Two pairs of opposites are the very backbone of his metaphysics: that of matter and form and that of the potential and the actual. The contrast of matter and form constitutes the structure of everything that exists except the divine being; the contrast between the potential and the actual is closely related to that of matter and form, but it concerns the process of becoming rather than the structure. In so far as Aristotle's metaphysics is a metaphysics of becoming, this second pair of opposites is even more central, more original, and more characteristic of his scheme than that of form and matter. The concepts of the potential and the actual gave him the tool by which he tried to unify the polarity of matter and form and to overcome the contradictions that otherwise would have arisen. The contrast of the potential and the actual is applicable to everything, inasmuch as everything is in a state of becoming; only the divine being is an exception to the rule. Everything else has to become what it essentially is, while the divine mind always is what it is essentially. Everything in the cosmos of Aristotle is in a state of change and process, is moved and moving, acts and is acted upon, grows or decays; in short, it is in a state of development. This is even true of the divine mind, but this mind does not develop or move in the strict sense; it does not grow or decay, but, as we shall see, it does act.

Since the divine mind of the world differs essentially from all other things, the *Metaphysics* of Aristotle is divided into two main parts, one dealing with everything except the divine, the other dealing with the divine. Plato's great division between the noetic sphere of the

Ideas and the phenomenal sphere of the individual things was accepted by Aristotle only in the transformed fashion of the division between god and world. The *Metaphysics* is divided accordingly into an ontology of the finite and into an ontology of the infinite; however, these terms are not those of Aristotle, although they are implied in his main division. This main division can also be characterized in terms of the duality of an analysis of being (or an ontology in general) and a theology concerned solely with an analysis of the divine being. I shall not discuss how these two parts are historically related to each other.[11] Systematically they fit with each other well, in spite of some obvious cracks and fissures. The general ontology that issues from the question, What does being mean?, treats Aristotle's two main principles, of matter and form and of potentiality and actuality, and speaks about their function with respect to the world, whereas his theology answers the question, In what sense can the two principles be applied to the comprehension of the divine?

The contrast of matter and form, though not occurring in Plato, is nevertheless derived from the contrast between the ideal and the phenomenal sphere. This latter contrast is transmuted in accordance with the new interest and intuition of Aristotle. Plato's Idea is now conceived as form, a principle that constitutes everything and makes it what it is to be or to become. The form as compared with the Idea is therefore not transcendent, but immanent within the things which it forms. It is not merely a pattern or model, but it is the active force that activates the proper shape of the thing and actuates the process by which it becomes that thing. The progressive nature of everything is therefore already predisposed in the structural concept of form.

The forms of Aristotle replace the Ideas of Plato; but they are no longer self-sufficient and self-dependent, dwelling in their own super-celestial abode; they now constitute the essences immanent in the things. Consequently, the forms themselves belong to the phenomenal world. To speak more accurately, there is no longer a phenomenal world in Aristotle's *Metaphysics;* instead, there is the contrast between the world and god. The *Metaphysics* is partly cosmological, partly theological; while the physics deals with the visible nature,

[11] The books of Werner Jaeger, especially that on the *Metaphysics*, have developed ingenuous and revolutionary insight into this problem.

the metaphysics deals with the invisible principles of the visible world. The forms are forms of those things that compose the world — not merely the physical world, though, but also the human soul and mind, man's activity and life, his cognitive as well as his volitional performances, his technical as well as his artistic productivity and creativity. All these various realms are dominated by the concept of forms; this concept explains and expounds the structure of all these realms in their specific modes.

The Platonic Ideas also could be interpreted as the essences of things, but this interpretation had to be qualified on account of the transcendence of the Ideas. Only in the metaphysics of Aristotle does the term " essence " assume its usual (since Aristotle usual!) sense. Aristotle ended the ambiguity of the Platonic Idea originating from its dual source: from the Socratic conception of virtue as an ideal and from the Existent of Parmenides as the true being. Plato had transferred the ethical ideal to the ontological realm and never consistently reflected upon the momentous chasm between the ethical and the ontological spheres, between an ideal never perfectly to be attained and the Idea as the essence which dominates the things. On the contrary, Plato conceived of the ontological relation between Ideas and things in terms of ethical striving and acting. He defined the Ideas as patterns or models which are imitated by things. Even the term " participation," often used by Plato to explain the relation between the Ideas and the actual things remained, if not interpreted ethically, in the dark. Aristotle, reflecting on such difficulties and unsolved problems, offered as a solution his own category of form (*eidos, morphē*) and the principle of the hierarchy of forms, already anticipated by Plato.

To Aristotle, not the ethical ideal but rather the technical and artistic form is the prototype of all forms. Thus he gave a new sense and significance to the term *" eidos,"* in contradistinction to the Platonic term " Idea." Aristotle thought of the organic form analogously to the technical and artistic process in which a material is actively formed by the conscious operation of mind and will. He could therefore also interpret technical and artistic creativity in terms of organic formation. Form always forms; it works within and upon a material conceived of as " matter." A comparison of the Platonic Idea and the Aristotelian *Eidos,* with respect to their affinity to the aesthetic sphere, discloses that the Idea (in so far as it had an aesthetic as well as an ethical connotation) corresponds more to the ideal vision of the artist, never completely and perfectly carried out in the real work; whereas the *Eidos* resembles the vision of the artist precisely as it is truly executed in the work. To Plato, the original pure conception in the mind was infinitely more beautiful than any material work could possibly be. The artist, in materializing his vision, has to enter the sphere of the material phenomena, which makes the original pattern somehow impure and blurred. As long as the vision lives in the soul, it is as it were ethereal and celestial; the moment it is materialized, it gets earthy and corporeal and loses its original spirituality and splendor. To Aristotle, on the contrary, the realization of the artistic vision brings out its full perfection and reveals its inner power and beauty. Accordingly the process, by which the vision is carried out and made visible in the world of actuality, is the most important and most intrinsic function of the form. Plato, in other words, regarded the original artistic design or project as superior to the artistic creation and performance, while Aristotle regarded creative activity as the very essence of the form, the channel by which form becomes the essence of the thing formed.

These two views, though rooted in the same soil of an artistic culture, are nevertheless worlds apart. To Plato, the pure ideal was the truly real (as it was to Socrates), in the ethical as well as in the aesthetic realm; to Aristotle, the actual activity, artistic as well as ethical, was the truly real. This difference is not only to be derived from the Socratic influence upon Plato, and the thoroughly and basically Greek feature of Aristotle's metaphysics; it was also conditioned by the philosophical milieu in which Plato and Aristotle philosophized. In spite of the fact that Greek philosophy had already undergone a long and remarkable development when Plato appeared on the scene, he was, nevertheless, a new beginning. The Sophists had destroyed the continuity of speculation and Socrates had not tried to restore the old systems. After the period of skepticism and relativism, Plato dared to recover the tradition. He initiated a new adventure by renewing the speculative mood and the metaphysical boldness of former times. His philosophy is accordingly characterized by its venturesome attempts at the conquest of speculative truth; by its variety of schemes, none of which was fully developed; by its ever new beginnings; by its visionary grasp of the Idea; by its fear to fix any intuition, and to materialize his vision. Plato was the great inspirer and instigator; Aristotle, the great performer and consummator. This momentous difference is itself mirrored in the difference between their general philosophical positions.

According to his own mission, Aristotle triumphed over the recalcitrant and tough material of thought. This triumph was the very soul of his *Metaphysics*. His philosophic creativity was that of the artist who forms the stubborn stone or wood and impresses his mind upon them. Of course, the two sources from which the difference between Plato and Aristotle can be derived, the ethicoreligious and the historical character of the two epochs, are inwardly related to each other. The deepest reason for the break between the first and the second period of Greek philosophy was the essential insufficiency of speculation when confronted with the supreme and ultimate problem: the nature of god and his creation. The first period came to an end because speculation failed to solve this problem in a satisfactory manner. The very plurality and rivalry of schemes indicated this fundamental failure. The rise of the Sophistic movement and finally of Socrates was the immediate consequence of this incongruity of philosophic speculation and religious revelation. The religious emphasis of Socrates, his humility and awe, his reluctance to penetrate into the mystery of the divine, all this was the necessary outcome of the speculative failure to create a substitute for the insufficient polytheistic religion attacked by the philosophers. Plato, the disciple of Socrates, inherited the Socratic sensitivity and metaphysical shyness. These basic features prompted Plato to exalt an ideal unattainable to man in the ethical, the aesthetic, or the philosophic sphere. Consequently, Plato became the utopian, the typical " idealist."

Aristotle, standing on the shoulders of Plato, continued the speculative conquest. He went as far as the older thinkers had gone and even farther in his confidence that he could reach the metaphysical goal. The breakdown of the earlier systems lay behind him in the far distance. Skepticism and the entire Sophistic movement were defeated by Socrates and Plato. The doctrine of the Ideas, as he knew and interpreted it, seemed to need correction, but it also made him believe that it is possible to use its truth in order to penetrate into the core of being. All helped to persuade him that, if the necessary correction were made, the door would be open to the " divine center." The failure of ancient speculations was due only to their one-sided principles, undisciplined and unmethodical thinking, the lack of proper distinctions, and their excessively mythological concepts. Having learned from Socrates and Plato how to proceed in a more methodical way, Aristotle could easily be tempted to use his superior discernment to resolve all unsolved problems and thus to give a completely satisfying substitute for the declining religion of the gods of old. Philosophy seemed to be called upon to perform and to finish the entire task of making the ideal real. Aristotle thereby became the " realistic " thinker who envisaged the world forms as the means of molding matter, an end finally and absolutely achieved by and in the divine mind.

How can the forms accomplish the formation of matter? How can matter and form so unite that their chasm is perfectly filled? This question was of paramount weight and consequence to Aristotle. If he did not succeed in answering that fundamental question, then he completely failed to solve the preliminary problem of ontology. The most penetrating and subtle discussion in the *Metaphysics,* is, therefore, dedicated to this problem; it is the pivot upon which the whole *Metaphysics* turns. The duality of the visible and the invisible spheres of the cosmos, which had caused all the difficulties and all the dissent in the first period of Greek philosophy and in the speculation of Plato, had to be overcome at its root. The polarity of form and matter was therefore of representative significance. How can this polarity constitute one and the same underlying substance? When we fashion the question in this way, we recognize at once that the concept of substance had to be the center of attention and had to be analyzed first. This is what we find at the beginning of the most serious exposition in the entire work. The best way to interpret this part of the *Metaphysics* is to reconsider Plato's concept of substance (*ousia*).

Plato understood the term *"ousia"* not so much in the sense of " substance," but, rather, in its original meaning, derived from the term " *einai* " (" to be ") and most correctly rendered by the Latin term " *essentia,*" a word derived from the Latin *esse* (" to be "). The Platonic Idea is not the substance of those things which participate in the Idea; it is their essence. To be sure, even this word has connotations that may mislead. "Essence" may be interpreted in an immanent fashion, as dwelling with things. This meaning was not entirely excluded by Plato since things "participate" in the Ideas; it was explicitly stressed in the dialogue *Parmenides*. But it was nevertheless secondary; the transcendence of the Ideas was primary. The term "essence" can be used also in this primary sense, according to which the Ideas are self-dependent and self-existent entities.[12] The Idea is *ousia* in the Platonic sense, inasmuch as it exists in itself and by itself. Aristotle used the same term but modified its connotation. To him "*ousia*" was in the first place an entity which cannot be predicated of something else. In the sentence, "This is an oak," the word "oak" does not purport a substance; rather, the word "this," pointing to the individual oak, purports a substance because this oak can never become the predicate of any other oak. To Aristotle the term "*ousia*" means therefore in the first place the individual thing which is composed out of matter and form. "This individual oak" is "this" and "individual," because of its matter; it is generic because of its form "oak." This modification of the meaning of "*ousia*" clearly changes the whole metaphysical outlook. To Plato, the generic and the universal, "oak" and "tree," are more real in the metaphysical sense than "this individual oak"; to Aristotle, the reverse is true.

This shift of meaning expresses the shift from the invisible to the visible sphere, from the Idea to the thing, from the self-existing essence to that entity in which the essence exists. One might say it was a shift from the metaphysical to the physical, but this statement would be misleading. The shift was made because of a metaphysical or ontological consideration; it concerned the metaphysical meaning of the term "*ousia*" and the metaphysical constitution of the physical thing (or indeed of everything in so far as it belongs to the visible cosmos, even when it is not visible in the physical sense of bodies). It was a fateful step when the Latin writers translated the term "*ousia*," in the Aristotelian sense, by "substance." Aristotle, taking over the term from Plato, still pointed to the original meaning which implies that the ideal constituent of the thing, i.e., the species or the genus ("oak" or "tree"), is the essense which determines what the thing is or is to become; whereas the term "sub-

---

[12] The German word *Wesenheit* expresses, in contrast to *Wesen,* this sense of an independent essence in contrast to an immanent one.

stance" points to the carrier of that species or genus, which is material and thereby individual.[13] The Latin translation, in other words, underscored the difference between Aristotle and Plato even more than Aristotle had done. Aristotle did not completely abandon the original meaning of *"ousia"* (" essence "). On the contrary, he applied the same term to the species, i.e., to the form itself, but he distinguished both the individual thing and the specific form by calling the thing " first," the species " second," *ousia,* thereby indicating that both are identical, in so far as the thing is " essentially " determined by its species or " is " that species *in individuo* (" an oak "). This ambiguous or alternate use of the term is a source of much misunderstanding, but it also points to an intrinsic difficulty.

If the thing is essentially its species, i.e., its essence or form, how does its matter and its form compose one and the same individual substance? This is the most thorny problem of the *Metaphysics.* Aristotle discovered that the most familiar, the most simple, and the seemingly best known thing in the world — namely, the thing that we perceive with our senses but also conceive with the thinking mind — contains the hardest of all metaphysical riddles: the composition or synthesis of two disparate elements or constituents, i.e., of matter and form. Not the realm of the supercelestial Ideas, but the unity of the metaphysical form and the physical matter, the " togetherness " (*synolon*) of two seemingly incompatible factors, one conceptual and the other sensuous, one general and the other individual, one cognitive and the other perceptive, is the greatest wonder and deserves the keenest attention of the metaphysical thinker. How can the opposites be united so that they are together one and the same thing?

Ousia as substance, i.e., as the composite of matter and form, is the unity of opposites each of which needs the other; only their synthesis makes the existence of the thing possible. Matter needs form to be the matter of a definite thing; form needs matter to be the essence of that thing. The existence of the thing demands both matter for its subsistence and form for its essence. Each depends upon the other and does not exist without the other. Although an oak is an oak only, because the species or form " oak " is its essence, this es-

[13] Aristotle has a special term for this carrier: " *hypokeimenon,*" mostly translated by " substratum."

sence would not exist without matter; it would be the species " oak " but not a definite existing oak. How is the form transmuted into an existing thing? How can matter and form penetrate each other so that they not only unite but become identical as this existing thing? This is the more problematic, because form, as such, is the same in different existing things in which it functions as their essence, while these things are many and differ from each other on account of their matter. The problem of identity is involved in this transmutation of the same form into many existing things. The distinction of substance in the primary sense (thing) and in the secondary sense (species) does not settle that problem. How can a thing remain the same thing when its matter changes, as is the case in an organic being? Is the form alone the identical element in the thing? If so, why does the form need matter? Is not matter rather an element that deprives the form of its self-identity? But how can we speak of the self-identity of the form, when the form does not exist outside the synthesis? What is, after all, the ultimate relation between essence and substance? On the answer to this question depends the answer to the question, What is substance in the primary sense? The final elucidation of all these difficulties is given only by the second pair of fundamental opposites: that of potentiality and actuality. Being can be understood only as Becoming.

But before I discuss this second principle, I must add some applications of Aristotle's theory of form which shed new light upon his whole metaphysical system. Matter as such does not exist. It is only a concept pointing at the abstract and fragmentary factor in existing things. Matter as such needs form to exist as such a factor. We should conclude according to the theory just developed that form, as such, is not able to exist either, since it needs matter to become the essence in the existing things. However, Aristotle teaches that form can exist apart, or in and for itself, and does so in the divine being. This seeming inconsistency will be elucidated later. Both matter without form and form without matter can be fully interpreted only after the contrast of the potential and the actual has been understood.

There is, furthermore, a hierarchy of forms; the form of the lower stage can become the matter on a higher stage. Flesh and bones are matter, but they are already formed, in so far as they presuppose an inorganic matter which itself is a genus only because it is formed matter. Wood is matter in a house, but it is itself formed by the species "wood." A statue is stone formed, but every stone is itself already formed, inasmuch as it is marble or granite. The animal body is matter on the stage of human life. Perceptions are matter within concepts. There is accordingly a conceptual matter differing in principle from the corporeal matter on lower stages. Matter is more of a function than something material which is already formed.

The final solution of the problem of substance is, according to Aristotle, only to be attained when we pay attention to the fact that there is no existing thing that does not become what it is to be. This process cannot be comprehended without the concepts of potentiality and actuality. Everything is potentially what it is going to become and it is actual only after it has become what it was potentially in the beginning. Aristotle has invented a new term in order to characterize this truth. The form, in so far as it is active and forms matter, is not an Existent as Parmenides had called it, but rather it is that being which answers the question, What was at the beginning? [14] In this way Aristotle combined Parmenides and Heraclitus. The Existent is conceived as something that develops itself by subjecting matter to the form. The form is ontologically prior to the thing formed or to be formed. The form is that initial and initiating power that works itself out through the process of forming matter. In this ingenuous fashion Aristotle used the artistic activity as the metaphysical pattern that comprehends the nature of everything. Form in his philosophy has a thoroughly aesthetic tone and function.

Matter is the potential thing which is actualized by the energy of the form. Matter and form are one, inasmuch as the actual is itself the potential in the state of maturity or completion. The marble stone which the sculptor hews out when he makes the form appear is the potential statue brought to actual existence by the work of the artist. Aristotle often avails himself of this example in order to illustrate his metaphysical theory. The Greek words for the potential and the actual both contain the suggestion of power. The potential is called "*dynamis*," a word that gave origin to the English "dynamic"; the actual is called "*energeia*," a word from which the English "energy" is derived. The energy of the form takes on a dy-

---

[14] In Greek, *to ti ēn einai.*

namic existence in the development out of which the end is materialized.[15] This statement combines the Greek words in their English rendering and makes plausible the artistic root of Aristotle's *Metaphysics*. The vision in the mind of the artist is the end of his activity as far as it concerns his final purpose and the completion of his work. It is the work's substance. But it is also its beginning. It is that which was before the work was made and which is materialized by and in the work. Everything is thus the work of a secret artistic power working in the world and producing the beauty of its forms. Aristotle located the artistic activity of Plato's demiurge within the world, but we shall see that this activity also needs a stimulus from outside the world.

Both the Eleatics and Heraclitus had challenged logic and offended common sense. Plato had unsuccessfully struggled to understand the synthesis of the visible and the invisible. Aristotle proposed to solve the riddle by the relative contrast and substantial identity of the potential and the actual or of form and matter in a work of art. The riddle of being can be penetrated only by the analysis of becoming. The Eleatic contradiction between being and becoming is thereby overcome. The paradox of Heraclitus is logically tamed. Heraclitus, like Aristotle, had taught both flux and the identity of the opposites, but Aristotle devised an ontological principle by which these two features were maintained without paradox. He replaced flux by an organic-teleological and an aesthetic-technical process, and he interpreted the identity of the polarity by the substantial identity of substance and accidence, form and matter, species and specimen, an identity generated by the self-actualization of the form within matter or more accurately by the material self-realization of the form which initiates and ends its own development. For the present I shall not consider whether or not this ingenuous and profound analysis of being and becoming is fully satisfactory and truly solves all the metaphysical intricacies. It is first necessary to study the culmination of the whole system: its theological doctrine. This doctrine puts the truth of his metaphysics to its supreme and final test.

Does the process, not merely of single things but of the whole world, ever reach its goal? In what sense can one speak of the cos-

---

[15] The Aristotelian term "*entelecheia*" ("that which has the end in itself") expresses the same.

mic process and what is its goal? And can philosophy ever perfectly comprehend this goal? If so, does philosophy then reach its own goal in this comprehension? What is the ultimate relation between comprehension and its objective? Has philosophic thinking itself a place in the cosmos? Is it perhaps itself the ultimate goal? All these momentous questions arise at the horizon of the *Metaphysics* after the analysis of being and becoming has come to an end. Aristotle answers them all. He is convinced that the thinking mind can penetrate into the innermost core of reality, because he is convinced that this mind itself is the ultimate form of all things, their highest form, which molds matter more energetically and finally than any other form. " Contemplation is the most delightful and the best " of all things. It " aims at no end beyond itself." It finishes its own process, and it can finish it only if it is capable of grasping the ultimate truth and all truth. The thinking mind penetrates matter so absolutely that all the darkness and toughness of matter ultimately dissolves and all opposition between matter and form disappears; the contrast between mind and body, between concept and perception, between thought and its object, between knowing and being, is triumphantly surmounted at the end.

To use Aristotle's own terminology the mind activates and actualizes its own possibility to the full. It attains the precious fruit of its labor and exertion, the supreme good: truth and happiness. To the philosophic contemplation, Aristotle ascribes a logical, ontological, ethical, and aesthetic and religious value. He feels justified in so doing because he thereby unconsciously fulfills the aesthetic dream of the Greek soul. Through the toil and creative energy of the thinking mind the supreme truth, which is also the supreme goodness and the supreme beauty, is attained: all desire is stilled. This highest end is achieved not merely through intuition and vision, but also through observation and investigation, through the logical effort and the methodical discipline of philosophic thought. It does not come like a sudden illumination or revelation, but only through the hard work of thinking. The very word " *energeia,*" which contains the word " *ergon* " (" work "), hints at this work.

Contemplation is not simply receptive; it is eminently active. Aristotle does not allow any doubt in this respect. He stresses greatly the active and creative aspect of contemplation. Sense impression may be merely passive; thought is the most vivid and vivacious life. For happiness is itself activity. The supreme happiness is the activity of creative contemplation, because contemplation attains the goal of all goals, the end of all ends. There is, of course, an intuitive element in thought that cannot be dismissed any more than impressions can be dismissed in order to activate the empirical comprehension. Consequently, Aristotle distinguishes the passive or receptive mind from the active and creative one (*nous pathētikos* and *nous poiētikos*). They are related to each other as the potential to the actual, as matter to form. But this distinction is surpassed in the course of philosophic development, inasmuch as the active and creative mind fully overcomes the resistance of the passive one and conquers victoriously the inertia of mere receptivity. On the highest level of contemplation the mind, therefore, not only grasps its objectives absolutely, but it also grasps itself. This is the zenith of all intuition and comprehension. Here all cognitive problems are solved. Self-understanding is perfect self-actualization. But does this not imply that the thinking mind is divine?

C. THEOLOGY

Active reason indeed is divine, according to Aristotle, for " the activity of god, which surpasses all other in blessedness, must be contemplative." [16] And man can and does attain complete blessedness himself when he envisages truth and lives accordingly; but " it is not in so far as he is man that he will live so, but in so far as something divine is present in him." [17] " If reason is divine, then, in comparison with man, the life according to it is divine in comparison with human life. But we must not follow those who advise us . . . being mortal to think of mortal things, but must, so far as we can, make ourselves immortal, and strain every nerve to live in accordance with the best in us; for even if it be small in bulk, much more does it in power and worth surpass everything. This would seem, too, to be each man himself, since it is the authoritative and better part of him. It would be strange, then, if he were to choose, not the life of his self, but that of something else . . . , since reason more than any-

---

[16] *Nicomachean Ethics*, X, ch. 8 (1178b22).
[17] *Loc. cit.*, ch. 7 (1177b26).

thing else is man." [18] Proud words, words that reveal the inward nature of the man who wrote them!

Reason is not merely human, but divine; man is essentially reason or mind, and therefore essentially divine. But man is also a composite being, matter and form, like all other beings and entities, and this composite nature differs from the nature of that being which is nothing but divine, the nature of god, i.e., the supreme god who stands at the zenith of the hierarchy of being and presides, as it were, over the world (we shall see presently what this means). The divine mind is no longer the mind of a composite being, but, as Plato's Idea of the Good was the good pure and absolute, the divine mind is mind pure and absolute. The divine mind is not both receptive and active; it is exclusively active. In man essence and existence fall asunder according to his double nature. Therefore, besides the " dianoetical " virtue, man also has ethical virtues, which are more material, because they are concerned with the handling of material things or material situations. The dianoetical virtue (we might call it spiritual, although this term is of a later date) is not determined by any individual circumstances and conditions; it is concerned only with the absolute, the ultimate, the unconditional, i.e., with the knowledge of the truth. It is the same as philosophic wisdom. The active mind is the divine part of man. Through it man reaches the truth which in the last analysis is identical with the self-understanding of mind.

Aristotle's theology is contained in Book XII of the *Metaphysics,* but his physics and ethics and other works point to the same theory. Werner Jaeger has made it very probable that this book of the *Metaphysics* was written in an earlier period than the *Physics* and *Ethics,* and that Aristotle was not satisfied with it in later times. But even if this proves true, a doctrine like the theology of Book XII is indispensable in the metaphysical scheme of Aristotle's system. This system collapses if one obliterates its theological apex. Aristotle later developed his doctrine of the celestial spheres and its star souls. But it is not to be assumed that these star souls completely eradicated the one god of the theology. The editors of the *Metaphysics,* who gave the books their present order, had good reason to place the theology after the ontology. Such a conclusive doctrine was required. Aris-

---

[18] *Loc. cit.,* up to 1178a8.

totle needed the concept of a supreme being as the zenith of the hierarchy of forms; he needed it especially because he had eliminated the transcendence of the Ideas and of the Good. He also needed it in order to give a substitute for both the demiurge and the world-soul of Plato, and to conclude his own cosmology.

The cosmos is not a whole and a unity without an ultimate principle which represents this wholeness and unity. Indeed, it is not a cosmos at all without a cosmic deity. Philosophy began with this consideration. Thales chose Water as this representative entity; Heraclitus, the Logos; Parmenides, the Existent; and even the so-called pluralists like Democritus had to think of an over-all necessity which holds together the manifold of atoms and brings about order and regularity. Since Aristotle was not an " idealist " who could put an abstract principle in the supreme place, like Xenophanes, Empedocles, Anaxagoras, or Plato, he had to conceive of a divine being that could represent the arche of the ancients, the first cause of all movements within the cosmos, if not the author of the cosmos itself. Because of his elimination of the mythical figure of the demiurge, Aristotle's theology did not have to include a creator. Instead, it had to comprehend a supreme governor and goal of the cosmic process, a god who would make the cosmos a cosmos by representing its unity and guaranteeing its order. To the very degree that Aristotle's philosophy was empirical and pluralistic, Aristotle was forced to construct an absolute and monistic focal point, capable of bringing together the diversity of facts and actions and gathering the vast variety of things and forms. As an army, he argues in the *Metaphysics,* is not an army without a supreme general, so the world is not world without a supreme head that directs everything and subjects it to law and order.[19]

In many ways Aristotle tries to prove that the divine being can be only one, while there are many stars and many movements of the stars. The supreme is not moved, since movement always presupposes a cause, but the supreme being is itself the supreme cause of all motion. This supreme cause furthermore cannot be what Aristotle calls " effective," i.e., a mechanical mover who has a place in space and time like Plato's world-soul. Rather the " unmoved mover " must

[19] *Metaphysics,* XII, ch. 10 (1075a14).

be beyond the limit of space and time; he must live a spiritual and eternal life. Only the mind can live such a life, and more particularly the thinking mind, for thinking is the best and the most blessed of all activities of the mind.[20] And since the form is the universal concept in Aristotle's metaphysics, mind is conceived as the form or essence of man. Mind is that peculiar form which makes man both a man and also divine. There must be a divine mind that is no longer human, since the human mind is bound up with the human soul as its matter and therefore is not absolutely pure and perfect. The human mind needs sensuous perception which informs it on the lower levels; the divine mind does not need such information, because it is not conditioned by any lower level but dwells eternally in its goal. The most perfect thinking can no longer be concerned with matter of any kind; it must be absolutely pure, i.e., it must be absolute form without any matter. Although man is essentially reason, it is not only his essence. Man is composite and is therefore a substance that exists. Man is needy and greedy, impelled by his desires and passions, which reason can only gradually and never completely discipline and subject. The whole sphere of ethical life depends upon this imperfection. There must be a supreme reason, no longer dependent upon matter and the material world but absolutely independent and sovereign.

The divine being is reason or mind in the state of perfection. Only god is the mind of the world, that mind on which " heaven and nature hang." [21]

Although the divine mind is pure essence, it is by no means a Platonic Idea, but rather a substance, and therefore active in spite of being unmoved. God is pure activity and actuality. Since he is eternally the goal of all striving and longing, he is no longer potential. His is the only activity that is not development toward an end. He represents and is himself the supreme end. He is therefore eternally blessed, happy, and active. Aristotle says in a naïve fashion that man has to sleep to gather new strength; the god never sleeps. He always

---

[20] Unfortunately the Greek word " *nous* " cannot be rendered accurately in English. It is something in between reason and mind. It is more rational and theoretical than mind, but it is more intuitive and creative than reason. The best translation would be " thinking mind."

[21] *Metaphysics*, XII, ch. 7 (1072b13).

thinks, for thinking is the summit of activity and the summit of joy. " If the god is always in a good state in which we sometimes are, this compels our wonder; and if in a better, this compels it yet more." And, he adds, " God is in a better state," because he never has to rest and to relax. " We say therefore that god is a living being, eternal, most good, so that life and duration continuous and eternal belong to god, for this is god." [22]

God is form and yet substance; he is thinking and yet he does not think material objects or anything restricted and limited. He is pure thought. But he can be pure thought only if he thinks nothing but himself. If he would think anything besides himself, he would be less perfect than he is. One might say that he is the perfect philosopher in whom thinking has become, or rather eternally is, the very substance and the true actuality of his being. Aristotle contributes to this god all the properties and characters that Parmenides contributed to his supreme and only true Existent and for the very same reasons: he is unalterable, indivisible, simple, not in time or space, complete in himself, impassive; and in him being and thought are the same. To this god there is nothing besides himself, as there is nothing besides the Existent of Parmenides. The world, as it were, becomes engulfed in the abyss of nonexistence, since it does not actually exist in the consciousness of the divine thinker because of its relative imperfection. If this consciousness comprises all truth, the world does not participate in truth. Does it live only in the forever imperfect mind of the human philosopher? This mind is imperfect precisely in so far as it is conditioned by the world and by matter and can therefore never absolutely actualize itself.

At the horizon of history all the future Aristotelians appear at this point: Aquinas and Duns Scotus, Nicolaus Cusanus and Giordano Bruno, Spinoza and Leibniz, Schelling and Hegel — all their systems seem in their own way to use, modify, and correct the scheme of Aristotle. But what is more surprising and appalling: Aristotle's theology came nearer Biblical revelation than any philosophy before him. It is a remarkable fact that the human intellect in Aristotle ascended so high; that human thought was able to approach revealed truth to such a degree. This speculative theology is indeed

[22] *Loc. cit.* (1072b25 f.).

superb and sublime. Aristotle was aware of this accomplishment; the words in which he speaks of the supreme god have a solemn tone, an almost ceremonial and sacramental accent. One feels that this theology was not only the product of his thinking mind, but had a quasi-religious reality and dignity. And yet how much less real and credible, how much less religiously true and holy, is Aristotle's god when compared with the living Lord of Biblical revelation! Here if anywhere the vast gulf between revelation and speculation is strikingly obvious. Aristotle reached the utmost limit of speculative theology; only Biblical revelation surpassed this height of thought.

But there is one other feature that I have not yet touched upon which seems to make Aristotle's god even more real and more religious; he moves, Aristotle says, the world by love. Aristotle's whole theology recollects and resuscitates all the past wisdom of philosophic thought. Hesiod had spoken of Eros as a creative power in the theogonic process which was also cosmogonic. Parmenides had put Aphrodite into the center of his " illusory " world and had said that she " governs all." [23] Empedocles had insisted that love or friendship holds together the cosmos as the principle of order and unity, in contrast to the principle of hate, which causes disunity and disorder. And Plato had explicitly spoken of Eros as that power which draws man toward the highest region of the divine, toward the Beautiful as such. It is especially this Platonic suggestion that Aristotle took up and elaborated upon.

Not only man, but the whole world, is drawn upward by love. God rules the world " as the beloved " rules the lover.[24] Unlike that of Hesiod, Parmenides, and Empedocles, Aristotle's " love " is not a deity; it is, as in Plato, a power that animates everything and prompts it to move toward the deity. Love is a general desire that motivates the world to reach out for the supreme and final end. The only relation between the world and god is therefore based, not on the activity of the divine being, but on the potentiality of the imperfect things; not on the perfection of pure form, but on the deficiency of matter which inclines to the form. But, of course, if there were not the supremely pure and perfect form, the material things could not incline to it. The world is thus moved by the existence of god, though

---

[23] Frs. 12 and 13.   [24] *Metaphysics*, XII, ch. 7 (1072a26).

not by the initiating love of god himself. In one place Aristotle uses the word " beloved " to explain the mode in which the divine moves; in another, he speaks of " desire " or " appetite," thereby disclosing that the biological trend of his thought also affected his conception of the relation between the world and god. Unlike so many other principles in his metaphysics, this central idea is unfortunately only casually mentioned and not elaborated upon. We are at a loss if we ask how this desire works in things and processes — whether it co-operates with the energy of the forms, or whether it is an impulse that belongs to matter as such. In any case it expresses the insufficiency and instability of all things that belong to the visible cosmos.

Aristotle probably felt that man's longing for truth and knowledge gives the clue to the interpretation of the relation between the world and god in general. In this longing the universal incentive of life discloses itself in its innermost truth. There is a tension between matter and form, between the potential and the actual, which ultimately is expounded as the tendency of the lower strata toward the highest one. The origin of his theory is best demonstrated when he argues that " the primary objects of desire and of thought are the same." [25] What the will wills is first conceived by the thinking mind as the objective of the will. Therefore the supreme objective of the will is at the same time the supreme object of knowledge. The supreme truth is the supreme good. Consequently, the supreme good is absolute knowledge, and if we think the supreme good, we think the knowledge of knowledge, or the thinking of thinking (*noēsis noēseōs*) [26] — the Aristotelian version of the identity of being and thought, first proclaimed by Parmenides. The divine mind thinks its own thinking: this is the complete fulfillment of thought, since in this supreme act of thought all thoughts are included and brought to fruition. In the divine mind longing no longer exists; its thinking is itself the goal of all longing, cognitive as well as volitional, human as well as cosmic, personal as well as impersonal, artistic as well as moral.

This act is not changing or passing; it perseveres notwithstanding its being an act or an activity. Inertia is caused by matter, and there is no matter anywhere in this highest activity of self-contemplation.

---

[25] *Loc. cit.* (1072a27).

[26] *Loc. cit.,* ch. 9 (1074b34).

Ethical and aesthetic motives join metaphysical and theoretical speculation in this consummate actuality. Greek philosophy thus reaches
its highest goal in this theology, inasmuch as the human mind of the
philosopher grasps and even represents the divine mind of the philos-
opher-god. Greek religion was already enervated and debilitated
when Aristotle dared to replace it by his own speculation. With an
air of superior knowledge, he says of the stars: " Our forefathers in
the most remote ages have handed down to their posterity a tradition, in the form of a myth, that these bodies are gods and that the
divine encloses the whole of nature. The rest of the tradition has
been added later in mythical form with a view to the persuasion of
the multitude and to its legal and utilitarian expediency; they say
these are in the form of men or like some of the other creatures." [27]
Aristotle will " save " what is true in this tradition and push aside
what is false. The idea that the divine somehow encloses the visible
universe is preserved in his concept of a supreme being outside the
visible sphere and " separated " (*chōristos*) from it, but nevertheless
embracing it in his thought. As to the star gods, Aristotle did not
completely abrogate faith in them.

He still believed that there are souls in the stars which control their
movement. These souls and these movements mediate between the
divine mind and the " sublunar " world. Their movement, being circular, is the most perfect, and it is eternal like the activity of the divine being. Mathematics, he says, deals with changeless figures or
numbers which are, however, not substances; physics deal with substances, but not with changeless ones. Only astronomy deals with
both the changeless and substances; it mediates therefore between
physics, mathematics, and metaphysics. Aristotle discusses accordingly the number and kind of celestial movements in the midst of his
theological considerations. So we must note that Aristotle, for all the
subtlety and refinement of his metaphysical thinking, was not yet
banished from the " paradise of the mind " in which all the Greeks
lived and thought. Concept and perception, thought and intuition,
intellect and sensation were not yet separated so radically as they are
with us. Speculation and imagination, observation and faith were
still inwardly and intrinsically united. In fact, philosophy is specula-

[27] *Loc. cit.*, ch. 8 (1074b1 f.).

tive only to the degree to which it is not analytical and critical, but intuitive and imaginative. Aristotle therefore insists that astronomy is to be regarded as the most philosophical of the mathematical and physical sciences.[28] Circular movement owes its excellence and divinity not only to its being continuous and infinite, but also to its being circumscribed and contained, going back into itself like thinking of thinking! It is the visible counterpart of that eternity which characterizes the actuality of the supreme immaterial form, although as a counterpart it is itself not altogether immaterial. It mirrors pure eternity as Plato had already proclaimed.[29]

But how can thinking be transformed into the circular physical movement of the stars and how can the movement of the stars be transferred to the world? And what is the ultimate relation between the physical movement of the world and the spiritual movement of the human mind toward the divine mind? It is obvious that there are some ultimate riddles that are not perfectly settled by the *Metaphysics*. Aristotle suggests a certain answer which is not explicitly carried through, but seems to be implied in the premises of his doctrine. Every substance is moved by the energy that constitutes its essence. Since his god is pure form, the essence of everything is in some way derived from this god; but inasmuch as the substances are material, their forms are also material, differing from the pure form and energy. But they can be known as forms only by the thinking mind, which, as it were, recognizes in them their divine origin and traces them back to the original mind from which they flow. This is the function of knowledge, and thereby our minds can attain the truth with respect to everything. For in the strict sense, only the forms are knowable, and the material things only inasmuch as they are formed. But in this way we can only know the forms, because we ourselves are longing for the absolute form inasmuch as we are striving after ultimate truth; this longing is the root of our cognitive activity. In this indirect way we know from within ourselves why and how all things are moved by desire or love. They are so moved, inasmuch as they are animated by indwelling forms which themselves long to return to their source and home. It is the very imperfection caused by the duality of matter and form, of the potential and

---

[28] *Loc. cit.* (1073b5).   [29] *Timaeus*, pp. 37 f.

the actual, that prompts the forms to move toward perfection and pure actuality; by this movement they form matter and make it as perfect and as spiritual as possible. It is the very imperfection of our own minds caused by the duality of sensation and intellection, of receptive and active reason, that prompts us to lead the forms back to the divine mind. In that way all processes in the world are return movements of the forms into their divine origin, culminating in the process of our thinking, which is itself a process of forming the world as a whole.

By its knowledge the human mind achieves within itself this return movement. It ultimately knows the forms by seeing them in the mind of god. In the human mind, by the actuality of its knowledge, the desire or appetite driving things toward god gains self-consciousness. By knowing and thinking itself and god the human mind fulfills the desire of all things: it enables them to return to their origin. The movement of the world is consummated in the movement of the human mind, and it can be consummated by this mind because more than any other form mind is divine in itself. The human mind can reflect upon this divinity by means of self-comprehension, which is itself the mark and excellence of the divine mind. Therefore, Aristotle says, in a startling sentence: " In some cases the knowledge is the object. In the productive sciences it is the substance or essence of the object, matter omitted, and in the theoretical sciences the definition or the act of thinking is the object. Since, then, thought and the object of thought are not different in the case of things that have not matter, the divine thought and its object will be the same, i.e., the thinking will be one with the object of its thought." [30] Here Aristotle seems to imply that in those cases there is no difference between human and divine thought. But this suggestion remains an open question. Perhaps we have already ventured too far in our interpretation of the ultimate consequences and implications of his system and its cosmotheology.

D. Transition from Aristotle to the Stoa

The system of Aristotle consummated Greek philosophy. It carried out all the former motifs and brought them to perfection. It seems therefore that the subsequent development could only mani-

[30] *Metaphysics,* XII, ch. 9 (1075a2).

fest the decline of Greek speculation and its slow exhaustion and agony. However, although this is certainly one aspect of the last systems before the rise of Christianity, there was still some strength left. Moreover, certain problems were not solved by Aristotle and continued to drive thought toward new horizons and — what is most important to us — toward the dawn of Christian revelation.

The system of Aristotle united the poles of many contrasting views. The latter broke asunder after the masterly art of synthesis practiced by Aristotle was no longer at work. As in the case of Hegel, so in the case of Aristotle, the extremes tied together by his metaphysical principles made themselves independent again. And thus there developed such inimical schools of thought as the Stoa, the Epicureans, the Atomists, the Idealists, the Academy, the Peripatetics, and so on. To understand this development and especially the origin of the most influential and powerful school, that of the Stoics, it is necessary to examine the problems not solved by Aristotle, and indeed not soluble at all on the basis of his principles and his system. This discussion will finally show that the logical, ontological, and theological difficulties that remained were at the same time those that point to the religiously dissatisfying features in Aristotle's whole conception regarding the relation between god and the world, and consequently to those that illuminate the relation between speculation and revelation. The rise and growth of the Stoic philosophy, which to a certain degree was itself a kind of religion, is most indicative and significant in this respect.

Aristotle's metaphysics was certainly of religious import. It had a religious origin and a religious consequence. It was the outcome of his pagan mind, although like his predecessors he disavowed the pagan religion in its traditional polytheistic fashion. The concept of god as propagated and demonstrated by his theology was by no means a merely logical conclusion from his premises; although it was also such a conclusion, it was, at bottom, the expression of his personal religion, which was of course the religion of a Greek thinker in whom the religious imagination of his national gods had been transformed into speculative contemplation. This contemplation was determined by the aesthetic as well as the logical predilection of the Greeks. Accordingly, the god of this contemplation was first of all " form " in the state of activity — he was the form of, and within, all forms; he was, secondly, a thinking mind, whereby thinking is to be understood in the Greek sense as based upon an intellectual intuition or a spiritual vision; thirdly, he was a self, but a self only in so far as he comprehends himself; in the fourth place, he was immaterial, but only in so far as he was " pure " form, i.e., form not obstructed or hampered by the resistance of an impenetrable matter; and, finally, he was a god who does not care about the world, but lives in perfect isolation and blessed perfection rejoicing in both, and not at all concerned about the imperfection and tragedies of this world of ours. All these features agree with the basically contemplative attitude of Greek religion and with the aesthetic nature of its gods. These gods, however, are more concerned about the events and sorrows of the human scene than the god of Aristotle, who is absolutely unconcerned. Of course, the Olympian gods are less perfect than Aristotle's god; with their passions and frailties, their shifting desires and their permanent quarrels, they are all too human. Their friendships and affections, their wrath and hate are even less serious than those of men; they are only superficial alterations of a life that is like a play, comparable to the storm of the sea or the rustle of the trees in the wind. There is no moral meaning and purpose in their deeds and emotions, except in so far as they reflect moral conditions of men. Only in the Biblical God the sublimity and perfection of Aristotle's divine mind is intrinsically conjoined with the humanity of the mythical gods.

The religious deficiency of Aristotle's god is mirrored and accompanied by the philosophical difficulties and unsolved problems of metaphysics. The logical cracks in its structure echo the religious debility of the faith that underlies that structure. Aristotle insists that god is both form and mind. Are these two characteristics compatible? Was not Plato more consistent when he did not dare to identify the Good with the world-soul or with the mind of the demiurge? How can the mind that contemplates the forms be itself a form? Is not the contemplating capacity different from the contemplated object, even if we grant that the form is active and forms matter? Aristotle would have answered that in the case of self-comprehension the mind and the object of its comprehension are the same, and that in self-comprehension the form reveals its innermost nature and its divine origin. But self-comprehension presupposes that peculiar capacity of the mind to comprehend an object, even when this object is the mind itself, and this capacity absolutely transcends the nature of the form and its activity of forming matter. Mind is more than form precisely because it possesses this capacity. The biological trend of Aristotle's whole system turned fateful when he conceived of the mind in terms of organic form. But even if form is interpreted in an aesthetic sense, it is not legitimate to identify the artist's mind with the vision or the aesthetic form that the artist impresses upon his material. The truth is that Aristotle did not yet understand the nature of the thinking and willing subject, the nature of the human self altogether. He understood only the nature of the object of perception and contemplation and comprehended mind in analogy to the object. His thought was limited by his fundamentally biological and aesthetic outlook.

This limitation had important consequences. If the mind is form and therefore no true self, then the divine mind cannot be a true self either. Indeed, Aristotle's god is not a contemplating subject, as man is, but he is merely an object of contemplation, in spite of his self-contemplation. This is evidenced by the relation between the divine mind and the world. I have said before that the forms originate from the supreme form and that they are brought back to its source by being known. But this statement has to be corrected; it is only half-true, or it considers only one aspect of the truth. It is true only with respect to the philosophical knowledge of the forms, but it is not true with respect to the knowledge ascribed to the divine mind by Aristotle. For since this mind is not only form but " pure " form, it is unable to contemplate and to know the manifold of worldly forms, which are always relatively material, and only thereby many and worldly. Here the problem of substance comes to the fore once more. Can a " pure " form be a substance in the Aristotelian sense, i.e., not only essence, but an acting and willing being? This is very questionable indeed on the basis of Aristotle's own principles and his ontology of becoming.

The form, according to the definition of Aristotle, is a substance only in so far as it actualizes itself in the medium of matter and thereby forms matter. What about a form that is not confronted with the task and end of forming matter? Does a " pure " form actually exist? Is it not rather in the rank of Plato's Ideas which are pure, but which therefore do not exist the way the human soul and mind, the human person and being, exist? To be sure, the human person exists as a self, and thereby does not contemplate material objects but is itself a subject that contemplates. Man is man and a self on account of self-comprehension (which Aristotle also assigns to his god). However, man can contemplate and comprehend himself as a self only because he is a composite substance, confronted by material objects from which he can distinguish himself as a self. Without such a contradistinction he would not be able to comprehend himself; he would not be a self. Self-comprehension is conditioned by the comprehension of something other than the self, by the knowledge of something (an object) that stands over against the self. The transfer of selfhood from man to god is a questionable undertaking, if god is defined as pure form separated from the world and its forms, as the Platonic Ideas are separated from the phenomenal sphere. This god cannot and does not know material objects and material forms, because this knowledge would impair his purity and very divinity. He is not a real subject, not a true person. He can therefore not explain the origin of the world and its forms by means of knowing them. Moreover, this god, unlike man, cannot redeem those forms because he has no relation to the material world. If god is form, then in what sense are the many forms themselves " forms " ? If god is not form, but person and self, how is he to be distinguished from man, who is always both form and matter?

I raise all these questions, not from a point of view alien to Aristotle, but rather from his own point of view. They grow out of the ground of his own principles and doctrines, and they concern the innermost kernel of his ontology and theology. Such questions make it clear that his metaphysics generated as many problems as it had tried to solve, and thereby they account for the further development of the history of speculation. The whole understanding of the relation between the world and god is at stake. If the concept of the divine being as pure form, pure act and energy, is not tenable, the entire edifice of Aristotle's philosophy is utterly in danger of falling to pieces, as it actually did in the subsequent centuries. If this concept cannot explain the duality of form and matter, as it obviously cannot; if the multiplicity of forms cannot be derived from the supreme form, then no reason is given for the duality of god and world; the knowledge of the world remains in the dark. The consequence seems to be inevitable that Aristotle's theology is insufficient so long as god is not conceived as the Creator of the world (a doctrine which the medieval Aristotelians tried to uphold, not without great difficulties).

Intrinsically connected with each other in this way are, on the one hand, the lack of a comprehension of selfhood and personality, and, on the other, the lack of an explanation of the duality of god and the world; both are accompanied by a lack of insight into the manifold of forms, and thus ultimately by a lack of understanding of the relation between form and matter. The great issues of theism and pantheism, of Platonism and Aristotelianism, of materialism and idealism, are here in abeyance. The greatest of all questions looms again high on the historical horizon: Can speculation anticipate revelation, or is revelation necessary in order to set speculation aright, and to guard it? So intimately and closely are faith and thought bound up with each other! So inseparable is the religious relation to god and the philosophical attempt to solve the ultimate problem of reality, of being and becoming, of knowledge and of mind! More particularly the question is urgent: Does the multiplicity of forms originate from the " desire " of matter to be formed, or is the pure form itself split up into the manifold of forms by matter? In other words: Is evolution of matter or emanation of form the ultimate reason for the hierarchy of the world? Is the materialist right who insists that matter develops to ever higher and higher levels, or is the theist right who believes that everything originates from the highest being? And furthermore such theological questions have to be decided upon: Is god existing as an individual substance and therefore a personal being, or is he an impersonal principle, a form or a power of some kind? Is he God or the god?

Aristotle has brought these questions to a brighter light than was previously possible. He is indirectly the founder of all the subsequent alternatives. But his own system does not enable us to answer the questions raised or to decide in one or the other direction. It was the history of philosophy that created answers and decisions, and thereby contributed to further clarification and illumination of the obscurities inherited from Aristotle.

The most formidable religious objection that can be made to Aristotle's theology concerns god's lack of knowledge and care of the world and man. In his endeavor to exalt the god above every restriction and deficiency, Aristotle did not realize that the very perfection he attributed to the divine mind, i.e., the concentration upon its own excellence and purity, is also the cause of ignorance. God, knowing himself alone, does not know the world and what happens in the world. His knowledge is in fact more imperfect than the knowledge of the human scientist and philosopher. The latter knows infinitely less, in so far as he is hampered by the resistance of matter; but he knows infinitely more, since he at least knows the vast range of the visible universe, its order, its various forms, and the human kingdom in all its branches and ramifications. Secondly, the lack of care for man is also a consequence of Aristotle's effort to exempt his god from all contact with the impurity and imperfection of the earthly scene. Unwittingly, Aristotle not only exempted his god from finitude and trouble, but he also deprived him of all power and authority over man's life. The Stoics corrected both deficiencies.

Aristotle, however, was not quite consistent. In his *Ethics,* whether or not the gods take care of man remained an open question. Of course he is here speaking of the gods, not of the god; i.e., he speaks in the traditional religious sense and not in the strict theological sense of the *Metaphysics.* " If the gods," he argues there, " have any care for human affairs as they are thought to have, it would be reasonable both that they should delight in that which was best and most akin to them, and that they should reward those who love and honor this most . . . ; that all these attributes belong most of all to the philosopher is manifest. He therefore is the dearest to the gods." [31] Here Aristotle seems to utter his own belief in a certain divine concern at least for the philosopher; but this passage also discloses how Aristotle affiliates philosophy and religion to the point where they are almost identical. But while his stern metaphysical god refuses to be drawn into the turmoil of human affairs, the religious need prompts Aristotle to admit that at least the philosopher may enjoy the hope that the deity favors him.

Although the god of Aristotle's theology is pure mind or spirit, even so he needs the world as his counterpart. Without the supreme

[31] *Nicomachean Ethics,* 1179a30.

being the world would not be a world; it would lack unity. Likewise, the supreme being itself would be of no functional utility if there were no world. The army cannot be an army without a commander in chief, but the latter cannot be a commander in chief without the army. From this perspective Aristotle's theology is as much a cosmo-theology as that of Plato and his other predecessors. In spite of the separation (*chōrismos*) of the world and god and the transcendence and isolation of the supreme mind, a mutual relationship exists between god and the world: god and the world belong together as form and matter. In the last analysis the pure form, for all its purity, is the form of the world. With respect to the world it performs the same task that the lower and less pure forms perform with respect to the single material substances and processes within the world. The pure act and energy is in this sense part and parcel of the cosmos. The latter embraces the material visible universe, as well as the invisible cosmic god, who presides and holds together the multiplicity of forms, things, and occurrences. The mind of man is immaterial, inasmuch as it comprehends the immaterial god; likewise the divine mind is immaterial inasmuch as it comprehends itself. But the divine mind, being the form of the world, cannot be immaterial in the same way. Of course, this trend of thought is not carried through by Aristotle; it is only implied at certain points. This reflection upon the implications of the system manifests, however, its " potential " pantheism, which was to be developed later by such Aristotelians as the Arab philosophers Avicenna and Averroës. The latter influenced the medieval Scholastics, some of whom were under the same spell. The same influence is present in Giordano Bruno and Spinoza, both of whom were of course also influenced by Stoicism and Neoplatonism.

If the cosmotheological view is thought out, the system of Aristotle again depicts the cosmos in an aesthetic manner, as did the ancient systems. And the " transcendent " god then belongs to the whole, as its form. It is, therefore, a cosmic god, an immanent god, as the term " world-mind " indicates. This god is endowed with the serene splendor of a majestic but icy light. The philosopher who attains the vision of the great cosmic panorama is more a spectator than a worshiper; he admires and enjoys the harmony and beauty of this divine cosmos, in which everything is in its prescribed place and develops according to the rules of the master plan. As the disharmonies of a symphony are finally resolved and reconciled from this point of view, even the imperfection of the sublunar sphere disappears in the perfection of the whole. Such a spectator does not expect that the picture he beholds will love, punish, and support him in his individual destiny, or accept him personally. Like a work of art, this divine cosmos is "blessed in itself." It lives its own life undisturbed by the tragedy and misery of men. It is not aware of our own grief or joy, of our guilt or merit. It does not condemn, nor does it save, the sinner. Aristotle did not worry about the origin of evil. In the last analysis he was and remained to the end the typical representative of a morally naïve and fundamentally artistic culture and religion.

Philosophic speculation after Aristotle had to become more ethical and religious to correct the deficiencies of such a culture. The Stoics discharged this task.

X

SPECULATION AND RELIGION IN STOICISM

THE classic thinkers Plato and Aristotle had penetrated to the
"divine center." By means of reflection and analysis they had
tried to grasp the object of religious faith. And on the basis of Greek
culture they had gone as far as the human mind could possibly go.
Under their influence the traditional polytheistic religion was transformed into a philosophic religion. True enough, the latter was constructed on the basis of the same contemplative and aesthetic culture,
but it also incorporated the ethical and ethicoreligious requirements
of a deeper spiritual feeling and a purer intuition. Unlike Plato, Aristotle no longer adhered to the ethical inwardness and the prophetic
vision of Socrates; nevertheless, Aristotle at least administered the
Platonic inheritance and created his own theology in devotion to the
teachings of his great predecessor. It was this theology, however, that
disclosed the limitation of the whole of philosophic speculation. Aristotle's theology made it evident that the spirit of Greek culture
established boundaries that could not be crossed in order to satisfy
fully religious demands. Likewise, certain intrinsic problems of
thought emerged which could hardly be solved within the scope of
speculation.

All these conditions and conclusions generated a philosophic atmosphere somewhat akin to that which existed after the breakdown
of the systems of the first period. There now arose a certain intellectual fatigue and a growing distrust in the ability of speculative
thought. Even in the Academy, the school of the Platonists, thinkers
soon came forward who doubted the ability of the human mind to
advance into the realm of metaphysical truth. Idealists became as
skeptical as the Sophists. They demonstrated systematically and
thoroughly that no knowledge whatsoever is possible. As at the end

of the first period, the very antagonism of so magnificent and penetrating systems as those of Plato and Aristotle contributed to the spread of speculative skepticism. Since the school of Plato continued to exist side by side with that of Aristotle, the issue between them was never settled, although later on syncretistic attempts were made to fuse the two systems and to assert that at bottom their doctrines were identical, or at least compatible.

The Sophists had paid special attention to the problems of human knowledge and life in general; once again epistemological and ethical questions unfolded and required intensive study, especially in the Stoic school. The Sophistic movement, however, did not revive. The personality of Socrates and his conquest of Sophistic relativism and subjectivism was not forgotten. The imposing and commanding figures of Plato and Aristotle prevented any renewal of the Sophistic frivolity and superficiality. The religious inclination and theological efforts of Plato and Aristotle were still remembered; their doctrines were still alive. A new Socrates was not to be expected precisely because no new Sophistic movement arose. The Stoic school, the result of all these spiritual conditions, renewed in some way the spirit of Socrates — as much as any school could. It stressed the priority of practical issues, the necessity of a congruity between thought and life, and the centrality of man's moral strength, in connection with his longing for happiness or blessedness. In short, the Stoics emphasized that kind of wisdom which would fulfill the goal of the whole philosophic enterprise. At first metaphysical and physical problems were still studied and new solutions were proposed. But the more the Stoic movement progressed, the more were the minds and hearts of the Stoic thinkers captured by the vital concerns of life, until at last their philosophy was more a religious creed than an academic doctrine.

Stoicism produced no personality comparable to Socrates and no speculative system builder of the stature of Aristotle. Nevertheless, to a certain degree the Stoics preserved the Socratic spirit and Aristotelian principles in their own new creations. Characteristically, Zeno, the founder of Stoicism, modeled his own ethics and interests after the Socrates of the *Apology*, whom he admired ardently.[1] At

---

[1] Cf. *Diogenes Laërtius,* Book 7, ch. 3.

the end of the history of Stoicism we meet a figure somewhat resembling Socrates but indirectly influenced by the Christian atmosphere of his time. I am, of course, referring to the great slave Epictetus. Like Socrates, Epictetus never wrote a book. In a fascinating, vivid, and straightforward manner, he taught to the unlearned of the street a doctrine aiming at practical wisdom. Epictetus sought to help the " common man " to bear the hardships of life and the inequality of destiny.[2]

Speculation was, therefore, more deeply guided by spiritual needs and longing than at any former period. It was, however, not eliminated as in Socrates. On the contrary, the Stoics tried to support man by a speculative religion based upon reasons and causes. It was its religious overtones that made Stoic speculation attractive in a period in which the official religion was no longer attractive to the cultured people. Stoicism, more than Plato and Aristotle, was able to guide people in their daily life and to elevate their minds, depressed by the degeneration of religion and the decay of culture. The Stoics saved the sense of human dignity and rescued the individual from despair in a time that no longer respected the values of ancient civilization, no longer gave a great place in life to the individual. It was a time in which the vast Roman Empire had absorbed and neutralized the individuality of the nations of the then known world, a time in which personal freedom was dwindling and personal creativity was dying out, in which the meaning of human existence and of existence in general seemed to shrink into nothingness; in which the ancient virtues were no longer practiced and no longer esteemed.

The Stoics were not skeptic, nor did they renounce metaphysics for ethical reasons. Instead, they cemented their ethical views by deriving them from supreme principles which they took for granted. They were, however, not dogmatic, as the thinkers of the third pre-Socratic period had been, but they were eager to prove the reliability and rationality of their supreme principles and of their own philosophic convictions. The Stoics laid great stress upon the analysis of logical thought, its origin, validity, and connection with sense per-

[2] Interestingly enough, a contemporary called Arrianus of Nicomedia, an admiring disciple of Epictetus who had composed the book in which his lectures are reproduced, a " new Xenophon," thereby indicating the similarity between Epictetus and Socrates.

ception. They emphasized rational inference and sought to detect a supreme criterion of truth which would assure them of the reliability of their speculative and ethical doctrine. Long before Descartes, they came to the conclusion that the " clear and distinct idea " is the surest basis on which to establish philosophic argument and theory.[3] Ironically, however, their own concepts were not so clear and distinct as those of Aristotle had been, but were on the contrary rather vague and hazy.

In the final analysis the Stoics were not basically theoretical thinkers, but kept theoretical thinking alive for the sake of practical conclusions. Characteristically, the Stoics used metaphorical language to distinguish between ethics, logic, and physics. Logic was compared to the fence of an orchard, physics to its trees, and ethics to its fruit. Such symbolism illustrates forcefully the primacy of ethics. The " fence " and the " trees " only make it possible to enjoy the " fruit ": ethical insight and practical wisdom. Like Empedocles and Anaxagoras, the Stoics were not original in their metaphysical principles but borrowed them from different sources, thereby using the entire past of philosophic thought and speculation. This feature is intensified by the multiplicity of Stoic philosophers who in succeeding generations amplified the principles and the doctrines without trying to systematize them into one great structure comparable to the system of Aristotle. The Stoic metaphysics can be compared to a medieval cathedral, built by many generations of architects whose names are forgotten, or at least are not so conspicuous as the names of great individual artists in other fields. The Stoic metaphysics was not the doctrine of one man but of a school, in which no outstanding figure of high rank ever produced an inner coherence and consistency. Such was the character of all the schools in this epoch, even of the Academy and the Peripatetics, the Pythagoreans and the Atomists. The great visions and thoughts of the past still prevailed; the hour of original creativity had passed.

An outer symptom of this condition is the remarkable loss of most books written in this last period of Greek pagan philosophy. No one cared to preserve them for posterity. Their doctrines are known only

---

[3] In Greek, *phantasia kataleptikē*. Of course the Stoics did not mean, like Descartes, the clarity and distinctness of mathematical concepts and symbols, since they were not mathematically minded.

from secondary sources and from fragments quoted by ancient historians and by authors of later date like Plutarch and Cicero. The latter wanted to instruct their contemporaries about the development of Greek thought, the variety of schools and their main doctrines, and so on. That we do not possess the original writings discloses an affinity between the beginning and the end of Greek philosophy. But the reasons for this loss are very different in the two cases. In the beginning it was the lack of organized learning and academic life that caused the negligence in preserving the writings, even of the most outstanding and most original thinkers. In the final period, however, science and studies, teaching and learning, were highly organized and methodically carried through. The schools were competitive, and one would assume that they would have eagerly kept the tradition by at least preserving the books written by the founders like Zeno and by the " headmasters " that succeeded him. The circumstances in this regard were very different from the ancient period and much more favorable to preservation, yet less is directly known of thinkers in the final period than is preserved in the fragments of the pre-Socratics.

The theoretical ideas of the Stoics are of less importance and worth than those of the preceding epochs; nevertheless, they are of great value and significance, if one looks at the history of philosophy from the perspective of the relation between speculation and revelation. The very reason speculation was in decline is an interesting phenomenon from this perspective. It was the advance of revelation and the religious motivation of thinking in this last period that generated a lack of creativity and did not permit the rise of great new systems. But there is an even more interesting fact: the modifications of the older structures of thought demonstrate and illustrate the shift of emphasis and the approach of Christianity. It is most remarkable that, especially by the alterations which they effected in theology and cosmology, the Stoics by speculative means prepared the ancient peoples for the acceptance of the new message. As if they had foreseen or guessed the trend of religious revelation, the Stoics created intellectual concepts well fitted to be used by the Christian writers who tried to express their new insight in a speculative language. It is this process that we must now pursue in more detail.

The general trend sought a philosophic foundation of a theistic view in which god was conceived in a much more personal and emotional manner. The Stoics worked hard to solve the problems left over by Aristotle. To a degree they were successful because they had neither the logical subtlety nor the metaphysical penetration of their great predecessor. But their continuation of his scheme was carried out on a higher religious level. Consequently even their speculative views were in some sense superior to those of the religiously less sensitive and less spiritual founder of metaphysical theology. That the very word " spirit " (*pneuma*) was introduced by them into philosophic language indicates that the Stoics satisfied a need not yet felt by Aristotle.

Stoic metaphysics, commonly called pantheistic and even materialistic, is usually contradistinguished from the theistic theology of Plato and Aristotle. If such labels were correct, the Stoics would not have contributed to the preparation of the gospel. They would then have been more remote from the Christian message and from Biblical faith than the philosophers of the classical period. It is therefore necessary to examine their innovations very carefully and to compare them with the doctrines of their predecessors. Undoubtedly the Stoics went back in some respects to the first period of Greek speculation, which in its very beginning and at its end had been more pantheistic and physically minded. It is also true that they adopted the term of Heraclitus for their theological doctrine, i.e., " Logos," and that this term was epoch-making because the Christian thinkers applied it in turn to Christ. But this very application again shows that there must be a certain intrinsic relation between Stoic thought and the Christian faith. All these facts point to historical connections and disconnections not easily disentangled and clarified.

The first striking feature in Stoic metaphysics is its stress upon the visible universe. Stoic metaphysics was even more physical than that of Aristotle. When the Stoics divided philosophy into logic, physics, and ethics, by the term " physics " they also understood metaphysics, and in fact taught physics in a metaphysical vein. They did not accurately distinguish physics and metaphysics but fused and confused the issues of both. To a certain degree all Greek thinkers were guilty of such confusion. Even Aristotle's physics dealt with matters we would call metaphysical, e.g., the nature of space and time, the finite and the infinite, motion and change, and nature and god. And his metaphysics analyzed the ontological structure of sensible substances and natural causality. It is true, moreover, that Stoic speculation, in so far as it is less methodical and less logical than the classical systems, puts us more in mind of the scheme of thought developed in the pre-Socratic systems. The Stoics thereby renewed a more pantheistic trend than is to be found in Plato and Aristotle. But this point must not be overrated and simplified. Greek thought was somehow pantheistic throughout. Even Plato taught the immanence of the world-soul and the divinity of nature as a whole. A potential pantheism was also concealed in Aristotle's metaphysics, inasmuch as the divine mind was the mind or the form of the cosmos and did not create the visible world but was co-eternal with it. Greek theology was, in all periods, a cosmotheology and it remained so in Stoic cosmology and theology.

The appearance of a more pantheistic tone in Stoic philosophy is deceptive for two reasons. The Stoics were less acute than classical thinkers, logically much vaguer and much less cautious. They could, therefore, easily mix the spheres of nature and of the divine, the cosmological and the theological. They could readily intermingle theistic and pantheistic versions of their theology, and physical and metaphysical thought. The Stoics were interested in such considerations only because they wanted to produce a background for ethical principles and for life itself. The second reason for their apparently pantheistic tendency was their inclination to transform their physics as well as their metaphysics into theology, because theology was nearer the ethical realm and nearer their heart. The Stoics talked theology, were inwardly prompted to talk theology, even when they talked cosmology or physics; their theological thinking was, at bottom, not physical and cosmological, but their physics and their cosmology were only pretexts for dealing with theological matters. Therefore, their theological speculation took on in form a physical and cosmological appearance. The Stoics wished to expand theology over all fields and spheres of knowledge; they were mainly and ultimately motivated to investigate nature and to philosophize only because of their religious ardor and their ethical aspiration. A similar spiritual and intellectual " climate," and therefore similar inclinations and results, is to be found in the Middle Ages.

The unique greatness of Socrates, lacking in the Stoics, was that he abstained from all metaphysical and theological speculations and concentrated solely on ethical discussions. The Stoics were not so deeply humble and devout. They had metaphysical ambitions and felt obliged to state their own opinion on the speculative issues that had been in the foreground during the classical period. They thought it necessary and worth-while to advance and to defend definite theses about the structure of the universe in general and the nature of the deity. But the eclecticism of their thought did not permit them to reproduce any definite doctrine of their own. Their doctrines were extremely fluid and differed from person to person and were never meant to be exact or precise in the same sense as the doctrines of Aristotle. We must also not forget that most Stoics were not of Greek origin. Zeno, the founder, was a Phoenician; others were born in Tarsus, where a Stoic school still existed when Paul was born.

There were also very strong theological reasons why the Stoics were not satisfied with the theology of Aristotle and consequently had to change his whole system radically. The Stoics felt strongly that Aristotle's god was not a god with whom they could live, and not even a god who satisfied the logical demands of thought. By isolating god too rigorously from the world, Aristotle made his god less perfect and less powerful than he intended. The Stoics were fundamentally motivated by the desire to remedy this defect. In seeking aid in the systems of the past, the Stoics discovered that Heraclitus had been less extreme in his logical consistency and method and therefore had a vision more satisfying than that of Aristotle. Heraclitus taught that the divine Logos does not merely know himself but actively regulates and orders the universe. The Logos is not merely good because he represents the truth but because he is actively just and eager to guarantee the harmony and beauty of the whole. This doctrine fascinated the religious and the theological spirit of the Stoics and thus influenced subsequently their metaphysical and physical views. They therefore proclaimed the Logos to be the innermost essence of the cosmic god.

The supreme god is not only " form " and " mind," not only thinking of thinking; he is rather a supreme will that commands and prescribes. He rewards and punishes, gives laws, and judges man and the universe, nations and individuals. The Stoic god is the sovereign legislator, administrator, and judge. He is therefore closer to the Biblical Creator than was the god of Aristotle. The Stoics went even farther in the direction of Biblical revelation; Stoic speculation and Biblical revelation approached each other astoundingly. The Stoics conceived of god as being a lover of man (*philanthrōpos*) and not only of the philosopher. Love was ascribed to the cosmic god for the first time not merely in a cosmological framework, but in the sense of charity and mercy. The Stoic god was also endowed with foreknowledge and providence so that knowledge and power were given to him on a much wider scale than in Aristotle. But what was most characteristic and of great consequence for the Christian comprehension, the Stoics called god or God (the capital should be reserved to the Lord of Biblical revelation) "*pneuma*," or spirit.

Why did they choose this word? Did they really do it, or did they do it primarily because their thought was more materialistic and less idealistic, more sensational and less strictly logical, than the thought of Plato and Aristotle? This is a crucial question. The word "*pneuma*" originally did not have a "spiritual" but a "material" meaning like the English word "spirit," which also meant originally something like "breath" and only later took on the meaning of the power or vitality of life, and finally of that flower of life which is related to the divine life or power. The Stoics selected this word (earlier used by the Pythagoreans) instead of mind (*nous*), preferred by Aristotle, precisely because it pointed to a more emotional, less intellectualistic, type of mind or life, but not for materialistic reasons. The word "*pneuma*," more than the word "*nous*," implied the concrete reality of God, instead of merely his thinking: it connoted his total personality, including his will and love, his vitality and his inwardness — features suppressed by the exclusively "theoretical" and contemplative thought of Aristotle. The word "*pneuma*" indicated that trend of thought which set in with the Stoics and marked the more religious and less rationalistic type of speculation.[4] The speculation of the Stoics tended toward Christian revelation when they adopted the term "*pneuma*"; the reinterpretation of this word by the Gospel writers was therefore not merely

[4] The successor to Zeno, Cleanthes, was a profoundly devout man, as is disclosed by the so-called hymn attributed to him. If the Stoics really had been materialists, it would hardly be understandable how they could also have been so sincerely and ardently religious. The god whom Cleanthes praises has many traits of the Biblical God.

a linguistic accident, but was the result of a religious development within philosophic speculation itself. No wonder that the first Christians who philosophized, e.g., the so-called Logos-Christologians and, later, Origen and Irenaeus, used Stoic terms to express the significance of their creed. The terms of the Trinity are the outcome of this Christian speculation, which, though based on Scripture, nevertheless can be traced back to Stoic cosmotheology. The first Christian philosophy was more Stoic than Platonic, as the works of Justin Martyr and Clement of Alexandria demonstrate, men whom no one would call materialists!

The very vagueness and ambiguity of Stoic concepts has also a speculative origin. To the degree that thought became less rational, it became more emotional and less capable of being molded in so methodical and scientific a manner as was generated by Aristotle. Aristotle had touched the utter limit of logical clarity and precision; the pendulum now swung back. It was only thereby possible to transcend the boundaries of philosophic thought by means of philosophic thought. It is certainly an ironical and paradoxical " progress " that was made by this abandonment of logical accuracy and refinement. But the course of the history of philosophy corroborates the inner necessity of that deterioration which implied at the same time an improvement and growth in the dimension of speculative inwardness and spirituality. This trend shows that the development of philosophical thought is not only a development from logically primitive to ever more refined and methodical thinking (although this is also an aspect of its development), but also an approach to the ultimate truth, which cannot be grasped any more by speculation alone but needs the support of religious revelation. Whereas the earliest Greek thinkers emerged from a mythological, polytheistic, artistic religion and labored by rational speculation to purify their idea of the deity, the Stoics found themselves in a very different, even in the directly opposite, situation. They broke away from an all too rationalistic speculation and returned to religion, but to a religion which in the meantime had undergone the process of intellectual examination and purification. This reverse movement led them back to the beginnings and explains their relative kinship with the pre-Socratic type of speculation. The ancients had believed that the thinking mind can penetrate the mystery of the divine; the Stoics were aware that not the mind but the spirit alone can approach this mystery.

This was the deepest reason why they transformed the theology of Aristotle into a seemingly more materialistic and pantheistic system and conceived of god as Logos, Pneuma, and Soul. All these designations were not logically clarified, but they indicated that the principles of the Pythagoreans, Heraclitus, and Plato seemed more appropriate for the comprehension of deity than those of Aristotelian theology. It is another ironic and formidable paradox that at the very height of the Christian culture, in the Middle Ages, Roman Catholic theologians and finally the Church authorities returned to Aristotle, made him the prince of all philosophers, and pressed the Christian faith into the principles of this most rational speculation.

Cicero reports that in order to prove the divine character of the cosmos the Stoics pointed to the beauty and goodness of things and to the spirit that animates and dominates all beings and all things.[5] This argument was obviously not the result of a scientific observation but, rather, an article of faith. The so-called cosmological proof of the existence of god is no logical proof at all but the expression of an underlying intuition or an inspired vision, most akin to revelation but clothed in logical form with the pretense of being a logical conclusion. As a matter of fact, the world gives as much occasion for the proof of its moral and aesthetic deficiency and imperfection as it gives occasion for the proof of an immanent goodness and beauty.

The intuition underlying Stoic philosophy is both of ethical and of aesthetic origin and it would be hard to decide which of the two was stronger and primary. Within the philosophic consciousness of the Stoics the ethical motive was by far the stronger, if not the only one that mattered. But beneath this consciousness there was, in their philosophy, the aesthetic motive at work, as it had been throughout Greek speculation. The cosmos was a beautiful whole and the cosmic life was therefore divine. In this respect there is hardly any difference in the three periods from Thales up to the Stoics. It was the common Greek mind or spirit that assured every thinker that the cosmos resembles a work of art in its regularity, order, and completion. And in spite of philosophic diversity, it was this common conviction that persuaded every thinker to believe in the divine government of this perfect whole. The Stoics, for all their religious devo-

[5] *De natura deorum*, Book II.

tion, did not deviate from this general line of Greek thought. Their very faith was grounded in this conviction. It provided the reason for their apparent pantheism, as it had for the pantheism of the Milesians, the Pythagoreans, Heraclitus, and Parmenides. It was the cause of the pantheism of the third pre-Socratic epoch and of the classical period. For in spite of their theistic tendency, even Plato and Aristotle, like the Stoics, believed in a divine world-soul or world-mind.

This aesthetic feature, coupled with the primacy of contemplation, intuition, observation, and speculation, was of course antagonistic to the ethical emphasis that began to unfold in Socrates and was in the foreground of Stoic philosophy. The two motives, the aesthetic and the ethical, necessarily clashed. The aesthetic is detached and impersonal; the ethical, involved and personal. In Stoic philosophy the two motives were assigned to cosmology and ethics. The antagonism between the motives therefore turned up as the antagonism between cosmological and ethical principles, i.e., as the antagonism between cosmic necessity and moral freedom. For the first time in the history of thought the abysmal opposition was deeply felt between these two equally powerful and indispensable ideas. And the attempt was made to ease the tension between them by means of speculation. Since cosmology as well as ethics culminated in their theology, the Stoics could believe themselves to be successful in assuaging, if not reconciling, the contrasting interests: the cosmo-aesthetic and the ethicoreligious. Only in later time — in full, only in Kant — was the true character of this clash recognized, and a new attempt was made to conquer this formidable obstacle of systematic speculation.

Stoic religion, aiming at the inward superiority of man in his struggle with the power of destiny, and therefore ethical in motivation, was nevertheless also based upon the aesthetic vision of the divine cosmos and expressed in terms of cosmology and theology. Man is virtuous and happy if he lives in agreement with " nature," i.e., with being as such. The term " nature " has this cosmic and ontic connotation in Stoic language, a connotation it already had in the Milesian and Eleatic schools. Moral evil necessarily entails human misery; it is, at bottom, a disturbance of the beautiful order of the cosmos. Man sets himself in opposition to that order when he transgresses against the moral law; such opposition necessarily provokes the hostility of " nature," thereby implying unhappiness for man. " Nature " connotes the rational because the cosmic order is the order of reason (Logos). Man is therefore " wise," i.e., he wills and acts rationally, if he thinks in accordance with the universal reason dominating the cosmos. The rational and the aesthetic are basically the same in Stoic speculation, as throughout all Greek philosophy. If man does not disturb the logical order of nature, he himself will not be disturbed. The inward calm and peace is thereby won. As in Socrates, so also in Stoic philosophy, the ethical, the rational, and the aesthetic join in the ideal of happiness and wisdom.

The Socratic thesis that virtue is based on knowledge or is knowledge itself (in the sense of wisdom, i.e., practical knowledge), and that the virtuous man is always and by " nature " happy, was more directly and more religiously reconciled to cosmological and theological speculation by the Stoics than by Plato and Aristotle. Aristotle had made philosophic contemplation itself the highest virtue; the Stoics on the contrary, made the highest ethical virtue contemplative and speculative. They renewed in this respect the " Socratic " school of the Cynics, which had anticipated the same trend without developing it elaborately. Zeno had been a disciple of the Cynic Crates, and a drop of " cynicism " was indeed always inherent in Stoic ethics. Within the development of the school this drop was magnified. The practical goal overshadowed more and more the speculative background, until it finally was almost the only thing about which the Stoics cared, as the soliloquies of Marcus Aurelius illustrate.

The " materialism " of Stoic cosmology has its origin in the aesthetic and ethicoreligious trend. It originated from the need to make cosmology more practical and more impressive. This " materialism " was therefore in its root a " spiritualism "; indeed, the " spirit " is more imaginative, and that implies more sensuous, than the thinking mind and its abstract notions. The presence of the divine power in every situation and in every perception was thereby urged and expressed. So paradoxically interrelated are speculation and revelation! The spiritual is much closer to the religious than the rational or the logical, precisely because it is attached to the " material " and not abstracted from it as are notions and concepts. God, according to the Gospels, is spirit and not mind (*nous*), because he is a living and acting God, not divorced from the visible world, as the philosophic god of Aristotle. The God of the Gospels reveals himself in the medium of the visible, i.e., by means of miracles and mystical presence.

"Happiness" (*eudaimonia*) now acquired a warmer and more personal meaning in the Greek language than it had in previous epochs. It even approached the Christian idea of religious salvation. The "wise" is saved from the evil of destiny and from the consequences of guilt because he is able to create within himself that state of perfect "apathy," the consequences of philosophic contemplation and speculation. There is, of course, a huge gap between Stoic and Christian salvation, between Stoic apathy, self-dependence, and self-sufficiency, and Christian obedience, charity, and hope. The Stoic sage seems to be concerned exclusively with his own happiness, while the Christian believer is concerned much more with the happiness of his fellow man. Even so, the Stoics did contribute to the preparation of the Christian community inasmuch as their ideal and their bond was cosmopolitan and transmundane: "Live a life hidden from society" was one of their precepts.

One other feature of Stoic doctrine prepared for the Christian doctrine of the Logos and transformed Plato's concept of the Ideas in an important and consequential manner. While Plato had taught that the Ideas exist in their own "supercelestial" realm, the Stoics began to think of them as immanent within the world Logos. This new interpretation was, of course, begun by Aristotle. Although Aristotle had conceived of the world-mind as pure form, and thereby excluded from it the ever material forms of the visible world, nevertheless he had brought the Ideas from their own isolated abode down to the world. Here, as in many other respects, the Stoics united Plato and Aristotle. They followed Aristotle in locating the Ideas, which they called "Logoi" (plural of Logos), in the world-substances, and even more than Aristotle thought of them as forces or powers operating in things and developing them toward their essential end. But, at the same time, the Stoics did not cut the connection between the cosmic Logos and these Logoi. Rather, the Logos itself permeated and governed all things actively and purposively. The Stoics conceived of the divine mind no longer as form, but rather as subject and person. As indicated by the grammatical relation between "Logos" and "Logoi" the Stoics emphasized the inner unity of the divine Logos and the mundane Logoi, in terms of their "panentheistic" cosmology. This cosmology had, as it were, two aspects: the one predominantly physical, the other religious and theological. The "Logoi" or the "seeds" (or the "seedlike Logoi"), in keeping with the more physical perspective, are the causes of change in nature. But according to the theological view, they are the divine ends operating in the world. By this device the Stoics prepared the possibility of an interpretation of Plato's Ideas in a completely new spirit: namely, as being the ideas in the mind of God. The Stoics did not yet go so far as to pronounce such a doctrine, but they opened the gate through which one of their adherents, who was also inspired by the Bible, could walk: the Alexandrian Jew, Philo.

In Philo, Greek speculation and Biblical revelation met for the first time to create a Biblical speculation which initiated the course philosophy was to take in the subsequent fifteen centuries. The philosophic gifts of Philo were not considerable, and his ideas were more imaginatively than logically fashioned; nevertheless, his undertaking was of fateful significance. He was a contemporary of Jesus, and anticipated Christian theology in a remarkable degree. This undertaking brought about a fusion of the most powerful and most determining factors in all European culture: the Biblical and the Greek. The whole movement of pre-Christian speculation, directed toward a more holy and ethical conception of the divine being than that offered by Greek religion, culminated and terminated in this great event. It was, as it were, providential that a Jewish scholar living in a Greek cosmopolitan community should combine his Biblical studies with his philosophical erudition. Philo was probably primarily influenced by Stoic speculation, which is very strong in his thought, but he also learned much from the Platonists and knew the works of Plato. But the Greek influence did not suffocate Philo's inherited faith, although it prompted him to speculate on the basis of this faith and to seek a reconciliation between these divergent spiritual powers. It is a strange coincidence that in the lifetime of Jesus, an Alexandrian philosopher attempted to bring about a theoretical synthesis of Greek and Biblical theological views, while some hundred miles away the greatest religious event of all times took place, an event which also issued in a synthesis of those two previously more or less separated worlds.

Philo pondered about the relation between the Creator God and the Stoic Logos. He was resolved to unify in terms of his personal acquaintance his Stoic learning and his Biblical knowledge: thought and faith. Thereby he instilled metaphysics into a hitherto unmetaphysical revelation and kindled a new spiritual light in metaphysical speculation. This was certainly an adventure of the first order, when one thinks of the long history of Christian thought which continued what Philo began.[6] Eugene de Faye says in his book on Origen that the effect of Philo's work upon the rise and content of Christian dogma and theology cannot be overrated. Indeed, without Philo there would be no Irenaeus, Athanasius, Gregory, and so on, up to Karl Barth or Donald Baillie.

Philo was not only a Biblical believer, scholar, and student of the Stoics and Plato; he was also a mystic. For the first time he emphasized the incomprehensibility of God, no matter whether God reveals himself or is comprehended by philosophy.[7] Man can unite with God only by complete surrender and a kind of ecstatic vision through which man may himself be deified. This doctrine or confession left ineffaceable vestiges upon the Christian soul and mind. Clement of Alexandria, Pseudo-Dionysius, and, indirectly, probably even Plotinus himself, the founder of Neoplatonism, were deeply influenced by this first mystic.

But the most significant contribution of Philo concerns his transformation of the doctrine of the Ideas. He taught that the Ideas are the thoughts of the living God, who has revealed himself in the deeds and words narrated in Scripture. Through this simple device Philo threw a bridge across the chasm dividing two spiritual spheres. The Stoics had paved the way by connecting the cosmic Logos with the Logoi at work in things. But even so the advance of Philo was new and momentous. Philo not only achieved thereby an intrinsic

---

[6] Philo had some predecessors who, however, were of lesser influence and importance. Zeller believes that the sect of the Essenes had already combined their religious creed with Neo-Pythagorean thought. This seems to be confirmed today by the Dead Sea Scrolls.

[7] *Nomōn hierōn allēgoriai*, 47a.

union between speculation and revelation; he also settled the difficult philosophic problem concerning the kind of being to be ascribed to the Ideas, in so far as they exist, as Plato taught, not in things but in a transcendent realm. It was hard to accept Plato's doctrine which made the Ideas not only transcendent but also independent of any mind. They seemed to hover in an imaginary heaven. Plato had only used mythological images when he spoke about this " supercelestial " abode. Philo, in substituting Biblical conceptions for such mythological conceptions, subjected the speculation of Plato to his own faith and thereby made his own faith speculative.

Philo thus began the long history of Biblical and Christian Platonism. He enabled later Aristotelians to reconcile the metaphysical theology of their master to the Christian faith. This potential reconciliation not only had a religious significance but also a philosophical one. It prepared for the solution of the problem unsolved by Aristotle as to how the divine mind can be divine and yet think or harbor the material Ideas which determine the essence and the development of temporal things and being. Only a living God can perform that task. Only a Creator can govern the world in spite of his own transcendence. Only a prescient and providing God can care for imperfect things and imperfect beings in spite of his own perfection and without impairing it. Only a personal Lawgiver, Judge, and King of Kings, as the Bible reveals him, can solve the ultimate problem with which Aristotle grappled in vain. To be sure, this solution was not philosophic but religious. But just this shift from the philosophic to the religious realm was needed to cope with the ultimate question, which for intrinsic reasons cannot be answered by human speculation alone.

Finally, Philo potentially started the modern reflection on the relation between the human mind and its experience of the world of appearance, to use the Kantian term. These reflections were possible only under the presupposition that the innate ideas, or the " transcendental categories " of the human intellect or understanding, condition empirical knowledge as well as they condition the objects of that knowledge. And this presupposition could be recognized only after the relation between the divine mind and the Platonic Ideas had been interpreted in the manner of Philo. It is a strange but an undeniable historical fact that man had first to learn from speculation and revelation that the mind of God harbors the forms of the world, in order to recognize the relation between his own mind and his own world in a critical fashion.[8]

Philo also accepted the Stoic theory that the Logoi are active forces working within the world. He called them messengers of God and compared them with the angels which God sends into the world to carry out his will.[9] For this purpose, he distinguished God the Creator and the divine Logos by understanding the one as transcendent, the other as immanent. The Logos is called by him the Idea of Ideas, the first Idea or the Word uttered by God. Even more astounding is that he spoke of him as the " second God," [10] thus anticipating the dogma of the second person in the Trinity, and provoking the Logos speculation of the Fourth Gospel and of the Logos-Christologists.[11] Finally he used the metaphors for the Logos which appear in the Epistle to the Hebrews, " High Priest " and " Image of God." [12] Only through Philo was the Stoic Logos fully personified and could thus be applied to Christ.

[8] The Stoics had already anticipated this insight by calling man "microcosm," thus acknowledging the cosmic significance of the human mind.

[9] Compare what Allan D. Galloway says about the imagery of the angels in his book, *The Cosmic Christ*, Ch. III.

[10] See Eusebius, *Praeparatio Evangelica*, VII, 13.

[11] Cf. C. H. Dodd, *The Interpretation of the Fourth Gospel* (1954), Part I, ch. 3. Also especially p. 276.

[12] These phrases point to the possibility that the author of the Epistle was directly influenced by Philo.

INDEXES

I. INDEXES OF NAMES

A. ANCIENT

Academy, 172, 215, 223, 226
Agamemnon, 71
Alcibiades, 138 f.
Anaxagoras, 26, 74, 79, 96, 117 ff., 120, 124–127, 128, 190 f., 207, 226
Anaximander, 47, 52 f., 55, 76, 80–86, 87, 94, 96 f., 106
Anaximenes, 80, 83, 87
Aphrodite:
  Hesiod, 76
  Parmenides, 109
Apollo (Apollonian), 25, 84, 113
Archesilaus, 124
Aristotle (Aristotelian), 26 f., 31, 33 f., 38 f., 61 f., 64 f., 74 f., 78 ff., 84, 90 f., 96, 111, 118, 124, 126, 146, 164, 170, 175, 178 f., 182, 183–222, 223 ff., 226, 228 ff., 232, 234, 236, 239
Arrianus of Nicomedia, 225
Athens (Athenian), 37, 48, 50, 60, 66, 133 f., 138 ff., 143, 145, 147 ff., 154, 185, 187, 190

Boethius, 177
Brahmanism, 19
Buddhism, 19

Chaos (Hesiod), 76, 108
Chleanthes, 231
Chthonic (cult), 26
Cicero, 227, 233
Confucianism, 19

Cynics, 148
Cyrenaics, 148

Democritus, 74, 80, 96, 117 f., 120, 127–129, 191, 207
Dike, 48
  Heraclitus, 97
  Hesiod, 49, 76
  Parmenides, 106, 108
Diogenes Laërtius, 125
Dionysus (Dionysian), 24 ff., 84, 113
Diotima (*Symposium*), 72

Eleatics, 78, 96, 152, 203
Empedocles, 23, 66, 69, 74, 79 f., 81, 96, 117 ff., 120–124, 125, 127 f., 178, 191, 207, 210, 226
Epictetus, 225
Epicureans, 215
Euripides, 60, 172

Greeks:
  aesthetic imagination, 45 f., 48, 96
  naïveté, 38, 59
  polis, 47 f.

Hades, 143
Harmonia (Hesiod), 76
Heraclitus, 24, 26, 33, 53, 55, 57, 66 ff., 70, 73 ff., 80, 84, 86 f., 92–101, 102 ff., 106 f., 112 ff., 117 ff., 120 ff., 124, 127 f., 131, 140 f., 153, 156 f., 160, 172, 178, 183, 186, 192 f., 202 f., 206 f., 228, 233 f.

Hesiod, 46, 49 ff., 57 f., 60, 68, 75 f., 81, 88, 97, 104, 106, 108, 152, 210 f.
Hippasos, 80
Homer (Homeric), 24, 45 f., 49 ff., 54 f., 57 ff., 60, 67 f., 69 ff., 75, 115, 172

Ionian, 25, 45, 47, 50 f., 52, 66, 168

Leukippos, 117

Megarian (school), 148
Melissus, 78
Metapontinus, 80
Milesians, 75, 102, 104, 234

Neoplatonism, 39, 221, 238
Neopythagoreanism, 238

Olympic gods, 24, 69, 75, 84, 140
Orphic religion, 24, 84, 87, 142

Parmenides, 23, 33, 55, 57, 65, 73 f., 75, 80 f., 84, 87, 100, 102–115, 117, 121, 123 f., 128, 131, 156 ff., 159 ff., 166, 169, 178 ff., 183 f., 186, 190, 202, 207, 209 ff., 234
Pericles, 45, 48, 50, 139
Peripatetics, 215, 226
Philo, Alexandrian, 114, 237–240
Pindar, 46
Plato, 36, 38, 56, 61 f., 64, 66 f., 73 f., 80, 83 f., 86, 91 f., 96, 108, 110, 116 ff., 119, 135, 140, 151, 152–182, 183, 185 ff., 190 f., 193 ff., 196 ff., 203, 207, 213, 217, 221, 223 ff., 229, 231, 233 f., 236 f., 239
  Apology, 133, 147, 149 f.
  Charmides, 131
  Cratylus, 132, 134, 141
  Crito, 147
  Euthydemus, 132
  Gorgias, 54, 132, 133, 141, 144, 146, 147
  Ion, 69
  Laches, 23, 59, 136
  Laws, 49, 69

Phaedo, 59, 124, 125, 141, 143, 144
Phaedrus, 131, 133
Philebus, 166 f.
Republic, 59, 69 ff., 78, 144
Sophistes, 170
Symposium, 139, 144
Theaetetus, 115, 142
Timaeus, 33 f.
Platonism, 71
Plotinus, 238
Plutarch, 65, 227
Pre-Socratics, 74, 77 ff., 80 f., 84, 87, 90, 103, 117, 118, 140, 152, 227, 234
Protagoras, 129, 132
Pythagoras (Pythagoreans), 23, 57, 74, 80, 87–92, 95 f., 102, 113, 122 f., 127, 142, 156, 178 ff., 186, 226, 233 f.

Sextus Empiricus, 124
Socrates, 23, 26, 59 f., 71, 73 f., 92, 96, 115, 118 f., 130 ff., 133–151
  and Christ, 134
  divinity of the soul, 143
  inner harmony, 136
  moral conscience, 140
  no doctrine, 149 f.
  religious significance, 139, 147
  selfhood, 142
  strangeness, 135
  virtue, teachable, 144
  wisdom, 137
Solon, 45 f., 50
Sophists, 66, 73, 96, 119, 123, 128–132, 135, 150, 157, 161, 196 f., 223 f.
Sophocles, 60
Stoics, 86, 215, 220 f., 222, 223–240

Taoism, 19
Thales, 24, 51, 67, 75 ff., 80 ff., 87 f., 92, 96, 104, 183, 233
Thucydides, 45, 48, 50

Xenophanes, 55, 66 ff., 70, 75, 81, 102, 124, 140, 172, 207

Zeno (Stoic), 227, 230
Zeus, 53, 71, 75 f., 97

B. BIBLICAL

Abraham, 21, 62
Amos, 21, 58

Essenes (Dead Sea Scrolls), 238
Ezekiel, 68

Isaiah, 18, 21

Jesus, 21, 62, 134, 147, 237
Job (Book of), 53

Moses, 21, 23, 62

Paul, 21, 39, 60, 65, 85, 145 f.

C. ANCIENT CHRISTIAN

Arian heresy, 178
Athanasius, 238
Augustine, 96, 115

Basil the Great, 165

Cappadocians, 164
Clement of Alexandria, 39, 60, 65, 71,
    232, 238

Dionysius Areopagita, 238

Eusebius, 60, 240

Gregory of Nyssa, 81, 114, 165, 238

Justin Martyr, 96, 134

Origen, 178, 232, 238

D. MEDIEVAL AND MODERN

Adam, James, 67
Aquinas, 35, 39, 209
Averroës, 221
Avicenna, 221

Baillie, Donald, 238
Barth, Karl, 238
Berkeley, 111
Bruno, Giordano, 40, 209, 221
Burckhardt, Jacob, 47, 55
Burnet, J., 110 f.

Caird, Edward, 67
Chen, Chung-Hwan, 181 f.
Cherniss, H., 78
Cornford, F. M., 110, 180 ff.

Dante, 61, 184, 192
Descartes, 28, 32 f., 120, 226

Diels, H., 26
Dodd, C. H., 240
Dooyeweerd, H., 24, 26 f.
Duns Scotus, 209

Fairbanks, Arthur, 105, 121, 124
Faye, Eugene de, 238
Fichte, 188
Fränkel, Herman, 46, 67, 105
French Revolution, 31
Freudenthal, Jacob, 67

Galileo, 27 f.
Galloway, Allan G., 53, 240
Gauss, Herman, 153
Goethe (*Faust*), 18, 54 f.
Gomperz, Theodor, 37

Hartmann, Nicolai, 181 f.

Hegel (Hegelian), 31 f., 34 f., 37, 55, 58, 65, 68, 74, 77, 102, 108, 181, 183, 188, 209, 215

Heidegger, Martin, 100

Hölderlin, 46

Hugo Victorinus, 120

Hume, 132, 190

Jaeger, Werner, 46 f., 49 f., 53 f., 67, 75, 91, 106, 114, 123, 147, 153, 160, 187, 189, 194

Kant (Kantian), 23, 28, 31 f., 53, 132, 142, 145 f., 187 f., 239

Knox, T. M., 68

Kroner, R., 108

Lange, Friedrich Albert, 31

Leibniz, 32, 120, 209

Lessing, 55

Lewis, C. S., 99

Locke, 132, 190

Melanchthon, 41

Moore, Hershel, 67

Nestle, W., 46

Nicholas Cusanus, 95, 157, 209

Nietzsche, 46, 84 f., 113, 122, 140

Pascal, 22, 34

Protestantism, 37, 41, 192

Ranke, 30 f.

Raphael, 190

Reformation, 29

Renaissance, 22, 192

Rintelen, F. J. V., 46

Roman Inquisition, 177

Schelling, 209

Schiller, 37, 90

Scholasticism, 27

Schopenhauer, 84

Scotists, 192

Shakespeare, 54

Solmsen, Fr., 174

Spinoza, 32 f., 106, 209, 221

Stenzel, Bertha, 155

Stenzel, Julius, 46 f., 154

Taylor, A. E., 135, 149

Thomists, 192

Tillich, Paul, 103

Whitehead, 41

Winckelmann, 55

Zeller, Eduard, 77

II. INDEX OF QUOTATIONS

(The Pre-Socratics are quoted according to the collection of Hermann Diels, *Die Fragmente der Vorsokratiker, Griechisch und Deutsch,* Vierte Auflage, Berlin, 1922.)

Anaxagoras, Frs. 11, 12 126

Anaximander, Fr. 9 94

Aristotle:

   De anima, p. 411, a 81

   Metaphysics:

     p. 938[c] 78

     p. 985[a] 79

p. 986[b] .... 80 f.

p. 987[b] 90

1034a 186

1072a .... 210 f.

1072b .... 188, 208 f.

1073b 213

1074b .... 211 f.

1075a 207, 214
Nicomachean Ethics:
  1177a 188
  1177b 188, 205
  1178a 206
  1178b 188, 205
  1179a 220
Physics:
  p. 187ᵃ 80
  p. 203ᵇ 80, 83

Basil the Great, ep. 38 165

Cicero, *De natura deorum,* II .. 233

Diogenes Laërtius:
  II, 10, 12 125
  VII, 3 224

Empedocles:
  Fr. 4, verse 16 121
  Fr. 11 123
  Fr. 14 123
  Fr. 17 123
  Fr. 23 121
  Frs. 27, 28 123
  Frs. 28–31 118
  Fr. 59 124
  Fr. 105 121
  Fr. 110, verse 10 121
  Frs. 112, 113 121
  Fr. 114 .... 69, 121
  Fr. 115 124
  Frs. 133, 134 68
Eusebius, *Praep. Ev.,* VII, 13 .. 240

Gregory of Nyssa:
  Against Eunomius:
  I, ch. 15 114
  I, ch. 19 165
  I, ch. 26 81

Heraclitus:
  Fr. 1 98
  Fr. 2 .... 93, 97, 127
  Fr. 3 105

Fr. 5 68
Frs. 14, 15 26
Fr. 16 99
Fr. 30 .... 53, 93, 95, 107
Fr. 32 97
Fr. 41 97
Fr. 45 131
Fr. 50 .... 93, 141
Fr. 51 .... 95, 107
Fr. 54 95
Fr. 67 95
Fr. 78 97
Fr. 79 104
Fr. 86 99
Fr. 94 97
Fr. 101 131
Fr. 102 .... 57, 95
Fr. 112 .... 98 f.
Fr. 113 .... 93, 141
Fr. 114 .... 93, 97, 99
Fr. 115 127
Hesiod:
  Theogony, verses 116, 600,
    889 f. 76
  Works and Days, verses 230,
    238, 256 f., 694 76

Justin Martyr:
  First Apology, XLVI 96
  Second Apology, X 134

Parmenides:
  Fr. 1 105
  Fr. 3 105
  Fr. 4, verses 6 ff. 106
  Fr. 4, verses 12 f. 108
  Fr. 5 .... 109 f.
  Fr. 8, verse 5 107
  Fr. 8, verses 34 f. 110
  Fr. 8, verses 38 f. 112
  Fr. 8, verse 43 114
  Fr. 12 210
  Fr. 13 210
Philo, *Nomōn hierōn allēgoriai,*
  47a 238

Plato:

Apology:

p. 20 149
p. 29 148
p. 36 155
p. 39 155

Charmides, p. 164 131

Cratylus:

p. 286 132
p. 386 132
p. 396 134
p. 428 141

Crito, p. 49 147

Euthydemus, p. 286 132

Gorgias:

p. 454 132
p. 469 146
p. 475 146
p. 489 146
p. 505 141
p. 508 . . . . 54, 147
p. 509 144
p. 521 133
p. 526 143

Ion, p. 530 69

Laches, p. 188 . . . . 23, 59, 136

Laws:

VI, p. 777 68
VII, ch. 19, 817B 49
X, p. 886 174
X, pp. 896 f. . . . . 175 f.
X, pp. 898 f. . . . . 174 f.
X, p. 902 176
X, p. 903 177
X, p. 909 177
XI, pp. 926 f. 177
XI, p. 932 177
XII, pp. 967 f. 156

Phaedo:

p. 61 59
p. 65 . . . . 141, 143
p. 69 144
p. 76 163
p. 79 141
p. 80 143

p. 91 141
p. 98 125

Phaedrus:

p. 230 . . . . 131, 133, 134
p. 247 . . . . 162, 173
p. 249 . . . . 163, 173

Philebus:

p. 25 167
p. 26 166

Republic:

II, pp. 377 f. 70
II, p. 380 71
II, p. 387 71
III, p. 401 59
VI, p. 506 173
VI, p. 507 163
VI, p. 509 . . . . 165, 188
VI, p. 511 . . . . 170 f.
VII, p. 517 170
X, p. 596 168
X, p. 597 . . . . 78, 163
X, p. 613 . . . . 144, 158

Sophistes, p. 258 170

Symposium:

p. 187 160
p. 211 . . . . 72, 163
pp. 215 f. 139

Theaetetus:

pp. 183 f. 115
p. 189 142

Timaeus:

p. 29 179
pp. 37 f. 213
p. 41 178

Sextus Empiricus, VII, 90 124

Thales, Fr. 23 82

Thucydides, II, ch. VI 48

Xenophanes:

Fr. 1, verse 24 68
Fr. 9 68
Fr. 15 68
Fr. 23 67
Fr. 25 67

III. INDEX OF SUBJECTS DISCUSSED

Absolute, the, 65, 82, 117, 130, 134 f., 166, 169, 178

Actuality, 202 ff.

Akosmia, 54

Arche, 27, 77, 79, 105

Arithmetical order, 88 ff.

Astrotheology, 176 f., 212

Atheism, 22

Atom (Atomists), 118 ff., 127–129, 215, 226

Autonomy, 27

Being:
  and goodness, 161
  Parmenides, 80, 102 ff., 109, 111, 114, 123 f., 127, 162 f.

Bible, 85, 140, 151
  Book of Job, 53
  faith, 61, 66, 146, 228
  Fourth Gospel, 53, 153, 240
  Genesis, 34, 67, 130
  God of, 19, 21 f., 38, 40, 53, 60, 66 ff., 70, 83, 114 f., 140, 166, 177 f., 216, 231, 238 f.
  insight, 6, 7
  language of, 35, 178
  Old Testament, 68
  position of, 52, 58, 175
  psalms, 72
  revelation, 19, 20, 23, 25, 96, 166, 178, 209 f.

Biblical Platonism, 239

Biblical speculation, 237

Biological teleology, 186

Bios (Aristotle), 191

Catholic theology, 233

Christian Platonism, 71

Coincidentia oppositorum (Heraclitus), 95

Conflict (Heraclitus), 95

Cosmic harmony, 40, 55, 57, 89 f., 90 f., 94 f., 137

Cosmocentric speculation, 53, 61, 74, 96

Cosmos, 49, 53 f., and *passim*

Cosmotheism, 62 f., 96, 120

Cosmotheology, 168 ff., 175, 221, 229, 232

Creation:
  denied by Heraclitus, 93
  Plato, 178

Cyclical movement, 86, 122, 212

Demiurge (Plato), 173, 178

Dialectic, 170 f.

Dogmatism, 118 ff.

Eidos, 195 f.

Energeia, 204

Entelecheia, 203

Epistemology:
  Aristotle, 204 f., 211, 213 f.
  Parmenides, 110
  Plato, 160
  Sophists, 131 f.

Eros:
  Aristotle, 210
  Empedocles, 120, 210
  Heraclitus, 210
  Hesiod, 76, 210
  Parmenides, 109
  Plato, 138, 210

Ethical cosmology, 86

Ethicotheology, 175 f.

Existent, 84, 106 ff., 123, 127, 153, 156, 158, 160, 164, 169, 181, 186, 191, 202, 207, 209

Existential, 115, 192

Flux, 93 f., 119, 128, 203

Form:
  Aristotle, 194 ff.
  and matter, 193 f., 198 ff., 202
  and mind, 216 f.

multiplicity of, 194, 201, 208 f.
pure, 34, 84, 209, 216 f.
Happiness, 146, 188, 205
Harmony, 40, 90 f., 95 f.
Hierarchy:
   Aristotle, 201
   Plato, 168
History of philosophy, 32 ff.
Holiness of beauty, 72 f.
Hypokeimenon (Aristotle), 200

Idea, 84, 152–182, 187, 190 f., 194 f.,
   197, 217, 239
   of the Good, 73, 162, 165, 169 f.,
   172, 188 f.
   origin of, 73
Ideas:
   in the divine mind, 237
   Idea of (Philo), 240
   innate, 190
   interconnection of, 170
Imagination, religious, 52
Infinite (Parmenides), 80 ff., 83 ff.,
   86 f.
Intuition, 18
   Parmenides, 105, 113
   Plato, 162, 173

Kalokagathos, 73
Kingdom of God, 155 f.

Last Judgment, 143
Logos, 53, 59, 63, 84, 92 ff., 97 ff., 100,
   102, 112 ff., 123 f., 127, 131, 153,
   157, 160, 186, 207, 228, 230, 233,
   235 f., 238
Logos and Logoi, 236 f., 240
Logos-Christologists, 232, 240

Materialism, 80 f., 118, 219, 235
Matter, 80, 195, 198, 201 f.
Metaphysical physicists, 118, 120
Metaphysics, 17 ff.

of becoming, 191
origin of, 184
principles of, 192
Microcosm, 240
Mind, 204 f., 208, 216 f.
Monarchianism, 62
Monotheism, 22 f., 62
" Mover, the unmoved," 207
Music, 89 f., 113 f., 136
Mysteries, 173
Mystery:
   Anaximander, 84
   Plato, 36, 171 f.
   Thales, 51
Myth (Plato), 172 f.
Mythological imagination, 69 ff., 105
Mythological polytheism, 62, 66, 120

Naturalism, 77, 80, 125
Nature, 52, 234
Negativity (Plato), 170
Neikos (Empedocles), 120
Nomos, 166
Nothingness (Parmenides), 107 ff.,
   112
Nous, 204 f., 208, 235
Now (eternal), 107
Number, 80, 88–91, 102, 123, 153, 178

One:
   Parmenides, 80 f., 110
   Plato, 182
Ontology, 102 ff., 110, 112, 128
   of the Ideas, 152–182, 189, 194 f.
Original Fall, 115, 130
Ousia (substance), 163 ff., 198 ff., 202

Pantheism, 22, 39, 56, 62, 66, 68, 192,
   229, 234
" Paradise of mind," 37, 68
Participation, 195
Philanthrōpos, 231
Philia (Empedocles), 120
Physicism, 85
Physics, 118, 228 (Stoic)

Physiologists, 118, 174
Physis, 77 ff., 92, 118
Positivism, 120
Potentiality, 202 ff.
Pure thought, 34, 84, 209, 216 f.

Recollection (Plato), 162 f., 173
Relativism, 119, 132, 196
Religion:
  of beauty, 55 f., 69
  of the cosmos, 57, 66, 122, 162
  of the soul, 143, 162
Roots (Empedocles), 119

Seeds:
  Anaxagoras, 119
  Stoa, 237
Skepticism, 119, 131 f., 135, 157, 196 f.
Speculation and religion, 22 ff., 52, 65
Spirit, 228, 231, 233
  and Mind, 235
Subjectivism, 119, 132

Syncretism, 119, 161
Synolon, 200

Taxis, 166
Teleology:
  Aristotle, 186
  Plato, 165
Telos, 165, 191
Theism, 22
Theōria, 25 f., 188, 204 ff.
Tragedy, 84
Trinity, 232 f.

World-mind, 65
  Anaxagoras, 120, 124 ff.
  Aristotle, 189, 206 ff.
  Plato, 156, 176 f.
  Stoa, 234, 236
  Thales, 82, 92
  Xenophanes, 67
World-soul:
  Aristotle, 189
  Plato, 174 ff., 178, 207
  Stoics, 233 f.